TRUE CRIME
CROSSWORD PUZZLE
BOOK FOR ADULTS

A KILLER CROSSWORD PUZZLE BOOK FOR
CLEVER TRUE CRIME FANS

JACK ROSEWOOD

ISBN: 978-1-64845-125-6

CONTENTS

INTRODUCTION... 1

CHAPTER ONE: WOMEN OF DEATH.. 3

  Aileen Wuornos 4

  Juana Barraza 6

  Miyuki Ishikawa 8

  Joanna Dennehy 10

  Beverley Allitt 12

  Dorothea Puente 14

CHAPTER TWO: EVIL MEN 17

  Pedro Alonzo Lopez 18

  Bruno Ludke 20

  Dennis Rader 22

  Javed Iqbal 24

  Harold Shipman 26

  William Bonin 28

  Joseph James DeAngelo 30

CHAPTER THREE: KILLIN' FOR LOVE 33

  Karla Homolka and Paul Bernardo 34

  Gwendolyn Graham and Cathy Wood 36

  Fred and Rosemary West 38

  Juan Carlos Hernandez and Patricia Martinez 40

  Gerald and Charlene Gallegos 42

  Carol Bundy and Doug Clark 44

  Faye and Ray Copeland 46

CHAPTER FOUR: KEEPIN' IT IN THE FAMILY 49

  Philadelphia Poison Ring 50

  Delfina and Maria de Jesus Gonzalez 52

  Ivanova and Olga Tamarin 54

Gang of Amazons 56

Briley Brothers 58

Hernandez Brothers Sect 60

CHAPTER FIVE: KILLER KIDS 63

Elmer Wayne Henley 64

Craig Price 66

Mason Sisk 68

Peter Zimmer 70

Jasmine Richardson 72

Edmund Kemper 74

CHAPTER SIX: HISTORICAL KILLERS 77

Amelia Dyer 78

Elizabeth Bathory 80

Bloody Benders 82

HH Holmes 84

Jane Toppan 86

Gilles de Rais 88

CHAPTER SEVEN: ART THEFTS 91

Isabella Stewart Gardner Museum 92

Mona Lisa 94

Montreal Museum of Fine Arts 96

LA Mayer Institute for Islamic Art 98

Breitweiser Thefts 100

Museu de Art de Sao Paolo 102

CHAPTER EIGHT: ROBBIN' THE BANK 105

Willie Sutton 106

Alvin Karpis 108

Father's Day Massacre 110

Anthony Hathaway 112

George Leonidas Leslie 114

CHAPTER NINE: HEISTS 117

Sentry Armored Car Company 118

Dunbar Armored Robbery 120

Pierre Hotel 122

Lufthansa Heist 124

Loomis Truck Trailer Heist 126

CHAPTER TEN: JEWELRY THEFTS 129

Antwerp Diamond Heist 130

American Museum of Natural History 132

Schiphol Airport Diamond Heist 134

Graff Diamonds 136

Carlton International Hotel 138

CHAPTER ELEVEN: PONZI SCHEMES 141

Charles Ponzi 142

Lou Pearlman 144

Reed Slatkin 146

Scott Rothstein 148

Greater Ministries International 150

CHAPTER TWELVE: CYBER CRIME 153

Colonial Pipeline Ransomware attack 154

NASA Cyber Attack 156

WannaCry Ransomware 158

Heartland Payment Systems 160

Equifax 162

CHAPTER THIRTEEN: KIDNAPPED! 165

A Busload of Kids 166

Jaycee Dugard 168

John Paul Getty III 170

Charley and Walter Ross 172

Nell Donnelly 174

CONCLUSION 176

SOLUTIONS 177

INTRODUCTION

Do you love crossword puzzles? Can't get enough of true crime stories? This book pairs synopses of true crimes in narrative form as the clues for crossword puzzles. Learn details of less notorious crimes while working your way through this puzzle book.

Please keep in mind these stories are true and graphic in nature. If you possess a gentle constitution, this may not be the book for you. When dealing with the evils of society, triggers will appear—and almost any trigger known will probably be mentioned in the following pages.

True Crime Crosswords covers female serial killers to killer kids to heists and today's newest crimes—cyber—plus a whole lot more! Grab a cup of coffee and a pencil. And turn on all the lights!

Chapter One
WOMEN OF DEATH

AILEEN WUORNOS

Aileen Wuornos (**1D**) worked in (**1A**) in the state of (**3A**) where she (**27A**) (**5A**) (**7D**) victims in (**31A**) year. She claimed (**2D**) when tried for the murders. She was executed by (**4A**)(**6D**) in 2002. She survived a traumatic childhood, (**8A**) by her mother, her (**20D**) convicted of (**9D**) and rape of a child, and incest by her grandfather and (**10D**). At fourteen, she became pregnant after being (**11A**) by a (**12A**) friend. She attempted (**13A**) six times, once shooting herself in the (**14D**). At 30 years old, Wuornos fell in (**15D**) with Tyria (**16D**), a motel (**17A**). Her fingerprint identified Wuornos after law enforcement found items stolen from a victim in a (**18A**) shop. Tried for each murder individually, Wuornos received (**19D**) death sentences.

7A. Larry, ___, and Curly. **22A:** Phonetic spelling of the letter "m". **25A:** Russian prison. **26A:** Girl's name meaning life. **30A:** 4th largest moon in solar system. **33A:** Adv. equally. **35A:** Not short **38A:** Prefix for wool. **41A:** Evil eye. **42A:** Repetition of sound reflected by sound waves. **44A:** Either/. **46A:** Temporary state of mind. **48A:** Fighting against the norm. **49A:** Use teeth to cut. **53A:** 4th note of the major scale. **54A:** A small chip. **55A:** Two, too. **56A:** Uncertain possibility. **62A.** Boy. **63A:** Chonan people of Tierra del Fuego off the Southern tip of South America. **65A:** Slang for unlucky. **67A:** Linseed. **68A:** Office of Public Instruction.

8D: Famous Boxer. **18D.** Discharge resulting from an infection. **21D:** Advertisement. **23D:** Instant Message. **24D:** Emotional Intelligence. **27D:** Container of beer. **28D:** Little. **29D:** Voodoo spirit. **32D:** Education for Employment. **33D:** Morning. **34D:** Slang for goodbye. **36D:** Fermented locust bean. **37D:** Dad. **39D:** Petroleum. **40D:** Omega Omega. **41D:** Disorderly retreat of troops. **43D:** What Santa says. **45D:** Felt sorry for. **47D:** Laboratory. **50D:** Slang for old. **51D:** Out of. **52D.** European Community. **57D:** Ouch. **58D:** Blood Alcohol Content. **59D:** Take a dim view. **60D:** Three. **61D:** Greek god of winds. **64D:** Combining forms. **66D:** United Nations. **69D:** Life. **70D:** Longitude. **71D:** Orange County. **72D:** Alcoholics Anonymous.

JUANA BARRAZA

From (**1A**) City, Juana Barraza worked as a professional (**2D**), known as the "Lady of (**3A**)" and "Little (**23A**) Lady (**4A**)". She preferred lucha libre, (**31A**). Her mother was an (**5D**), frequently trading Juana for three (**6D**). The man routinely (**7A**) her, resulting in a (**8D**). Her victims were (**9D**) (**3D**) years old or older in which she strangled or (**10D**) prior to robbing them. At least three victims possessed a copy of (**6A**) *in a* (**20A**) *Waistcoat* by Jean-Baptiste Greuze, which threw investigators for a loop. Witnesses described the killer with (**11A**) features wearing women's (**12A**). Police (**54A**) the culprit male and focused on (**15A**) prostitutes until Barraza was caught trying to (**22D**) the residence of a victim. With close-cropped dyed blond (**24A**) and a (**14D**), the composite drawings closely resembled Juana. A Mexican court found her guilty of (**16A**) counts of murder while she was suspected of at least forty more. She received a prison sentence of 459 years. While incarcerated, she supported her family by working as a (**13A**) instructor and selling (**70A**).

26A: Bending at the waist. **28A:** Father. **29A:** Alabama. **30A:** Clue. **32A:** To such a great extent. **36A:** Ford Mustang. **37A:** Supposition. **38A:** Title for a man. **39A:** Boston University. **43A:** Masculine form of Renee. **44A:** Frozen water. **45A:** Sour substances. **46A:** Abbreviated form of Nancy. **47A:** Used as a function word to indicate movement. **49A:** To handle or touch to explore some quality. **50A:** Confidential Informant. **51A:** Hardy cabbage with curled, fine, incised leaves. **52A:** Me. **53A:** Spoken form of has. **56A:** North Carolina. **58A:** Illinois. **60A:** Courtney ____, star on *Friends*. **61A:** Overeaters Anonymous.

1D: Supernatural powers. **4D:** Knockout. **12D:** Domestic Violence. **16D:** Imitate. **17D:** Regarding. **18D:** Special occurrence. **19D:** Either/. **21D:** Sister. **22D:** Enter. **23D:** Occupational Therapy. **25D:** Held. **26D:** Two. **27D:** Notice of Intent. **28D:** 3.14. **29D:** President Lincoln. **33D:** Mixture of invisible, odorless, tasteless gases surrounding the earth. **34D:** Vehicle manufactured by Jaguar 1996-2012. **35D:** Stylish. **40D:** Naked. **41D:** Mantra used in contemplation of reality. **42D:** Spanish for media. **48D:** Phonetic spelling of the letter "f". **51D:** Male ruler of a country. **57D:** Voodoo spirit. **62D:** Donkey. **63D:** Run away to get married without notice to others. **64D:** Notation indicating a known mistake. **65D:** Railroad. **66D:** Advertisement.

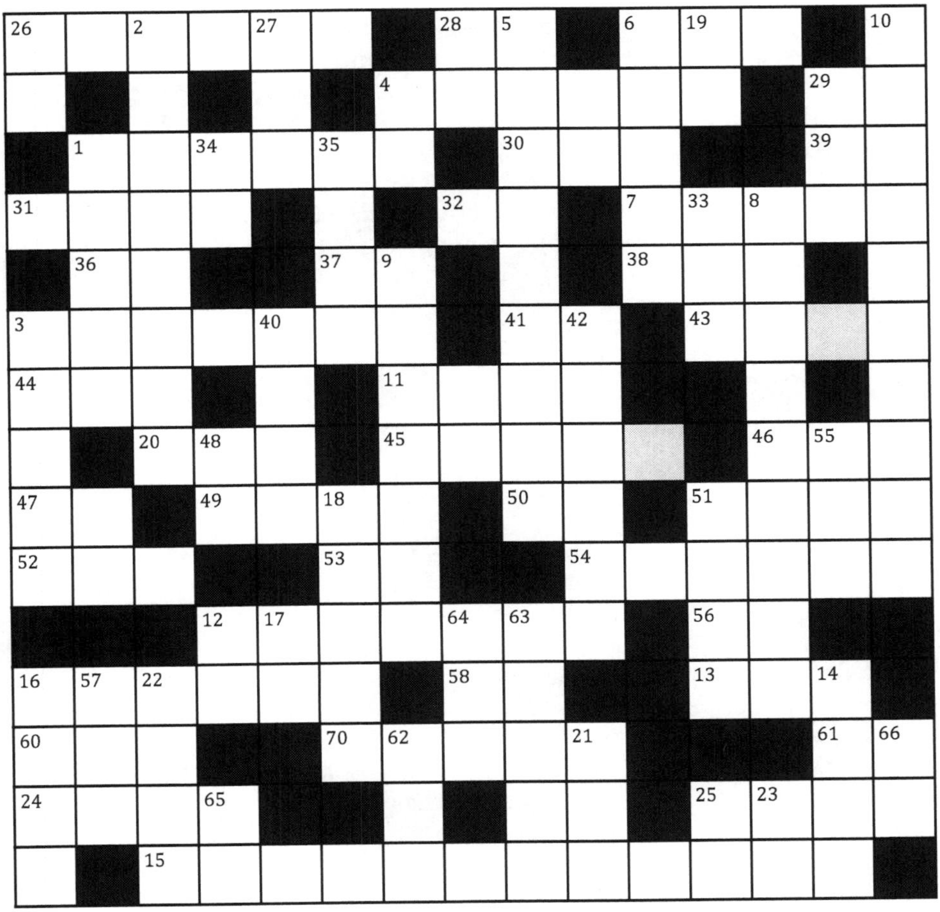

MIYUKI ISHIKAWA

Miyuki Ishikawa worked as a real estate agent, (3A), and serial killer in (4D) after WWII. While the US occupied Japan, she acted as a midwife and caretaker for many (5A) newborns. Unwanted babies (6D) by (7D) mothers and (8A) families populated the maternity home. Her (9A), an unemployed sergeant in the military police and a police officer, had a (44A) in neglecting the babies, resulting in the death of at least (1A) newborns, out of (2D) deaths in a (106A) of four years. Law enforcement became aware of her activities when officers discovered the remains of (15D) victims. Further investigation revealed the (21A) of remains for forty babies at the home of a (22D) and thirty more in a (10D). A (23D) assisted the couple in creating death (24A) for the infants. Ishikawa and her husband each received "(52A)" sentences of eight and four years, respectively. Upon appeal, their sentences were reduced to four and two years, respectively. After further investigation of (25A), authorities discovered it appeared to be common practice to actively (12A) chosen (26D), resulting in their death. Ishikawa blamed the birth parents for (82D) their children. Authorities argued she practiced discrimination against abandoned children. The action—or non-action—of caretakers resulted in the (11A) of (20D) in Japan, entitled the Eugenic Protection Law. Today, it's known as the Mother's Body Protection Law. After discharge from prison, Ishikawa worked selling (13A), cream, and (14D) before starting her own real estate agency. She continued using the address of the former maternity home until her death in 1987.

7A: What a plant grows from. **23A**: Across. **29A**: On. **30A**: One who touts. **31A**: Sparkle. **33A**: Milk's favorite cookie. **36A**: Follows orders. **38A**: National Lawyers Group. **39A**: Out. **40A**. National Guard. **41A**: Receive. **42A**: Artificial Intelligence. **43A**: Send to another country. **45A**: Do away with. **46A**: Laugh. **48A**: Period. **49A**: Narcotics Anonymous. **50A**: Federal Aviation Association. **51A**: Outstanding. **54A**: Associated Press. **67A**: Him. **69A**: Musical recording containing more tracks than a single but less than an album. **70A**: Lunar Excursion Module. **71A**: International Diagnostic and Admissions Test. **72A**: Suffix forming names of appliances or instruments. **73A**: ID. **76A**: California. **77A**: Obituary. **79A**: Hemoglobin. **80A**: Exclamation of understanding. **81A**: Alright. **82A**: Stag. **83A**: Old. **84A**: Technetium chemical symbol. **85A**: Borrowed. **86A**: Long song in an opera. **87A**: Mechanical, technological person. **88A**: Biography. **90A**: 10. **91A**: Loud exclamation from an animal typically meant to intimidate. **92A**: 3.14 **93A**: Air conditioner. **94A**: Life energy circulating through all things. **95A**: Optical Transport Network. **103A**. Senior. **111A**: South America.

1D: It is. **3D**: Imperial dynasty of China from 1368-1644. **11D**: Deadly. **12D**: Short sleep time. **16D**: Anger boiling over. **17D**: Soldier in the US Army. **18D**: Sign into a computer. **19D**: Prince of Wales motto in German. **21D**: Wooden box. **32D**: A woman belonging to a religious order with vows of poverty, chastity and obedience. **33D**: Viagra treats this disorder. **34D**: Yuck! **35D**: Noise. **37D**: Meat juice. **46D**: Pile. **47D**: Audio Visual. **55D**: Small trickster. **56D**: Irish for Wolf. **57D**: Exclamation. **58D**: Gorilla. **59D**: Honey-making insect. **66D**: Thick oil. **68D**: Someone who served in the armed forces. **74D**: Similar. **75D**: Whole, universal. **89D**: Emotional Intelligence. **90D**: Involuntary movement. **93D**: Expressing location in a particular place. **96D**: Extra Sensory Perception. **97D**: Cheer! **98D**: Non-Alcoholic brain freeze drink. **99D**: Structure of a plant underground providing foundation. **100D**: Those consuming nutrients. **101D**: Performing an action. **102D**: Nebraska. **104D**: Washington. **105D**: Superman, Batman, Wonder Woman. **107D**: Also. **108A** Bachelor of Arts. **109D**: Suspicious Activity Report. **110D**: Plant substance to treat sunburns. **112D**: Stopping in a car.

JOANNA DENNEHY

In 2013, an (**1A**) mother of two children, Joanna Dennehy killed three men, (**2D**) (**23A**) others, and intended to kill a total of nine men, like (**3A**) and Clyde. She left their bodies in (**5D**) in (**4A**). She dressed one victim in a black (**6A**) dress after killing him. A male (**7D**) drove her around in a (**33A**) while she searched for more victims. A third man was (**9D**) in the car with them. The two men who (**54A**) through the (**1D**) were (**8A**) walkers. Dennehy stole one of the dogs. Once incarcerated, Dennehy was diagnosed with psychopathic, (**10D**) and borderline personality disorders. In (**64D**), Dennehy pled (**12D**) to the murders and (**11A**) frequently throughout the trial. The judge sentenced her to life in prison and stated she should never be released due to the premeditation of each murder. The judge described her as sadomasochistic and remarked that she failed to possess normal human emotions. Dennehy had been on probation for assault and owning a dangerous dog during the time she committed the murders. While incarcerated prior to the trial, prison officials discovered plans to (**13A**). Dennehy intended to (**14D**) a (**15D**) and cut off a finger to fool the (**17A**) scans utilized to secure the prison. She was moved to solitary confinement. Later, she filed a claim stating her human (**16A**) were violated when placed in solitary confinement. The judge disagreed. In 2018, as a last (**70A**) for love, she asked permission to marry her (**17A**). That same year, the couple entered into a suicide (**22A**). In 2020, she began a relationship with another inmate. But a year later, the wedding was back on with the first (**31A**), as she'd been released.

10A: Advertisement. **23A**: More than one. **30A**: Policeman. **32A**: Spanish aunt. **33A**: Osteoarthritis. **34A**: Informal 1. **35A**: Taxi. **36A**: Arkansas. **41A**: Mesopotamia. **42A**: Hear what someone says. **44A**: Abbreviation for Lake. **45A**: Ouch. **46A**: Unhappy. **47A**: Old-fashioned pen. **48A**: Vehicle. **49A**: Red colored horse. **52A**: Estimated Time of Arrival. **53**: Herb used in making pickles. **55A**: Electronic Fuel Injection. **57A**: Seats in a restaurant. **59A**: Los Angeles. **60A**: Slice. **61A**: Spanish "Hey!" **62A**: Individual Retirement Account. **63A**: Instrument to write with. **67A**: Internet Protocol. **68A**: Clock worn on the wrist. **69A**: Rock, jewel. **71A**: Phonetic spelling of the letter "l".

16D: Regarding. **17D**: Cabbage or kale. **20D**: House. **22D**: 3.14. **24D**: Yuck. **25D**: 12:00PM. **26D**: Cut tree. **27D**: Manager. **28D**: Small. **29D**: Train on an elevated railroad. **36D**: Of or relating to the anus. **38D**: Uniform Resource Locator. **39**: Outer layer of corn. **40D**: Executive Order. **43D**: Greek letter "n". **50D**: Overdrawn. **51D**: Pointy-eared mystical being. **52D**: Spanish he. **56D**: Affirmative. **58D**: Drummer for the Beatles. **61D**: A long poem of ancient oral tradition about heroic deeds. **65D**: Scale measuring acidity. **67D**: Intensive Behavioral Intervention. **68D**: Us. **72D**: Phonetic spelling of the letter "m". **73D**: Multiple bad. **75D**: Environment Protection Agency.

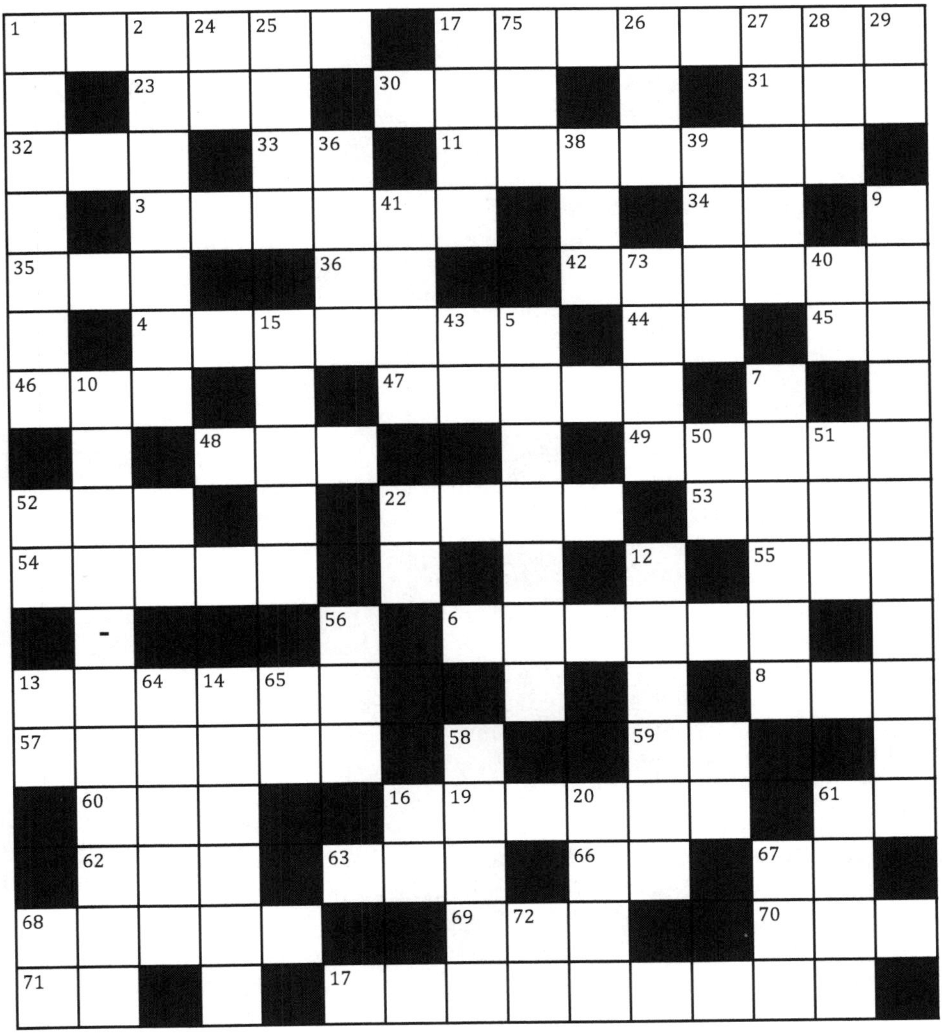

BEVERLEY ALLITT

An (42A) court (43A) nurse, Beverley Allitt, with the (11D) of four infants, attempting to murder (16A) others, and (34A) bodily harm to six more in a (31A)-month killing (13D) in 1991. She received (23A) concurrent life sentences and became eligible for (18A) in 2021. She (62A) (8D) doses of (5A) to two victims. An air bubble was discovered during the autopsy of one baby. Medical staff became (29D) after the significant number of cardiac arrests on the (37A) and informed law enforcement. Police quickly discovered Allitt worked every shift a child died and had unfettered access to the medications. In a bid to avoid prison, Allitt confessed to all her crimes, hoping to be institutionalized in a mental hospital. Treating professionals didn't think she would benefit from a commitment. Her motives were never discovered but some authorities believed she suffered from the factitious disorder (11A) Syndrome by proxy. The disorder is (49A) by a caregiver creating medical symptoms in a child to draw attention to themselves. While incarcerated in the mental (2D), she fell in love with another patient who was convicted of attempted murder. He earned the nickname, "(4D)" after drinking his victim's blood. The couple married in the asylum. She (63A) still incarcerated in the hospital. She must be transferred to prison prior to parole.

1A: Dual, double. 3A. Audio-Visual. 14A: Gore. 15A: Former name of Russia. 17A: "Et __, Brutus?" 19A: Raised platform. 20A: Angered. 21A: Christmas carol. 25A: River. 26A: Spanish you. 27A: Atrial Fibrillation. 30A: Greek letter "m". 39A: Age, period. 40A: Appendage attached to your head, aids in hearing. 41A: Prefix: early, primeval. 46A: India Pale Ale. 48A: Humanoid of lower intelligence, ugly, mean with horns and/or tusks. 58A: Paddle. 59A: A measure of the duration of events. 60A: Prefix meaning "in". 61A: Ducks Unlimited.

1D: Large passenger vehicle. 3D: Exclamation of understanding. 5D: In other words. 6D: Neural network. 7D: Frustration or disappointment. 9D: Anger. 10D: Necessity. 12D: Smash. 22D: Hawaiian underwater plants. 27D: To serve. 28D: Type of pin. 32D: Weight. 33D: Judge on OJ Simpson murder trial. 34D: Past tense of grate. 35D: Hold up; stop and rob. 36D: Snake looking sea fish. 38D: New. 43D: Powdered chocolate. 44D: Article of clothing covering your head. 45D: Latin for man. 47D: Plural of cactus. 50D: Past tense of has. 51A: Appendage on the upper torso. 52D: It is. 53D: Emergency Medical Technician. 54D: Most modern technology uses as catalysts and in magnets. 55D: Hello. 56D: Phonetic spelling of "z". 57D: Beginning.

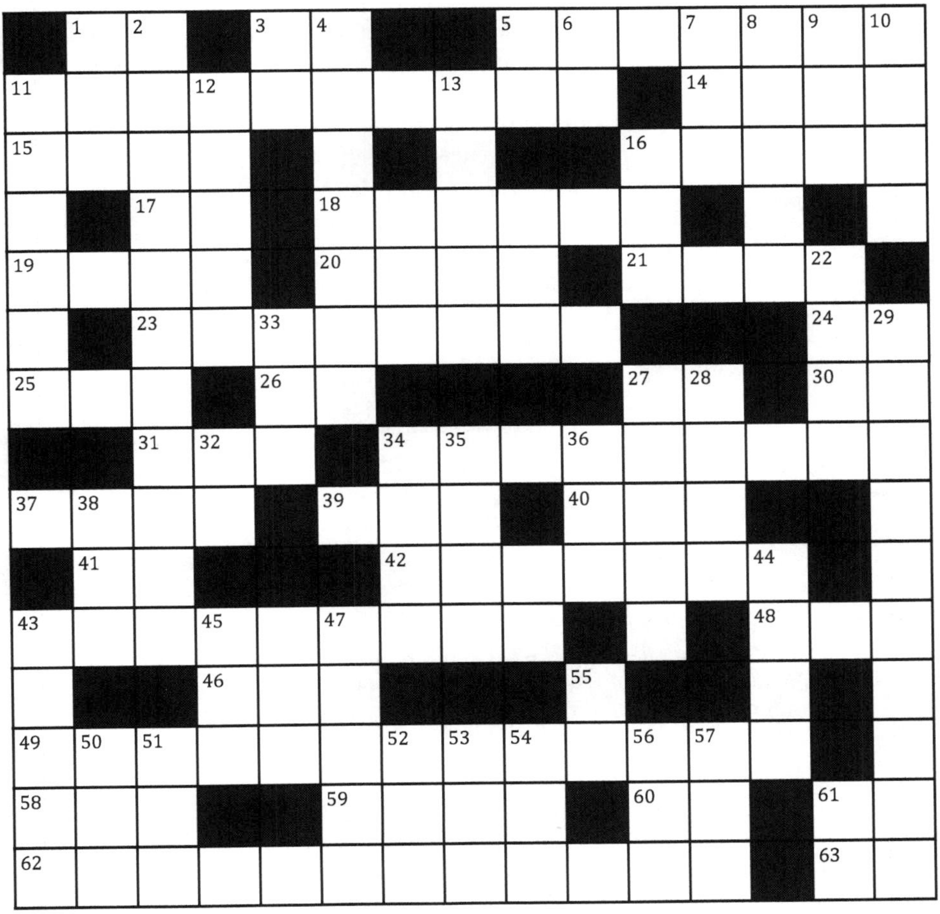

DOROTHEA PUENTE

Dorothea Puente operated a boarding house for (**4D**) and (**6D**) adults in California. A jury convicted her on three murders (**57A**) hung on six others. She (**1A**) her tenants and continued to cash their Social Security checks. She suffered a horrific childhood: both her parents were alcoholics, her father suffered from (**1D**) illness and threatened to kill himself in front of the children frequently. He died of tuberculosis. After his death, her mother turned to (**10D**) to support the children. She died in a motorcycle accident the same year. Puente and her siblings resided in an orphanage where she was (**26D**) abused. In 1960, she was arrested for operating a (**58A**) under the guise of an accounting firm. Her husband committed her to a mental hospital for drinking, lying, criminal activity and suicide attempts. Mental health professionals diagnosed her (**22A**) a pathological liar. She portrayed herself as an (**17A**) to the community by offering AA meetings and (**66D**) housing for young women and aided disabled people in applying for Social Security benefits. In 1978, she was convicted of cashing thirty-four benefit checks belonging to her tenants. Even while incarcerated, she continued to (**43D**) her boarding house. In 1988, a number of her residents went missing under mysterious circumstances. An officer began digging in her yard, where the ground had been disturbed. By the time the first body was found, Puente disappeared. (**31A**) bodies were found on her property. Some had been dismembered. Her (**56D**) (**45A**) entailed serving victims drug-ladened (**47D**), resulting in death. All of her victims had significant amounts of numerous (**52A**) (**40A**) found following (**12A**) samples of their (**24A**). The (**37A**) deliberated for 35 days before finding her guilty on three out of nine murder charges.

7A: Group of soldiers. **15A**: Arkansas. **16A**: A traveler without a home base. **18A**: Ethylene oxide. **19A**: Old fashion alcoholic beverages. **21A**: Talk back. **23A**: Egyptian sun god. **25A**: Pass tense of lead. **28A**: Calm period. **29A**: Electronic Fuel Injection. **30A**: Beside. **36A**: Right. **41A**: European Union. **42A**: Artificial Intelligence. **43**: Ancient. **44A**: Actively encourage. **48A**: Work steadily. **49A**: Emergency Room. **50**: Gear to blend in with the background. **51A**: Affirmative. **53A**: Idiots. **59A**: Life energy. **61A**: Ra, the Egyptian god of the ___. **63A**: Sound a dove makes. **64A**: Upper side or back of an animal. **65A**: To such a great extent.

2D: Type of tomato. **3D**: Knob allowing selection. **5D**: Estimated Time of Arrival. **7D**: Pharoah of Egypt. **8D**: Regarding. **9D**: Sowing your wild ___. **14D**: Video game company. **20D**: Female Pig. **32D**: Tehran. **46D**: Clothed. **48D**: Political Action Committee. **50D**: Consumer Technology Association. **55D**: Computer of our bodies. **60D**: Among other things. **62D**: Negatory.

Chapter Two

EVIL MEN

PEDRO ALONZO LOPEZ

Born (**51A**) Columbia in 1948, Pedro Lopez became one of the most (**10A**) serial killers with over 110 confirmed female victims, girls to young women. His father was murdered prior to his birth and he claimed his mother worked as a (**46A**). Kicked out of his home at age eight after attempting to (**36D**) his (**26D**), he became a victim of rape numerous times before joining a street (**54A**). An American immigrant family adopted him at age twelve but he ran away after being sexually abused by a teacher. Convicted for auto theft, Lopez was (**42D**) in prison by three different men who he later killed. Upon his release, he wandered around South America, eventually reaching Peru. Lopez estimated (**28A**) over one (**15A**) (**41A**), mostly (**23A**) street (**45D**). A local tribe caught him attempting to abduct a young girl. They stripped him and buried him in the sand up to his neck. A missionary convinced the tribe to turn him over to authorities. The police expelled him from Peru. He continued his killing spree. Authorities noticed the uptick in missing (**13D**) but assumed it was due to human (**1D**). (**16A**) revealed the bodies of several missing girls, prompting police to re-open and investigate the disappearances. A mother and daughter walked to the local market. Lopez attempted (**35A**) (**55A**) the girl. Merchants intervened and held him until the police arrived. When interrogated, he admitted nothing. But unbeknownst to him, his cellmate was actually the police captain. He boasted of murdering over one hundred girls. He described luring them away using a (**1A**). Then he raped and strangled his victims. He stated he lost his innocence at age eight and wanted to make as many girls pay as possible. He (**8D**) authorities to fifty-three bodies, with one hundred ten confirmed kills. He only served fourteen years in prison before being released for good behavior. Lopez (**44D**) now a fugitive and his whereabouts remain unknown. Numerous murders bearing his modus operandi populate South America.

14A: American Football League. **21A**: Bad mood. **22A**: Something preventing escape. **27A**: Fiddle made with coconut resonator impaled by a stick with one string. **30A**: Distinct theory. **31A**: Remains of burnt wood. **32A**: In other words. **33A**: Senior. **34A**: Leave. **38A**: Frozen water. **39A**: Woven fabric with soft surface created by clipped yarns. **43A**: Angry. **52A**: Regret. **53A**: Gray color horse. **57A**: Bees defense against attack. **58A**: Extent of a surface. **59A**: Substance to cover the smell of a dead body.

2D: Mass of land surrounded by water. **3D**: Kitchen Porter. **4D**. Emergency Room. **5D**: Implement to assist with work. **6D**: Hawaiian rare and precious. **7D**: Appendages on fish. **11D**: Fear, uncertainty, and doubt. **12D**: Certificate of Deposit. **17D**: Minion. **18D**: Abilities. **19D**: Payment for services. **20D**: Smell. **22D**: Not coffee. **24D**: Small chunk. **25D**: University. **29D**: Part of the eye. **37D**: Exclamation of understanding. **40D**: Attempting. **47D**: Ugly humanoid of lower intelligence. **48D**: Egyptian king. **49D**: Slang for university. **50D**: How chickens reproduce. **56D**: Urinary bladder. **60D**: Garment women wear covering breasts. **61D**: Sexual relations by force.

BRUNO LUDKE

Allegedly, Bruno Ludke was a (**31D**) (**7D**) killer with (**33A**) victims attributed to him in a (**5D**) period. Ludke suffered from developmental disabilities. After the interrogation, witnesses noticed indications of physical abuse. Ludke stated, "They will kill me if I don't (**21D**)!" Due to his (**18D**) limitations, Ludke was sent to the (**41A**)-run Institute of (**68A**)(**10A**) in (**4D**). He wasn't tried for the crimes as professionals dubbed him (**34D**). "Treating professionals" carried out medical (**1D**) up until his death in 1944, when (**61D**) experiment went awry. He spent about a (**43D**) in custody. Most of his (**9D**) victims were (**54A**). Authorities discovered a woman in the woods who had been strangled with her own shawl. Familiar with Ludke due to his reputation as a peeping tom (**14D**) petty thief, the police immediately brought him in for questioning. Due to low intelligence, many thought Ludke couldn't have (**8D**) authorities for fifteen years, if he was the killer. After all this time, (**35A**) will know who the (**37A**) killer was.

1A: Test. **5A**: Advocate of free open-source software. **11A**: Kilmer. **12A**: Colorfully jumbled. **13A**: Royal Academy of Dramatic Art. **15A**: Yes. **16A**. Slang for nothing. **17A**: To no longer have life. **19A**: _, white and blue. **21A**: Canada. **22A**: Advertisement. **23A**: English. **24A**: It is. **25A**: Osteoarthritis. **26A**: Snake-like fish living in the ocean. **28A**: Days To Expiration. **29A**: Mom. **30A**: Refers to one or some of a thing. **31A**: Judo garment. **32A**: Education. **40A**: Trademark. **42A**: Exclamation to get one's attention. **44A**: Creator. **47A**: Stories of heroic achievement. **52A**: Irish Republican Army. **53A**: Ensuing. **58A**: Reverse Osmosis. **59A**: Down. **60A**: Forcemeat. **64A**: Regarding. **66A**: A short French tale told in octosyllables regarding Arthur or the Round Table.

2D: Reparations. **3D**: Fear. **6D**: Off. **20D**: Estimated Time of Arrival. **27D**: Urban slang; Hey you. **30D**: Yes. **33D**: Field Officer. **36A**: German grandmother. **38D**: Ate. **39D**: Alaska. **46D**: Egyptian sun god. **52D**: Out of. **55D**: Are, hour, ___. **56D**: French for me. **57D**: National Provider Identifier. **62D**: Spanish for he. **63D**: Organization. **67D**: 3.14. **65**: Emotional Intelligence.

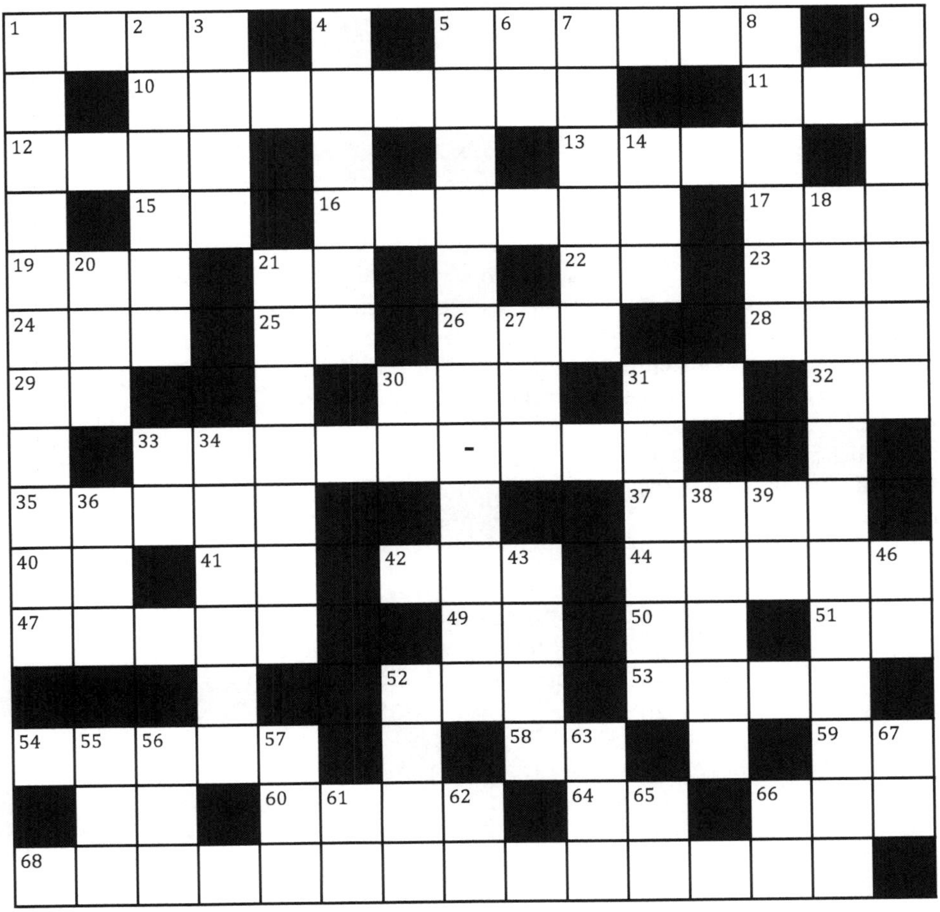

DENNIS RADER

Haunting Kansas for fifteen years, Dennis Rader targeted women, killing (**7D**) least ten victims. Given the moniker BTK, he preferred to (**61D**), (**32A**) then (**1D**) his targets, while sending letters (**13A**) law enforcement and the media, taunting their inability to find him. He stopped killing for thirteen years. Frequently, he utilized items from his victims' homes to bind and strangulate or (**58A**) them. Rader kept (**13D**) from his kills: panties, licenses and personal items. During his formative years, his parents worked a lot and ignored the children. Rader fantasized about (**38D**) sexual fantasies, (**17A**), (**11A**) (**43A**), and (**40A**) while (**6D**). Typical for serial killers, he took part (**59A**) (**10D**), killing animals. During breaks, Rader dressed in women's clothing, female masks and (**42D**) himself. He took pictures, imagining himself as one of his victims. After his arrest, he confessed to killing four members of a family: mother, father, son and daughter. His (**53A**) was found next to the partially clothed body of the (**26A**)-old daughter. One victim he took to the church where he served as president of the church council. He staged her body in numerous bondage poses, taking pictures. He planned and stalked his victims prior to attacking them. He dealt with others in the home before focusing on his primary victim. After committing numerous murders, Rader sent a letter to police and the TV station. Knowing he would be watching, law enforcement put a subliminal message in the newscast hoping the (**1A**) would call. But it didn't work. Local media received boxes with photos, mementos and detailed information eleven times. Rader kept his fetishes hidden, fitting well into everyday life. Craving attention, Rader re-emerged in 2004 after learning a book was being written about his crimes. His daughter has forgiven him but has difficulty reconciling her normal childhood with her father being a notorious serial killer. He is serving ten consecutive life sentences.

7A: Tagalog for ouch. **14A**: Toss softly and high. **15A**: Spanish for you/he/she heard. **16A**: European currency. **21A**: Not Otherwise Specified. **23A**: European Union. **24A**: You. **25A**: International Phonetic Alphabet. **29A**: High Definition. **30A**: A business to pamper women. **31A**: 7. **36A**: Untruths. **37**: Decay. **62A**: Speaks. **39A**: Sadomasochism. **41A**: Intelligent Mail Barcode. **48A**: Advertisement. **49A**: Unemployment. **50A**: Individiual things considered complete but can also be part of a larger group. **51**: Chinese for all or both. **56A**: Cut food into smaller pieces using a metal instrument. **60A**: No longer having life. **64A**: Average Monthly Balance.

2D: Laboratory. **3D**: A trivalent metallic element of rare earth. **4D**: Eat. **5D**: Foundation of a plant. **8D**: Rhode Island. **9D**: Highest and lowest card in a deck. **12D**: 3. **17D**: Cost for service. **18D**: Extreme Ultraviolet. **19D**: Organ used for sight. **20D**: Area where two pieces are joined. **22D**: Energy. **27D**: A bed. **28D**: To imbibe food. **30D**: To provide for. **33D**: Difficult. **34D** Urinary Tract Infection. **35D**: Trees with round serrated leaves and papery seed cases. **44D**: Large Japanese wrestler. **45D**: A cute paw. **46D**: Vietnamese aluminum coin. **47D**: Artificial Intelligence Research Institute. **52D**: Mule. **54D**: Phonetic spelling of the letter "m". **55D**: New Hampshire. **57D**: Erectile Dysfunction. **63D**: University. **63D**: Text message eyes.

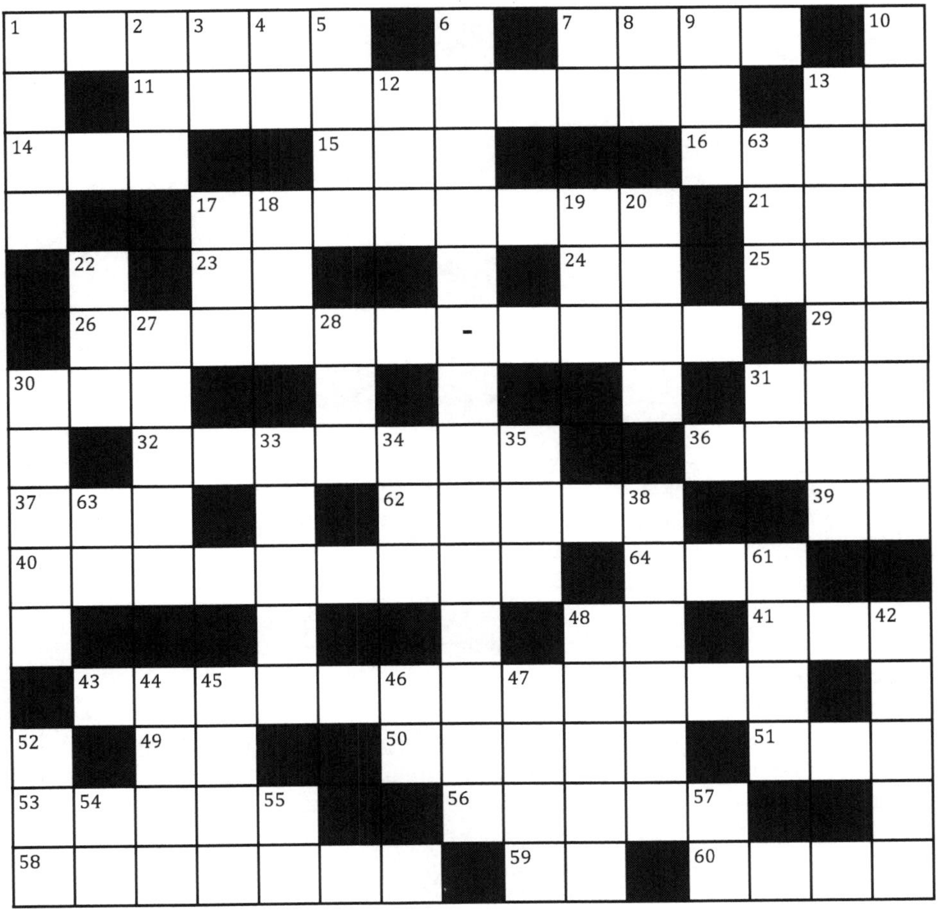

JAVED IQBAL

A (26D), Javed Iqbal confessed (45A) (21A) (3D), (2A), (39A) and (9D) in (50D) one hundred boys ages (14A) to (2D). In December 1999, Iqbal sent a letter to local law enforcement and the media describing his crimes. He targeted (15A) and (36A) living on the streets. After he sexually assaulted (27A) killed them, he dismembered them and put the remains into a (22D) of (62A) acid. He would (35D) the vats into a river. Inside (11D) villa of torture, police found bloodstained walls and floors, the chain used to strangle victims, and (49A) detailing the names, ages and photos of each victim. Iqbal left two vats filled with acid and partially dissolved bodies for authorities to (58A), adding evidence to his confession. He left a note detailing his (56A) and intimated he intended to drown himself in the river. After the police searched the river, they conducted the largest manhunt in Pakistan and found Iqbal living with four young boys in a flat. One of the boys died in custody. His postmortem showed signs of abuse. (48A) enforcement stated he jumped from a window while in custody. Iqbal stated he committed his crimes after the police arrested him for sodomy against a young boy who bludgeoned him into unconsciousness. Due (45A) the investigation, Iqbal lost his social, economic and symbolic status, leading his mother to suffer a fatal heart attack. He vowed to make one hundred mothers (57A) for their sons. He (8D) not been charged in the incident. He turned himself into the media, fearing the police. At his trial, the judge ruled, "You will be strangled to death in front of the parents whose children you killed, your body will then be cut into one hundred pieces and put in acid, the same way you killed the children." The interior minister contradicted the sentence, stating Pakistan was a member (20D) the Human Rights Commission and such punishments weren't allowed. Iqbal and another accomplice were found dead in their cells. The official report stated they hung themselves with bedsheets. Their autopsies revealed they suffered extensive physical abuse (43A) to death.

10A: 21st letter of Greek alphabet. 12: Native American tie. 13A: Species of palm tree with grape-like fruit bearing antioxidant effects. 18A: Internet slang for Dear Son. 19A: Star Trek Online. 23A: Phonetic spelling of "f". 24A: Nope. 25A: Large monkey. 28A: Implement used for work. 30A: Tooth. 34A: Point of View. 42A: Indefinite article used before a word beginning with a vowel. 44A: Coming. 55A: Emergency Nurses Association. 60A: Chinese: Absolute principle underlying the universe. 61D: Return On Investment.

1D: Adult Protective Services. 4D: Zero. 5D: Pharmaceutical company GSK. __ SmithKline. 6D: Massive compound stratovolcano in Indonesia. 7D: Psychologically manipulated to doubt their beliefs, memories and/or events. 16A American Automobile Association. 17D: Chemistry. Suffix used for radicals. 24D: White cloud. 29D: Operations. 31D: Left eye. 32D: Chinese circulating life force. 33: Hangs. 36D: Or Best Offer. 37D: Public Relations. 38D: Non-Government Organization. 40D: Emergency Room. 41D Part of major scale in music. 42D: Also. 46A: Ethnic group North Edo of Nigeria. 47D: Calming mantra sound. 48D: Right 51D: Mister. 52D: Latin for pine. 53D: Jacob's first wife and older sister of his second wife. 54D: Permanent mark on the skin. 59D: Designated Hitter.

HAROLD SHIPMAN

(20A) (26A) doctor, Harold Shipman holds the record of (45A) of the most prolific killers with two (28D) (1A) (22D) – elderly patients he over-prescribed or administered (54A) doses of (67A). After a two-year inquiry into suspicious deaths, he was convicted of murdering (1D) patients. Four years later, in 2004, he hung himself in his cell. He is the only physician convicted of (40A) patients in England. At seventeen, Shipman watched his mother (59A) at home (2D) lung cancer. Her treating professionals (13D) morphine which alleviated her pain (52A) she passed away. This became the (65A) (15A) for Shipman. Another doctor became aware of the high death rates for the patients in Shipman's care. She addressed her concerns with the coroner. In particular, she noted the high number of cremation forms requiring a countersignature. Law enforcement investigated but found nothing. A few months later, a taxi driver expressed concerns regarding twenty-one patients he transported to the clinic who appeared in good health but (49A) while under Shipman's care. His final victim proved to be his undoing. He was the last one to see her alive. Her daughter, (51D) attorney, seemed skeptical. Another attorney stated that she had created a new will, leaving just under four hundred thousand pounds to Shipman, cutting her children out entirely. Shipman claimed she was a heroin (7A) when a (10D) report indicated (8D) in her system. His records backed up his report. However, further investigation revealed he altered the records after her death.

11A: Whiskey is made from. **12**: Old-fashion alcoholic beverage. **14A**: Executive Order. **17A**: Highest point. **19A**: Ancient book. **21A**: Ozone Monitoring Instrument. **23A**: Dimensions measured in microns. **29A**: Nay. **30A**: Take back. **31A**: Unique Physician Identification Number. **33A**: Police Department. **34A**: Moves all the rocks away. **35A**: Chapter. **36A**: Slang for whore. **37A**: Number of cartons on a pallet and number of layers of cartons. **38A**: Example. **39A**: Rodent. **47A**: Equal Rights Amendment. **48A**: Significant Other. **61A**: Phonetic spelling of "m". **62A**: Harvest your crop. **68A**: Personal Computer. **69A**: Vegetable that grows in a pod.

3D: Using fingers on a keyboard to make words and/or numbers. **4D**: You. **5D**: Recognition of faith and deeds in Islam. **6D**: Plural of man. **9D**: Phonetic spelling of "c". **16D**: Sharp blows or knocks. **18D**: Suffered. **21D**: Either/. **22A**: Vice President. **24D**: To scam. **25D**: Internet Protocol. **27D**: Best. **32D**: Physical Education. **41D**: Utah. **42D**: Diversity, Equity and Inclusion. **43D**: Infrared. **44D**: $1000. **46A**: Male castrated cow. **50D**: Plural for dice. **53D**: Portable device used to store information. **54D**: Lunar Excursion Module. **55D**: Suffix used as a significant contrastive unit. **56D**: Phonetic spelling of "o". **57D**: Half circle. **58D**: Open, grassy arable land. **60D**: Emergency Medical System. **63D**: @ **64D**: 3.14. **66D**: Down.

WILLIAM BONIN

William Bonin raped and (**69A**) at least (**20D**) boys and (**70A**) men. He admitted to (**1D**) (**31D**) but was suspected of many more. He lured (**5D**) into his van under the pretense of (**54A**) (**32D**). After he finished with (**1A**), he dumped their bodies along the southern California freeways, (**21A**) different counties from where he picked them up. Bonin was the first person (**7D**) receive (**16A**) (**46A**) in California. He was (**22A**) (**53A**) 1996. His (**3A**) years proved grueling, between alcoholic parents, an (**9D**) mother, gambling father who lost the family home, a (**57A**) grandfather and a series of Catholic schools that didn't spare the rod. He showed a proclivity early (**37A**) for homosexual pedophilia. Bonin molested his younger brother and was victimized by many men in his life. He joined the Air Force and served in Vietnam where he earned a number of medals and (**63A**) a couple soldiers under his command. Once released, he targeted adolescent boys and young men who he found hitchhiking. He offered them rides, questioned them about homosexuality, handcuffed and raped them. (**53A**) 1969 he was committed to a mental hospital (**6D**) a mentally disordered (**38A**) offender. He was released five years later even though he disclosed he'd kill future victims to ensure he didn't get caught again. He served three years for kidnapping and raping several young boys, which again, he told authorities there wouldn't be witnesses next time. He was only out for about a year before returning to prison. Upon his release, he began killing his victims, often strangling them with their own (**34A**) and a tire iron. He had one (**43A**) four accomplices help him with (**19D**) least twelve of the murders. Bonin used a Ford Econoline (**8D**) as a rolling torture chamber. He removed the handles from the passenger and back (**25D**). He stored an array of implements in the van to further his attacks.

10A: Amazement. **12A**: American Auto Association. **14A**: Administrative Services Only. **15A**: Morning. **19A**: Alabama. **20A**: Fine Needle Aspirations. **26A**: Active stratovolcano in Sicily, Italy. **27A**: A boy named ___. **28A**: To such a great extent. **29A**: Universal Product Code. **30A**: Television. **33A**: Belonging to us. **36A**: Appendage attached to the head aiding in hearing. **40A**: Estimated Time of Arrival. **42A**: Hawaiian for good to eat. **44A**: Vegetable processed into sugar. **45A**: About three. **56A**: A large beer or wine cast. **68A**: Wild pig. **71A**: Everybody sucks here.

2D: Sexual attraction to the opposite sex. **3D**: 4th note of musical scale. **4D**: Overeaters Anonymous. **17D**: Uncultivated land consisting of heather and coarse grasses. **18A**: Hatchet. **23D**: Charismatic new religions targeted at removing personal identity. **24D**: Unemployment. **35D**: Frozen water falling from the sky. **39A**: Struggle to support one's self. **41D**: Spanish for tea. **48D**: Roman goddess married to Jupiter. **49D**: Hints to solve a mystery. **50D**: Low class, brassy, cheap. **54D**: Wildlife refuge in Costa Rica. **55D**: Greek for dream. **58D**: Vehicle that glides through snow. **59D**: Light. **60D**: International Bitterness Units. **61D**: Anonymous. **62D**: Implement to impede speech placed over the mouth. **64D**: Paid. **66D**: A suffix transferring a verb into a noun meaning the person who benefits from the verb. **67D**: Eye Movement Desensitization and Reprocessing.

JOSEPH JAMES DEANGELO

Known for (**66A**) different crime (**35D**) (in) California, Joseph James DeAngelo racked up (**49A**) least thirteen murders, fifty-(**17A**) rapes and one hundred twenty (**2D**) before authorities caught him (**9D**) 1986. (**He**) served as a (**25D**) officer and was known as a peeping (**37D**). He (**20A**) victims and police using (**40A**) phone calls and letters. DNA linked his crimes in different areas and time periods, as did his modus operandi, while he (**44D**) his skills. DeAngelo's crimes were one of the main factors contributing to California's (**64A**) of a DNA (**16D**) compiling data from all arrested and convicted felons. In 2018, law enforcement charged DeAngelo for eight murders using DNA evidence via his (**58D**) through forensic DNA (**10D**) using the GEDmatch website. Police tied all of DeAngelo's (**36D**) sprees together for the first time. The statute of limitations ran out on his rapes but California charged (**50D**) with thirteen related crimes of (**4A**) and attempted abduction. In exchange for removing the death penalty from the table, DeAngelo pled guilty to multiple (**51A**) and kidnapping charges. (**60D**) confessed to a number of uncharged crimes of rape. He committed most of his offenses while married and raising a family, with his children describing (**63A**) as a "perfect father." DeAngelo began his life of crime by breaking into homes, stealing minimal amounts and (**34A**) the house. Later, he evolved into targeting couples and single women with children. He changed his modus operandi based (**18A**) the profile law enforcement developed. The FBI offered a $50,000 reward in 2016 for information leading to his arrest. He blamed his crimes on an inner personality named "Jerry".

11A: Unallocated Loss Adjustment Expenses. **12A**: Ordinary. **13A**: Beige, pale gray, yellow or brown.**15A**: Paid. **19A**: Encourage strongly. **22A**: Chemical iron. **23A**: Illinois. **26A**: Bendable. **27A**: Ontario Hockey League. **28A**: Scary, weird, freaky. **29A**: Bachelor's Degree of Arts. **31A**: Pakistani for potato. **32A**: VI. **38A**: Singular have. **39A**: Conversion Electron Yield. **43A**: Water fell from the sky. **45A**: You. **47A**: The control center of a ship. **53A**: Milwaukee Symphony Orchestra. **56A**: Norse trickster god. **59A**: Mischievous child. **60A**: Hello. **61A**: 3.14. **70A**: No longer.

1D: French for blue. **3D**: Hint to solve a mystery. **4D**: Past tense of keep. **5D**: Nurse Practitioner. **6D**: Much. **7D**: Having panes. **8D**: Colorfully jumbled. **21D**: None, zero. **24D**: Beer. **30D**: Refuse to allow. **41D**: Boyfriend. **42D**: Company. **46D**: Alabama. **47D**: Therapy for AIP. **48D**: Human Resources. **49D**: Gold. **51D**: French for me. **52D**: Data Manipulation Language. **55D**: German for grandpa. **57D**: Exclamation of surprise. **62D**: Thing. **65D**: English Language Arts. **67D**: Extra-large. **68D**: Stumble.

Chapter Three

KILLIN' FOR LOVE

KARLA HOMOLKA AND PAUL BERNARDO

Acting (**24A**) an accomplice (**43A**) her husband, Paul Bernardo, Karla Homolka assisted (**21D**) the (**59A**) and murder of three female (**13A**), including her own (**37D**). Once apprehended, Homolka worked out a plea deal with Canadian officials to testify against Bernardo. Prior to the trial, video of the slayings surfaced, showing Homolka participated far more than she confessed to investigators. Homolka blamed her part on fear of (**1D**) violence from her husband. Bernardo (**1A**) an attraction to her younger sister in the summer of 1990. Homolka stole (**20A**) from the (**10D**) clinic she worked (**7D**) and they (**29D**) the teenage girl. She aspirated (**44D**) her (**10A**), never regaining (**35A**). The couple cleaned up the (**56A**) prior (**6D**) calling for (**7A**) ambulance. Bernardo found opportune victims as he drove around. He notified Homolka and the two worked together to rape, torture and sodomize the victims, all the while, recording themselves. They (**70A**) one victim, placed body parts (**33A**) (**27D**) and threw them (**40A**) a body of water. Another, they dumped on the side of the road. (**48A**) interesting fact is that Bernardo tried to (**15D**) two victims, one being his wife's sister. The judge attempted a public ban during Homolka's hearing. However, due to the proximity to New York and Michigan, and the internet, the ban proved ineffective. Bernardo's attorney gained possession of the (**72D**). The prosecution was unaware of their existence. He withheld the tapes for over a year, intending to use them to impeach Homolka's testimony, (**49A**) she maintained the façade of acting under (**29A**). The tapes revealed Bernardo raped the victims, but Homolka killed them. Due to the plea agreement, Homolka was sentenced to twelve years. Bernardo received (**63A**) in prison. Homolka obtained a bachelor's degree in psychology during her incarceration. The tapes no longer (**50A**), as the judge ordered them destroyed.

8A: Autonomous Vehicle Software. **9A**: Form of "a" to use prior to a word starting with a vowel. **17A**: I. **18A**: Internet slang for eyes. **19A**: Extra-Terrestrial. **23A**: Schutzstaffel. **25A**: Employers Reference Number. **26A**: 4. **28A**: Them. **30A**: Indium Tin Oxide. **31A**: Encourage action. **34A**: Commercial. **45A**: Freshwater fish with long cylindrical body covered in diamond-shaped scales. **47A**: Solid smoke. **51A**: North America. **52A**: Donated a set amount to a church monthly. **55A**: Phonetic spelling of "n". **58A**: Head Nurse. **62A**: Exclamation of understanding. **67A**: It is. **71A**: Preposition denoting attachment or support.

2D: Doors to leave. **3D**: Popular vehicle for killers. **4D**: Dad. **5D**: Phonetic spelling "n". **11D**: Satellites orbiting planets. **12D**: An atom or group of atoms having a positive or negative charge. **14D**: German granny. **16D**: Secure Digital. **17D**: Mom. **22D**: Greek woman's name meaning peace. **32D**: Turn round and round. **36D**: Quiet. **38D**: Stannous Oxide. **42D**: 2000 pounds. **43D**: Field Officer. **54D**: Noise made to quiet someone. **56D**: Unhappy. **60D**: North Atlantic Treaty Organization. **61D**: Needle. **64D**: Inspired by. **65D**: Iron. **66D**: Anno Domini.

GWENDOLYN GRAHAM AND CATHY WOOD

Gwen Graham and Cathy Wood worked together as nursing (**51A**) (**7D**) a care facility in (**13A**). Their relationship evolved into a romance. Fear of breaking up, the couple "(**65A**)" by killing (**34A**) of the facility. They killed (**54D**) elderly (**63A**). According to Wood, Graham (**1D**) the victims with a pillow while Wood kept watch. All the women suffered from (**56A**) (**39A**) and lacked the physical abilities to defend themselves. Due to their age and (**4A**), their (**17D**) were initially ruled as natural. But after Graham broke up with Wood and moved to Texas, Wood told her story to law (**31A**.) Two of the victims were (**44D**) but it was impossible to tell if they had been murdered. The medical examiner ruled their deaths as (**22A**) based upon Wood's account. Wood struck a deal with prosecutors and served thirty-two years. While in prison, she bragged to her cellmate how she got revenge against her ex for breaking up with her by sending her to prison for life. She was released in 2020. Graham is still (**10D**). After Graham's conviction, people who knew the couple disagreed with Wood's story, stating Wood was the dominant force in the relationship. Many believed that Graham lacked the intelligence to carry out the murders. Her conviction was based upon the word of her latest love whom Graham bragged to of killing five people. Graham was sentenced to life (**21D**) and (**36A**) still incarcerated.

1A: Large body of water. **15A**: One distinct from another previously mentioned. **16A**: Someone who craves something to a detriment. **19A**: Look. **20A**: Assistant Sub Inspector. **30A**: Requirement to breathe. **32A**: Police Officer. **35A**: Make a mistake. **37A**: Latin for thing. **46A**: Falls behind. **47A**: Sheep offspring. **48A**: Rating Percentage Index. **50A**: Also. **52A**: Homo sapien. **53A**: Latin for year. **54A**: Futility Based Off-spring Sizing. **55A**: Advertisement. **60A**: Him. **61A**: Said to scare someone. **62A**: All. **66A**: Mountain.

2D: Engineer in Training. **3D**: Automated Clearing House. **4D**: Institute for Intergovernmental Research. **5D**: Nanogram. **6D**: Fabulous. **8D**: Manufactured. **9D**: Tonal SE Asian languages including Thai and Lao. **11D**: Singular present tense of eat. **12D**: Stop Loss. **14A**: Having to do with the anus. **16D**: Study a situation. **23D**: 1. **24D**: Mobile Financial Service. **25D**: Indication of Interest. **26D**: Central Registry Depository. **27D**: Frozen water. **28D**: Where a fox sleeps. **29D**: Emergency Medical Technician Services. **33D**: OR. **36D**: Unable to reach an agreement. **40D**: Influenza Like Illness. **41D**: Unhappy. **42D**: God of Summer. Personification of Summer. **43D**: Abdominal muscles. **45D**: Where the weapons are kept. **49D**: Out. **51D**: The Association for the Study of Animal Behavior. **55D**: Hindi word for potato. **57D**: Gently throw. **58D**: A place where wild animals are exhibited. **59D**: Environmental Enteric Dysfunction. **64D**: 12th Greek letter. **67D**: The highest level.

FRED AND ROSEMARY WEST

Fred and Rose West committed at least eight murders together, with Fred killing three more on his own and Rosie killing Fred's eight-year-old (**24A**) while he was incarcerated. They buried most of the bodies on their (**51A**), either in the cellar or the garden. The (**39A**) the couple performed together satiated their (**14A**) gratification, involving (**27D**), (**7A**), bondage and (**2D**). Fred (**1D**) himself while in custody in 1994 shortly after being charged with three murders plus nine more with Rosie. Rosie was convicted of the nine joint murders as well as the murder of her (**6D**) and received ten life sentences. Rosie's turbulent life began prior (**21D**) her birth with her mother treated with (**12D**) (**42A**) while pregnant. Her father suffered from schizophrenia and molested Rosie. Rosie, in turn, (**37D**) her two brothers. At age fifteen, Rosie met Fred at the bus stop. He was twenty-seven. Rosie gave birth to a daughter at age seventeen. (**32A**) was suspected that her father was the biological father of the baby. Rosie (**61A**) for Fred's daughters while he served time for petty crimes. (**45A**) of the girls (**64A**). Her (**58A**) were found on the property later on, with finger, wrist, toe and ankle bones missing. It is believed these may have been trophies. Rosie performed sex work out of the house. The couple sexually abused and (**20A**) their six children, forcing the oldest into prostitution at age 13. Another child of theirs "disappeared."

1A: City named for Lord Jeffrey Amherst, a colonial-era military hero. **13A**: Highest point on a mountain or hill. **15A**: Physical Therapy. **16A**: Emerging Business Enterprise. **18A**: Phenylbutazone. **19A**: Hawaii. **22A**: Orange County. **23A**: Young Lives. **29A**: Helps identify sources of metal emissions. **30A**: An operation where missionaries tried to convert natives in Ecuador. **31A**: Odorless, tasteless non-smelling gases encircling Earth. **33A**: Ultrafast Transmission Electron Microscopy. **34A**: Representative. **36A**: Sighting in on targets. **38A**: Abbreviation for Army soldier. **41A**: Two, to. **43A**: Sign up help. **44A**: Angels wear upon their head. **47A**: Ancient long heroic story. **50A**: Phonetic spelling of "s". **53A**: Text slang for "ok". **54A**: Latin for cactus. **56A**: Text slang for surprise or shock. **57A**: Regarding.

3D: Text slang for high maintenance. **4D**: Reign of an emir. **5D**: Rhode Island. **8D**: Like an ox. **9D**: A rare polyvalent metallic element of the platinum group. **10D**: A flat piece of furniture to place things on. **11D**: Blade used by native Alaskans. **14D**: To convince to have sex through positive actions. **17D**: Pretty things. **25D**: 3rd letter of the Greek alphabet. **26D**: Fabric towels are made of. **40D**: Lower. **44D**: Exclamation for attention. **48D**: Advanced Placement. **49A**: Had fond feelings for. **45D**: Optimal Production Offshore Satellite Platform. **46D**: New. **51D**: Vegetables that grow in a pod. **52D**: Rip. **55D**: Area Median Income. **59D**: Suffix forming states and disorders. **60D**: Nurse Practitioner. **62D**: About, concerning.

JUAN CARLOS HERNANDEZ AND PATRICIA MARTINEZ

Both born in (**15D**), the couple (**6D**), raped, killed, dismembered and (**1A**) ten to twenty victims from 2012 to 2018 in their (**49A**) town. Their relationship lasted ten years and they had three (**35D**) together. Hernandez, raised by a single (**15A**), watched (**2D**) she worked as a prostitute. She dressed him (**10A**) a girl, in dresses during his early years. He suffered a severe traumatic brain injury and was raped by a female caregiver, as a child. Martinez suffered an (**4D**) (**43A**) and worked as a prostitute. They (**52D**) (**47D**) women into their home, promising money and jobs, or selling food, phones or clothes. Once inside, Hernandez raped and (**5D**) the victims. He (**58A**) to killing them by slitting their throats or stabbing them. Afterwards, Martinez fried up the victims in (**41A**) and salt, and served them as steak, (**1D**), tamales and chili. The pair were (**14D**) while transporting body parts in a baby (**13D**). Nearby, officials found remains covered in (**35A**). Human remains were also located in their fridge. Hernandez told authorities (**7D**) was used for fertilizing the (**39D**) and dog food. They each received sentences of 327 years for over twenty murders and human trafficking for selling the infant of (**11A**) of the victims and human bones. Their arrests sparked protests in support of women's safety in Mexico.

12A: Prefix that refers to the womb. The third-person singular present tense form of to be. **17A:** End forward momentum. **18A:** Scottish for "no." **19A:** Office of Energy Efficiency and Renewable Energy. **20A:** Arkansas. **21A:** European Energy Exchange. **22A:** Louisiana. **23A:** Period. **25A:** Coast on the winds high in the sky. **26A:** Moved very far off-topic. **29A:** Text slang for too long. **30A:** A small spring. **31A:** A snake-like creature living in the sea. **32A:** Used after a measurement of time. Prior to the present. **34A:** Compact Disc. **37A:** Singular form of "did". **38A:** Expressing location in a particular place. **39A:** A sound telling others to be quiet. **40A:** Past tense of "run". **48A:** Beer. **50A:** Learning Disability. **51A:** 4th Largest moon in the solar system. **53A:** Game hacking language for undetected. **54A:** New Orleans. **55A:** More cute. **63A:** Nodules. **65A:** Intentionally setting an illegal fire. **66A:** A rock with crystals in the middle. **68A:** Chapter.

3D: White cloud. **8D:** Astronomy. High point. **9D:** Calamity. **16D:** Used to express hesitancy. **24D:** 8. **27D:** Chemical symbol. Erbium. **28D:** American Endowment Fund. **31D:** Relating to the environment. **36A:** Teaching Assistant. **42D:** A Chinese unit of distance equal to .3 mile. **43D:** Someone who donates. **44D:** Very important religious figure as a statue. **45D:** South America. **46D:** Involuntary facial movement. **56D:** Appendage attached to the foot. **57D:** Former name for Tokyo. **59D:** 4th note in a major scale. **60D:** Suffix for adj or adv. Used to form comparative degrees. **61D:** Secret Service. **62D:** Sex Offender. **64D:** Southeast. **64D:** Emergency Room.

1 2 3 4 5 6 7 8 67 9
10 11 12 13 14
15 16 17
18 28 19 20
21 22 23 24 25
26 27 68 29
30 31
32 33 34 35 36
37 38 39 40
41 42
43 44 45 46 47 48 52
49 50 51 53
54 55 56 57
58 59 60 61 62 63 64
65 66

GERALD AND CHARLENE GALLEGOS

Gerald and Charlene hunted a short (**13A**) from the Sacramento area between 1978 and 1980 claiming at least (**7A**) lives, focusing on (**50A**) they kept as (**52D**) (**63A**), then (**19A**). A prostitute, Gerald's (**28A**), was physically abusive. Her clients sexually abused him numerous times. His father was the first person to be (**62A**) via gas chamber in Mississippi. Well-known by law enforcement, he (**15D**) his daughter and her friend. He (**39A**) seven times. As a teenager, Charlene began using drugs and alcohol. She developed a reputation as a (**10D**). Charlene married twice prior to meeting Gerald. (**1A**), they appeared (**33A**): she proved subservient to his (**1D**) needs. Gerald brought home a sixteen-year-old (**56A**) dancer. But the two females weren't allowed to touch each other- only him. When he came home from work, he found them in bed. He threw the girl out the window, then beat Charlene. He refused to have sex with her for about a year. Then he disclosed he needed sex slaves to perform. Charlene proved willing to acquire them. They drove around, typically looking for one to two teenage girls. Charlene coaxed them into the van. Gerald repeatedly raped the victims while Charlene drove. After reaching a remote location, Gerald bludgeoned the victims and shot them. He placed their bodies in shallow graves. While abducting their last victims, a witness caught their license plate number. Gerald was convicted of murdering four people and received the death sentence in Nevada and California. While awaiting execution, Gerald died of cancer. Charlene's family paid for attorneys and arranged plea agreements allowing her to testify against Gerald for a reduced sentence. She received sixteen years and eight months. She was released in 1997.

11A: Main means of mass communication. **12A**: Overeaters Anonymous. **15A**: Study of a body after death. **18A**: Advanced Placement. **21A**: How long something is. **22A**: Month, day, year. **24A**: Georgia. **27A**: Pose a question. **29A**: Nonpolar substance composed of hydrocarbons. **31A**: Bind Torture Kill. **32A**: Iowa. **38A**: A hot oven for cooking clay. **40A**: International Business Machines. **41A**: Overdraft. **42A**: Ill or in pain. **45A**: Special Edition. **46A**: Once known as Persia. **49A**: Fruit from a palm tree high in antioxidants. **53A**: California. **54A**: Covered in ice. **55A**: Take. **61A**: Daily tasks.

2D: Extended Memory Specification. **3D**: Universal Event Tracking. **4D**: A proverb expressing a short truth. **5D**: An interior removable cover protecting an outer shell. **6D**: A resinous substance produced by insects. Non-Executive Director. **8D**: Toilet. **9D**: Organ that aids in hearing. Suffix that is used to form continuous verb tenses. **14D**: Education and Economic Development Act. **16D**: Act of putting food in your mouth and chewing. **17D**: The minute information that determines hair color, eye color, etc. **20D**: A kingdom. **23D**: A discussion is put on hold. **25D**: A leg **26D**: Spanish for mess. **30D**: A type of pine tree. **34D**: After noon. **35D**: Alcoholics Anonymous. **36D**: Determines the most import patient to treat first. **37D**: Biography. **44D**: Tree bearing beechnuts. **42D**: Air conditioning. **43D**: Intelligence Automation. **47D**: Anger. **48D**: Rope knitted together used to catch fish. **51D**: Early Years Outcome. **57D**: Chemical symbol for Xenon. **60D**: Highest and lowest card in the deck. **58D**: Text slang. Of Course. **59D**: Text slang. Thank you. **63D**: Forbidden.

CAROL BUNDY AND DOUG CLARK

Bundy and Clark met each other later in life. Clark moved in with Bundy and her two sons the first night they met in a bar. They killed (**8D**) least seven women together and both admitted (**32A**) individual kills as well. Authorities suspected the duo in other murders of girls and young women. They enjoyed picking up (**1A**) or teenage (**2D**), engaging in (**4D**), then Clark shot them. But Clark's fun didn't stop there. After he decapitated his victims, he engaged in (**13A**), and kept the (**42D**) as (**61A**). Bundy described putting (**18D**)-up on (**3D**) head and Clark used the head to pleasure himself before finally dumping it in an alley. He grew up as a military brat and joined the military himself. After his discharge, he wandered around a bit, cozying up to older women. He moved in with them, (**41D**) as much (**60D**) possible. Both of Bundy's parents were (**17A**). Her mother died and her father started to (**9D**) sexually (**39D**) her at age eleven. After he remarried, he put her into foster care. Bundy married several times to abusive men. The couple entered into a (**10D**) relationship. Then, Clark began eyeing a young neighbor girl. Bundy assisted him in (**16D**) the girl. It was a quick evolution from pedophilia to killing a woman while having sex with her. Clark received the death penalty for six murder charges. He died on death row last year. Bundy received life in prison after being convicted on two counts of murder. She died in 2003.

11A: Dull grayish-brown color. **12A**: A hot drink made from infused crush leaves. **18A**: Mom. **19A**: Besides. **20A**: Long stretch vehicle used by celebrities and wealthy people. **23A**: To wake up. **25A**: What a balloon is filled with. **26**: Ocean and freshwater creature who lives in a flat-ish shell. **27A**: Phonetic spelling of "k". **28A**: The part that remains alive after the body dies. **29A**: Killer whale. **30A**: Variation of "y". **35A**: Finished after the ninth spot. **37A**: Gut. **40A**: Stick to. **43A**: Energy Policy and Evaluation Branch. **45A**: Law of Armed Conflict. **47A**: Electronic Travel Authorization. **49A**: Strontium Unit. **50A**: Against Medical Advice. **52A**: Indeclinable. **53A**: The expression of creativity. **55A**: Slice. **56A**: College and Career Initiative. **57A**: To act. **58A**: Ankle Brachial Index. **59A**: Crushes. **63A**: To _ or not to _. **66A**: A follower of a distinct practice, ideology or system. **67D**: Dessert with crust on top and bottom, filled with fruit or berries. **68A**: Color of leaves and grass. **70A**: Inca sun god. **71A**: To one side. **72A**: Downfall.

5D: Bottoms. **6D**: Deep red-brown Pacific sea bream fish. **7D**: Sexually Transmitted Infection. **14D**: On Line Nuclear Orientation. **15D**: A person's well-being. **18D**: -up on **21D**: Indefinite Leave to Remain. **22D**: Nickname for MacDonald. **32D**: Bottom. **38D**: Nipples on a cow's udder. **44D**: Collected, obtained. **46D**: Swear to. **48D**: Group of soldiers. **50D**: Scottish. 1. **54D**: Rescued. **62D**: Unique Item Identifier. **64D**: Indefeasible Right of Use. **65D**: Chinese. To love others. __ & Stimpy show. **69D**: Negatory.

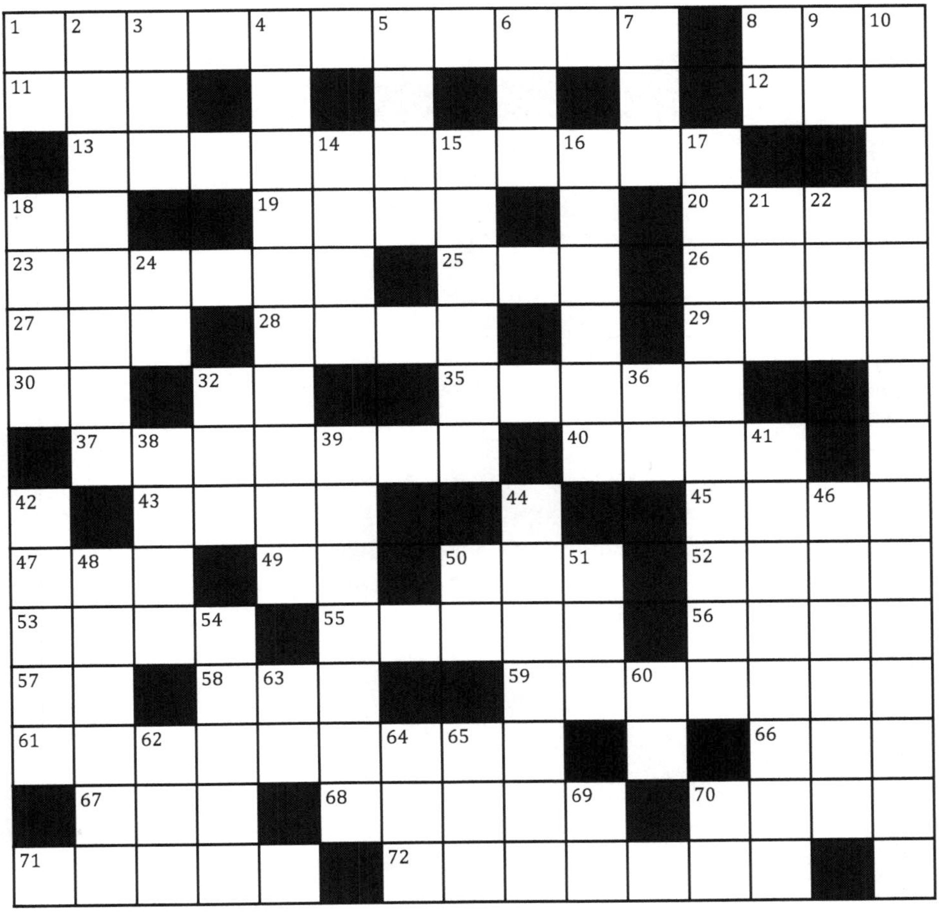

FAYE AND RAY COPELAND

The oldest couple ever sentenced to death in the United States, Faye (**31A**) and Ray (**3D**) Copeland hired and killed at least (**12A**) (**2D**) (**52D**) their ranch in Missouri. With a well-known petty criminal past, Ray's (**19D**) to (**3A**) locals was greatly impinged. To overcome this, Ray hired men passing through. (**17D**) had them buy cattle at auction, then would (**25D**) with a bad (**8C**). He then sold the (**18A**) before the check bounced. Eventually, he got caught and went back to prison. Upon his release, he decided to change (**32A**) (**1A**) (**26D**) to ensure a (**45A**) wouldn't be linked back to (**17A**). He continued to hire a lone (**51A**) or drifter, but they never left the ranch. After a Crime Stoppers special, a former employee reported seeing (**11D**) (**16A**) on the ranch and Ray tried to kill him. Skeptical, law enforcement swarmed the ranch. They found three dead bodies in a barn and others scattered around the property. All had been shot with a .22 (**29D**) authorities located inside the Copeland farmhouse. Tried individually, the two were both convicted of five counts of murder and (**23D**) to death. When Ray heard of Faye's conviction prior to his trial he replied, "Well, those things happen to some, you know." Ray (**48A**) in prison prior to (**27D**). Faye's sentence was commuted to life in prison. After suffering a stroke, the (**54A**) granted her medical (**36D**) and she died in a nursing home.

7A: Forming a noun of the person affected by the verb. **10A**: Type of tuna. **14A**: Cup for coffee. **15A**: As a possibility. **20A**: Endangered goose of the Hawaiian islands. **22A**: Used in comparsions to refer to the extent of something. **24A**: Vegetable sugar is made from. **25A**: Parent Teacher Association. **26A**: 1. **27A**: One of the first online auction sites to buy and sell items. **30A**: Alabama. **33A**: Regret an action. **35A**: Phone home. **37A**: Spicy Indian Tea. **38A**: To educate one's self. **40A**: Belonging to me. **41A**: Forever. **42A**: Private parts below the waist. **46A**: Induced Human Intestinal Organoids. **55A**: Taking notice of.

1D: I. **4D**: Carbon Copy. **5D**: Alaska. **6D**: Large. **7D**: Greatest. **9D**: Short for honey. **10D**: Area Median Income. **12D**: Correct size of shape for a situation. **13D**: Extraterrestrial Biological Entity. **21D**: Large body of water. **28D**: Bluetooth. **30D**: Denotes the noise made when one clears their throat to gain attention. **42D**: Breaker, breaker one nine. **43D**: Famous Malaysian shoe designer. **44D**: Hello. **48D**: Department of Transportation. **49D**: Employer Identification Number. **50**: Googly eyes in a text message. **53D**: Use deodorant to treat this condition.

Chapter Four

KEEPIN' IT IN
THE FAMILY

PHILADELPHIA POISON RING

During the (**62A**), Italian Immigrants flooded into Philadelphia. Cousins Herman and Paul Petrillo started their own little crime syndicate, morphing into the Poison Ring. In 1938, authorities uncovered their activities and the cousins met their end at the electric chair after being convicted of murder. Herman focused on (**11D**) and arson, with numerous criminal contacts. Paul took advantage of the cheap insurance rates, preying on the fears of the new immigrants. He dealt with double (**6D**) (**7D**) scams. Immigrant gang member Louie the Rabbi snitched to the cops. Gang members, associates and "dupes" (**1A**) Italian women the media dubbed as poison widows, were convicted and (**10D**) to be (**3D**) which many were later commuted. In 1931, Paul arranged with local thugs. Paul carried double indemnity accident insurance on the victims. The local thugs killed them in a manner that appeared accidental, allowing Paul to rake in the dough. On separate fishing trips, two men were bludgeoned and drowned. The cousins headed up the informal gang, adding Italian wise women and witches to their rolls. Unhappy immigrant women came to the wise women and witches prescribed powders, (**35D**) and poisons to cure their ails. The (**41A**) consisted of arsenic and antimony. Along with the witches' wares, the gang took out double indemnity insurance on the victim with one of the gang members as the beneficiary. An undercover cop and an informant attempted to snare Herman in his counterfeiting activities. The informant was enlisted to kill someone. Herman wanted him (**61D**) steal a car and run over the victim. The informant and cop wanted Herman to give them counterfeit bills to buy a car to use in the murder. The informant stopped by the victim's house. He found the man gravely ill, with bulging eyes, unable to speak and immobile. He returned with law enforcement. Herman later told the informant that the matter was being handled. At the autopsy, a large amount of arsenic showed up in the toxicology report. Police became aware of a familiar modus operandi: high levels of (**55A**) in Italian immigrants with a large double indemnity insurance policy benefiting one of the Petrillo cousins where the victim dies in a violent accident.

12A: United Nations. **13A**: Belonging to or on behalf of yourself. **14A**: Zero. **15A**: Sat. **17A**: Autograph. **18A**: Take without permission. **19A**: Tall bird prized for its eggs and oil. **21A**: Attention. **22A**: 12th Greek letter. **23D**: Long fiberglass or wood planks attached to feet, used on snow. **24A**: Visual hallucination. **26A**: To such a great extent. **28A**: Given. **31A**: Anno Domini. **32A**: Disagree. **34A**: Excursion. **36A**: Vehicle. **37A**: A semiconductor with two terminals allowing charge to flow in one direction. **38A**: Move towards me. **40A**: Garfield's best friend. **46A**: Business Object. **47A**: Belonging to more than one. **48A**: Not temporary. **52A**: Charlton Heston is my President. **53A**: Unable to reach an agreement. **54A**: Used to attract someone's attention in a rough or angry way. **56A**: 6. **57A**: The head of the Mafia family. **58A**: Regard as likely to happen. **63A**: A song or poem celebrating a person or event.

1D: Alleged. **2D**: Prefix meaning not. **4D** Past tense of sit. **5D**: Even score. **8D**: Ocean Observatories Initiative. **9D**: Remove a gag. **16D**: Exclamation of understanding. **20D**: Spanish for my. **21D**: Agriculture. **29D**: Lemon-, Lime-. **30D**: Ate. **41D**: Enter a statement into court regarding guilt. **39D**: Satellites orbiting a planet. **42D**: Affirmative.

43D: Fruit from Florida bearing same name as a color. **44D**: Herbal and plant condiments added to food to boost flavor. **45D**: Enterprise Resource Planning. **46D**: Elementary. **49D**: Phonetic spelling of "m". **50D**: Expert. **51D**: Zero people. **57D**: Past tense of "do". **59D**: 11. **60D**: Purchase Order.

DELFINA AND
MARIA DE JESUS GONZALEZ

Guiness World Records called the Mexican Gonzalez sisters the most prolific group of serial killers. Operating a brothel, (**8D**) discovered the bodies of eighty women, eleven men and several fetuses. While convicted for ninety-one murders, officials believe they probably killed more than one hundred fifty. Their father, a police officer, imposed strict rules while growing up. If they broke a rule, he placed them in jail. To escape home, the four women opened a tavern but failed. They turned to prostitution to survive and instantly became successful, franchising to three more Mexican cities. A procuress arrested by law (**10D**) disclosed the names of the sisters and their brothel. When law enforcement (**1A**), they began finding the bodies. The women advertised for maids. When young women applied, they (**53A**) them with (**45D**) or (**27A**). Once the (**12D**) lost their beauty, failed to please, (**29D**) became ill, the sisters killed them. If a man showed up with large amounts of money, he never left. Tried (**64A**) 1964, the sisters received forty years in prison. Delfina died in prison when a construction worker dropped a bag of concrete on her head while trying to catch a peek of the infamous killer. Maria finished her sentence and disappeared. Carmen died of cancer while (**1D**) and Maria Luisa went insane, fearing attack.

13A: French for Christmas. **14A**: Mix for a long time to make butter. **15A**: Physician's Desk Reference. **16A**: Clickthrough Rate. **17A**: Swamp bird similar to an egret. **19A**: To overcome with fatigue. **21A**: The fifth element filling the space between the universe and the terrestrial sphere. **22A**: Those who shoot. **23A**: Baseball. Runs Batted In. **24A**: Type of brown bean. **26A**: Detective. **28A**: A mythical enormous bird that could pick up an elephant with its talons. **30A**: Pakistan Inter-Services Intelligence. **31A**: Enrollment on Arrival. **32A**: None. **33A**: Anger. **34A**: Central Standard Time. **35A**: Finnish. ruokalusikallinen. Tablespoon. **36A**: Wonderful. **38A**: Past tense of meet. **40A**: Really smart. **42A**: Humans' creative output in numerous forms. **44A**: An upward warm wind used to gain height. **50A**: Creepy. **51A**: Past tense for sit. **52A**: Associated with a thing easily identified or mentioned prior. **55A**:Second-closest angel to god. **57A**: Of the penis. **62A**: Smallest. **63A**: One who corrects grammar. **65A**: Therefore. **66A**: Coiffed look on the head.

2D: Bound paper for writing with a pen or pencil. **3D**: Up and down. **4D**: Train. **5D**: Not awake. **6D**: Implantable Collamer Lens. **7D**: Apparition. **9D**: Translator. **11D**: formal speech delivered to an audience. **15D**: Able to guess an outcome with fairly high certainty. **18D**: WNBA player arrested in Russia. **25D**: Hawaiian goose. **37D**: Exclamation of wonder. **39D**: Things that scare. **41D**: Warm sea carnivorous fish. **43D**: Revocable Living Trust. **46D**: Explode and eject lava. **47D**: Abnormally large or great. **48D**: Boy-like behavior with misogynistic views. **49A**: To make noble. **54D**: Denoting an inhabitant. **56D**: Metropolitan Transport Authority. **58D**: Erectile Dysfunction Syndrome. **59D**: Insect associated with lice. **60D**: Laugh Out Loud. **61D**: Before.

IVANOVA AND OLGA TAMARIN

In 1912, somewhere around Estonia, Ivanova Tamarin and her (**7D**)-old daughter, Olga, lured at least (**41A**) people to their deaths. Law (**32A**) officials began hearing rumors of people missing near the Tamarin home. A search of the woods near the home revealed numerous decaying bodies, (**2D**) beyond recognition. Authorities discovered twenty-seven bodies in a storeroom, waiting to be butchered. Then, they found the eating room. A (**56A**) lay in the floor, dropping to the storeroom where the victims remained until butchered. Clearly, the women engaged in (**24A**) and their home became a (**51A**). Further investigation revealed a group of thirty townspeople worked with the Tamarins and took part in the feast. Police rounded up almost everyone involved in the grisly activities, nine people escaped. Police found numerous mementos: watches, purses, jewelry, wallets, clothing belonging to males and females. The Tamarins fought valiantly against arrest. Over forty people were killed in the small Russian village.

1A: Publicize a business or service in the media. **13A**: Jewel from an oyster. **14A**: Uniformed security police of the Russian Army in the 19th and 20th centuries. **17A**: Pulmonary Function Test. **18A**: Italian pasta stuffed with sausage, hamburger and/or cheese. **19A**: To the same degree or amount. **20A**: Executive Office for Immigration Review. **21A**: African Elephant Research Unit. **23A**: Arch. **29A**: Livestock Marketing Association. **30A**: Angry, threatening. **31A**: California Highway Patrol. **34A**: Information Technology. **35A**: Spanish for goodbye. **36A**: Simplicity. **37A**: Made for iphone/ipod/ipad. **38A**: Regarding. **39A**: Canada. **40A**: Ethylene Oxide. **48A**: Yes. **49A**: People who experience auditory and visual hallucinations. **53A**: Overemployed. **54A**: A patriot of the US. **61A**: United Service Organizations. **62A**: In certains sports, helping a teammate score points. **63A**: Good fortune due to a higher being.

1D: Ask for reconsideration of an authority's judgement. **3D**: Italian for the Vatican. **4D**: Exclamation of confusion. **5D**: Text slang for real life. **6D**: Independent Grocery Alliance. **8D**: Experimental Network Intelligence. **9D**: Hearing with attorneys and judge to decide a legal issue. **10D**: Calming mantra used in meditation. **11D**: Manual device to change gears in a vehicle. **12D**: Making a guess without all the information. **15D**: Teams of two playing against each other. **16D**: Alabama. **22D**: Earned Income Credit. **24D**: Picked. **25D**: Area of Responsibility. **26D**: National Security Council. **27D**: International Iron Metallics Association. **28D**: Latin copper or bronze. **33D**: What you yell as you hit a golf ball. **35D**: Aortic Stenosis. **37D**: Cartilage in the knee, acting as a shock absorber. **39D**: An abnormal growth. **41D**: Old French for tile maker. **42D**: Wireless Emergency Alerts. **43D**: Total Petroleum Hydrocarbons. **44D**: Supply Chain Risk Management. **45D**: An expression denoting a range of emotions in a conversation: shock, embarrassment, disgust, etc. **46D**: Preposition: before, in front of. **47D**: A small ornamental case for holding needles, cosmetics, etc. **48D**: Latin. Debauchery. **50D**: Stop. Quit an action. **52D**: Supreme rulers. **55D**: Move your head up and down in an affirmative motion. **57D**: For instance. **58D**: 16th Greek letter. **59D**: Overtime. **60D**: Operating System.

GANG OF AMAZONS

A Russian family decided to quit their day jobs as a nursery (**1A**) and (**20D**) to begin killing police and security officers and stealing random items from their victims. Inessa Tarverdiyeva, (**25D**) (**40**) the family, developed an extreme hatred of police after her (**41A**) lover dumped her for another woman. Authorities suspected her second husband, Roman Podkopaev, killed her first husband to marry her. Tarverdiyeva included both her daughters in the murders and robberies, making it the family business. Her youngest daughter, Anastasia, was 13 years old. From 1998 to 2007, the Gang of Amazons killed at least eighteen victims. They stole guns, passports, candles, a hairdryer, women's boots, and a camera, for example. As (**12D**), they sucked. Oftentimes, they left gold jewelry and items of higher value behind. A son-in-law, an active police officer, kept them informed of law enforcement's investigation endeavors. The name "Gang of Amazons" came about from the media when an unrelated knife inscribed with "My Favorite Amazon" was found near one of their crime scenes. The media investigated the crimes of the family as law (**53A**) attributed many crimes to them that weren't likely. The family committed their crimes under the guise of camping. Their spree ended when Tarverdiyeva and Podkopaev attempted escape from a scene on a (**62A**). Podkopaev was killed and his wife, seriously wounded in a (**1D**). Police found the girls at a campsite, surrounded by stolen items from numerous crime scenes. They (**25A**) their victims using (**57A**), knives and even gouged out the eyes of their victims.

14A: Feeling better due to exercise. **15A**: Eastern Michigan Office of Cardiology. **17A**: Female. **18A**: Head of a monastery. **19A**: Office of Disability Adjudication and Review. **21A**: Fixable. **23A**: Belonging to the Teiidae lizard family. **26A**: Japanese demon. **27A**: Bully. **29A**: Northern Kentucky Rabbit Breeders Association. **31A**: UT. **32A**: Acute Tubular Necrosis. **34A**: Spotted Lanternfly. **35A**: Stannum. **36A**: Annoy. **42A**: Combining form used in biology as a prefix meaning egg. **43A**: Luminous spheroid of plasma held together by self-gravity. **45A**: Latin. Inter alia. **46A**: Doctor. **47A**: Not small sized or large sized. **54A**: Father. **55A**: Yellowish fossilized resin. **56A**: Robust. **59A**: None. **61A**: Suffix. Used to form third person singular. **63A**: Cast a ballot based on opinion.

2D: Common Era. **3D**: From Hawaii. **4D**: Nigerian for queen. **5D**: Out of The Money. **6D**: Landing Helicopter Assault. **7D**: Chemical element Sn. **8D**: Extended Essay. **9D**: Building where the weapons are kept. **10D**: Existential place your soul goes if you've been good. **11D**: Leave. **13D**: A unit of digital information containing 8 bits. **16D**: Animals who require heat to be active. **21D**: The Muslims of the branch of Islam that adheres to the orthodox tradition and acknowledges the first four caliphs as rightful successors of Muhammad. **22D**: Learning Disabilities. **24D**: Person in charge of a DND game. **28D**: Not later. **30D**: Able to pay, so it's ___. **33D**: Large roast off a pig's leg. **36D**: Mythical woman changed to a cow when Jupiter and Juno argued. **37D**: Tellurium. **38D**: Thanks. **39D**: Thing with distinct and independent existence. **41D**: Confess. **43D**: Spanish. Yes. **48D**: Dept of Resources. **49D**: Assessment of Environmental Effects. **50D**: Texas Medical Association. **51D**: Suffix. Denoting concern or involvement with an activity. **52D**: Special Needs Trust. **53D**: Tall, flightless Australian birds. **55D**: Amount of time lived since birth. **58D**: Knockout. **59D**: Nope.

BRILEY BROTHERS

In 1979, the Briley brothers, Linwood, James and Anthony, (**47A**) on a killing, raping and robbery spree, where they killed twelve to twenty-one victims. They randomly targeted people as they cruised around town. Their weapons included guns, knives, baseball bats, a cinder block and a fork. Linwood first killed a neighbor at age sixteen. He served one year in a juvenile (**1A**). A fourth (**6D**) (**65A**) against them for a reduced sentence. The brothers (**32D**) a seventy-six year old woman and a woman 8 months (**38D**). Their youngest victim, aside from the unborn baby, was a five-year-old. One of the murders and (**1D**) gained them $6, the amount in the victim's wallet, which they split. For their (**23D**), Linwood and James received the (**45D**) penalty. Prosecutors failed to prove Anthony actually (**34D**) anyone. He received life in prison. The accomplice is eligible for parole, but continues to be denied. Prior to their (**2D**), Linwood and James planned an escape from death row taking four other death row inmates with them. The group took over the unit. Other inmates stopped them from (**34A**) guards and raping a nurse. They (**13D**) and spent almost three weeks on the run. The day James was executed, the inmates tried to delay the execution by attacking guards with shivs. Nine guards and one inmate were injured. The brothers died by the electric chair.

11A: Take, hold or deploy as a means of achieving a result. **14A**: A binary compound with oxygen and another element or group. **15A**: Members of the largest Christian church. **17A**: Favorably. **18A**: Air Conditioner. **19A**: British Columbia. **20A**: Old English. **21A**: Period of time. **22A**: A subclass of ascomycetes having the asci borne in an ascocarp. **29A**: Right. **30A**: Tear. **31A**: Nowadays. **33A**: 2. **36A**: Bottom of dog's foot. **37A**: Early Opportunity Program in Medicine. **39A**: Italy. **42A**: Signal to Noise Ratio Lineal Equalizer. **43A**: Continual Education. **44A**: Scored or corrected a school assignment. **46A**: Early Life Stress. **48A**: Aufrecht, Melcher and Großaspach. **52A**: Groove in the ramus of the mandible. **59A**: Entrepreneur of the Year Award. **60A**: #1 ship in a fleet. **61A**: Feral, not cultured. **66A**: Change the color of.

3D: Appendages on a fish. **4D**: Wrote the 1937 play *Golden Boy.* **5D**: Referee. **7D**: A member of any Thai speaking peoples. **8D**: Over the Air. **9D**: Russian Hockey League. **10D**: Scandanavian pagan season feast celebrating the new year and the sun's return. **11D**: User Interface. **12D**: A permanent mark due to a wound. **16D**: Suffix. Having the qualities of. **24D**: Flattering speech. **25D**: The city where Jesus performed his first miracle. **26D**: English Language college major focusing on the Anglo-Saxons. **27D**: Thank you in text slang. **28D**: Phonetic spelling of "m". **35D**: Individual unit on a list. **40D**: Organized. **41D**: iShares US Insurance ETF. Stockmarket abbreviation. **48D**: Make changes. **49D**: Top rated hospital in the nation. **50D**: Gigabytes. **51D**: Louisisana Highway Patrol. **53D**: Islamic State of Iraq and Syria. **54D**: Love for Low Frequencies. **55D**: Hawaiian nobility. **56D**: Utterly destroy. **57D**: Office of the Secretary of the Defense. **58D**: Large town. **62D**: Chief Executive. **63D**: Vermont. **64D**: Being one more than one.

HERNANDEZ BROTHERS SECT

The High (**1A**) of Blood, Magadelena Solis, proved to be one of the few women serial killers sexually motivated to kill. She orchestrated the murders of many people, culminating (**26A**) the drinking of the victims' blood. Convicted in two murders, authorities believe she performed eight and may have killed as many as twelve before her arrest. She demonstrated hedonistic, organized and visionary (**9D**). Petty scammers, two brothers started a cult in hopes of getting rich. The sect required followers to provide economic and sexual tributes, ingest drugs during orgies and forced some members into (**1D**). To further their agenda, they befriended Solis and her brother who acted as her pimp from an early age. They claimed to be prophets of Incan gods and promised to lead their followers to hidden Inca gold. Through a smoke and magic trick, the brothers introduced Solic to the sect as the (**15D**) of the Inca Goddess Cōātlīcue, who birthed the moon and stars. After a time, she began to believe the ruse, suffering from a theological psychosis, resulting in major religiously oriented delusions of grandeur, along with (**57A**) disorders demonstrated by consuming the blood of her victims, sadomasochistic tendencies, fetishistic practices and pedophilia. When Solis took control of the cult, two members desired to leave, tired of the sexual abuse. Fearing repercussions if the members left, Solis ordered they be detained. The group lynched them. Solis' bloodlust grew and she developed a blood (**20A**) ritual. One evening a teenage boy explored the noises he heard at the cave. Witnessing a sacrifice and orgy, he ran 25 km to the nearest police station. The police didn't believe him. The next day, the officer took him to the village. They never returned. Law enforcement ventured out along with the army. The (**42A**) uncovered at least six decaying bodies in the caves, around the village and the farms. One brother was killed resisting arrest, the other, a sect member killed. Solis and her brother served fifty years for the murders of the teenage boy and officer.

9A: Head Cook. **12A**: Indestructible bug. **13A**: Observe. **14A**: Preposition used to introduce more information. **16A**: A system of radio navigation in which any bearing relative to a special radio transmitter on the ground may be chosen and flown by an airplane pilot. **18A**: Cherish. **21A**: Jewish scholar or teacher. **22A**: Syllable representing the 7th tone in the diatonic scale. **23A**: Maine. **24A**: Yellowish fruit. Bartlett, D'anjou. **27A**: Freedom. **30A**: District of Columbia. **31A**: Delaware. **32A**: Seventh Day Adventist. **33A**: Impartial. **37A**: An implement that attaches to a mixer. **38A**: Phalanges on the feet. **39A**: Institute of Personality Assessment and Research. **41A**: Betty Ford's given first name. **45A**: Parallel-banded variety of chalcedony, a silicate mineral.**46A**: Present tense verb. To compose words. **47A**: Digital Audio Tape. **49A**: Spanish. 7. **50A**: An interface between two binary program modules. **51A**: Thespians. **54A**: 61. **56A**: Kangaroo baby. **59A**: Greyish brown. **60A**: Socio-Economic Research Applications and Projects. **61A**: One who plays the bass.

2D: Citizen of Rome. **3D**: Instrument Absolute Neutrophil Count. **4D**: Enforcement Case Information Report. **5D**: Prawns. **6D**: Education and Workforce Needs Index. **7D**: San Antonio Gun Club. **8D**: Tea bag placed in hot water. **10D**: Estimated Fuel on

Board. **11D**: Restricted, not allowed. **17D**: India. Artists. **19D**: Challenge someone to a task. **25D**: Phonetic spelling of "n". **28D**: Behavior not directly associated with the psychology of sex, which individuals associate with their sex lives, in an attempt to avoid the anxiety they feel, caused by sexual repression. **34D**: Not. **35D**: Group. **36D**: Number. **37D**: Angry mood. **40D**: Kneecap. **43D**: Silly or annoying people. **44D**: People from Ireland. **48D**: Regarding. **51D**: Large primate. **52D**: Vehicle. **53D**: Teachers Retirement Association. **55D**: 14th Greek letter. Plural. **58D**: International Baccalaureate.

1	2	3	4	5	■	6	7	8	■	9		10	11	■
12					■	13				■		14		15
16					17				■	18	19			
20									■	21				
22		■	■	23		■	■	24	25		■	26		
27		28				29				■		30		
	■	■		■	31		■		■		■	32		
33	34	35				36	■	37						
38				■	■	39	40			■		41		
42				43	44							■		
45				■	46						■	47	48	
	■	■		49					■		■	50		
■	51	52	53				■	54	55			56		
■	57						58					59		
60						■	61							■

Chapter Five
KILLER KIDS

ELMER WAYNE HENLEY

(**34A**) seventeen, Henley shot Dean Coril, the man he spent 2 years delivering young men to be (**38D**), (**37A**) and killed. Coril used a combination of guns and (**1A**) for the kills. Afterwards, he assisted in moving the dead bodies to one of three boating sheds where the bodies were stored. Paid $200 per male, Henley brought or helped dispose of twenty-eight young men. Henley took part in some burglaries and Coril paid him small amounts. Henley helped support his mother and three younger brothers after dropping out of high school. His friend, David Brooks, introduced him to Henley initially. Henley suspected Brooks and Coril engaged in sexual relations. The second time Brooks took him to Coril, he was meant to be a victim. But Coril offered him the same setup as Brooks, $200 per kid. Coril told him they were sold to a child sex slavery ring. By the second victim, Coril informed Henley the men were being raped and murdered. This didn't dissuade Henley from bringing friends and (**3D**) to their doom. Prior to working with Coril, Henley noticed a significant number of young men disappearing from his neighborhood and school. One night, Coril brought (**45A**) acquaintance and his (**64A**). Coril, incensed a girl was brought over, demanded Henley cut off the girl's clothing and rape her while he raped the boy. The girl asked Henley if he was really going to rape her. Henley grabbed Coril's gun, shooting him multiple times. He then called law enforcement and admitted to everything. He even showed them where the bodies were buried. Literally. During the trial, the victims testified about the (**1D**). Convicted on six counts of murder after the jury deliberated for an hour, his attorney appealed the convictions and they were overturned. (**46D**) the second hearing, he was again convicted on six counts. He has routinely been denied parole. Brooks died in prison of COVID. Henley sparked (**14A**) by selling original paintings through art shows while incarcerated. He offered to help pay for a monument to victims of violent crime.

13A: No longer. **16A**: Equals. **17A**: Anti Meridiem. **19A**: Beyond belief. **21A**: Prefix meaning away from. **23A**: Observation. **25A**: Norse Trickster god. **26A**: Used to refer to the persons being addressed as the object of a verb or preposition when they are also the subject of the clause. **31A**: Gold. **32A**: North Dakota. **35A**: Latin for I have come. **36A**: Street. **41A**: To make a motor roar. **42A**: Instrumental music. **43A**: Manages to support oneself. **44A**: Iron. **46A**: Alternating Current. **47A**: Cold-blooded, cold-hearted. **48A**: Not able to be accepted. **54A**: Juice made from limes. **55A**: Italian locale. **56A**: Abrupt, short. **57A**: Time off in lieu. **59A**: Advanced Distant Learning Network. **60A**: Senior. **61A**: To rub raw. **63A**: Tax Increment Equivalent Grant.

2D: Treatment. **4D**: Naught. **5D**: Gnarled. **6D**: A species of bird in the family tyrannidae, found in Cuba and the northern Bahamas. **7D**: Listener Regisration. **8D**: Authorized On-Site Soil Evaluator. **9D**: Television. **10D**: In other words. **11D**: Deposits in the earth's crust with one or more minerals. **12D**: Not Sufficient. **15D**: You. **16D**: Entrepreneurs Organizantion. **18D**: Largely. **20D**: Take advantage of. **22D**: Corsage for a man. **23D**: Under. **24D**: Receiving advantage from. **27D**: Grain popularized by Quakers. **28D**: Mesopotamian sun god. **29D**: Look for. **30D**: Las Vegas. **33D**. Spot. **39D**: One who recalls. **40D**: Breakable, sensitive. **49D**: Antimicrobrial

Resistence. **50D**: Latin for blind. **51D**: Appendage on a flower. **52D**: Staff used in karate. **53D**: Rhaeto-Romanic language that contains some words and sounds similar to Italian and Latin. **58D**: On. **62D**: Human Resources.

CRAIG PRICE

Deemed the youngest serial killer in US history, Price (**60A**) four people before he turned sixteen. In 1989, Rhode Island criminal laws hadn't evolved to deal with minors committing atrocities. He could only be held in a juvenile facility until age (**13D**, **43D**), then his record sealed. He bragged he would make history upon his release. His first murder occurred at age thirteen. He broke into a house in his own (**15D**) and (**11D**) the young (**1A**) (**25A**, **28A**) times. Two years later, he committed his next murders, a mother and her two daughters. High on (**16D**) (**52A**) LSD, he stabbed the mother (**7D**, **32D**) times, (**35A**, **36A**, **38A**) daughter sixty-two times and crushed the skull of the seven-year-old. He used numerous knives as the blades broke due (**42A**) the viciousness of his attack. He murdered the mother in front of the girls, leaving the youngest for last. Price admitted to his crimes, showing no remorse. Rhode Island re-vamped the laws pertaining to juvenile offenders because of Price. Due to continued violence behind bars, his sentence has been extended and he hasn't been released. In 2019, he received another twenty-five years for assaulting an inmate.

12A: Nothing. **16A**: Friend in Australia. **17A**: Past tense of xear. **19A**: Similar, like family. **20A**: Last survivor of massacre of Panara people over Brazil. **21A**: Royal Air Force. **22A**: Disagree in a verbal vote. **24A**: Reach out and take. **30A**: Female version of Joe. **31A**: Inca Indians that fled the Spanish. **33A**: Recedes, tide rolls out. **34A**: Common era. **40A**: First-, second- and third-person plural present of to be. **44A**. Greek for six. **45A**: Operate a motor vehicle. **47A**: Nanotechnology. **48A**: Daughter of my sibling. **51A**: Take notice of. **53A**: Forever. **54A**: Cow says. **56A**: Roentgenium. **57A**: Belongings for an activity. **58A**: Italian American who wrote 25 operas. **59A**: For each, for every. **63A**: That is. **64A**: Phonetic spelling of "m". **66A**: Regions or areas characterized by some specific quality. **67A**: Burro. **68A**: An indefined amount of time. **69A**: Ate.

2D: Third-most populated city in Japan. **3D**: Decorative design. **4D**: Word at end of prayer. **5D**: New England. **6D**: Idiopathic Hypersomnia. **8D**: To cut or thrust with a knife. **9D**: Michigan Discovery and Recovery of Taxes. **10D**: Hatchet. **14D**: Having more farts than others. **18D**: Regarding. **23D**: Spanish for oh. **26D**: Frozen H2O. **27D**: The style of script when typing or writing. **29D**: Great Britain. **34D**: To show a commercial. **35D**: Gave. **37D**: Akaike Information Criterion. **39D**: Fib. **41D**: A sequence, series, or scale between limits. **43D**: Uno. **46D**: The most edgy. **48D**: Neon. **49D**: Input/Output. **50D**: Aquatic plant reaching above the surface. **53D**: Upper appendage on a human. **55D**: 1. **61D**: Israeli machine gun from WWII. **62D**: Do Not Interact.

MASON SISK

At fourteen years old, Sisk shot and killed his entire (**20A**) while they slept in bed: Father, (**10D**), six-year-old, four-year-old, and six-month-old. His reason? He was sick of the fighting. Due to his age, the death penalty wasn't (**21D**) option. Circuit Judge Chadwick Wise described the crime as "ghastly, disturbing, and draped in (**35A**) evil." Initially, he told (**1A**) he was playing (**31D**) in the basement and saw a car drive away. He stated he didn't check on his family members and called his girlfriend prior to calling 911. Eventually, he admitted his (**56A**). After his conviction in 2018 he appealed. He (**26D**) police (**65A**) him extensively without reading his Miranda rights and an adult wasn't present to represent him. During the trial, the judge refused to allow a witness to testify regarding coerced confessions. He wasn't allowed to speak before the jury. The court refused to allow Sisk to show evidence of paternity issues with one of the children and discuss family dynamics that may implicate someone else. While awaiting trial, Sisk maintained an electronic device where he regularly texted his girlfriend. Unaware his texts could be used against him, he admitted to killing his family but stated someone forced him at gunpoint. The judge denied the motion for a new trial. His first trial ended in a mistrial after evidence from his stepmother's phone came to light. He was sentenced to life in prison without parole.

12A: Northeast. **13A**: Step. **14A**: Prefix for away from. **15A**: Tax Collected at Source. **17A**: Southwest. **18A**: Massively, largely. **22A**: Legendary, the best ever. **23A**: Capital of this country is Tehran. **25A**: Female garment worn on the torso. **27A**: Maid of Honor. **28A**: Telephone. **30A**: The first woman. **32A**: Request For Offer. **34A**: Unrealized Gains and Losses. **39A**: Experiencing negative issues. **40A**: Trick-taking card game made up of teams. **41A**: Inclusive Education Unit. **42A**: When blood leaves the body through unnatural means. **44A**: Electrical and Electronic Engineering. **45A**: Over the Top. **46A**: Orange Juice. **47A**: Dance Dance Revolution. **48A**: Interpreting visually. **53A**: Birth Control. **54A**: Ante Cibum. **60A**: Allow off the ground. **62A**: Latin for give out. **64A**: Goddess of the Moon. **68A**: Color of the sun.

1D: By an institution. **3D**: Phonetic spelling of "s". **4D**: Main trunk of a plant. **5D**: Cabs. **6D**: Industrial Investment Trust Limited. **7D**: Color between white and black. **8D**: A weapon emitting an electro-shock. **9D**: Broad sash worn around a kimono. **11D**: Drug that alters reality and/or causes hallucinations. **19D**: Positive. **20D**: Ramifications. **24D**: Remorse. **29D**: What drink goes with rainbow stew? **30D**: European Music Exporters Exchange. **33D**: Met an obstacle head-on. **36D**: National Lacrosse League. **37D**: Industrial Engineer. **38D**: Engineer. **43D**: Disc Jockey. **49D**: High-strength welding electrode great for repairing all grades of aluminum bronzes. **50D**: Illinois. **51D**: Text slang for. No Problem. **52D**: Bean used in refried beans. **53D**: In close proximity to. **57D**: Hit with a stick. **58D**: Animal's home. **59D**: Tennessee. **61D**: Slang for To the Next Level. **63D**: Song or poem in someone's honor. **65D**: Heat transfer and doing work in chemistry. **66D**: Underinsured. **67D**: Exempli gratia.

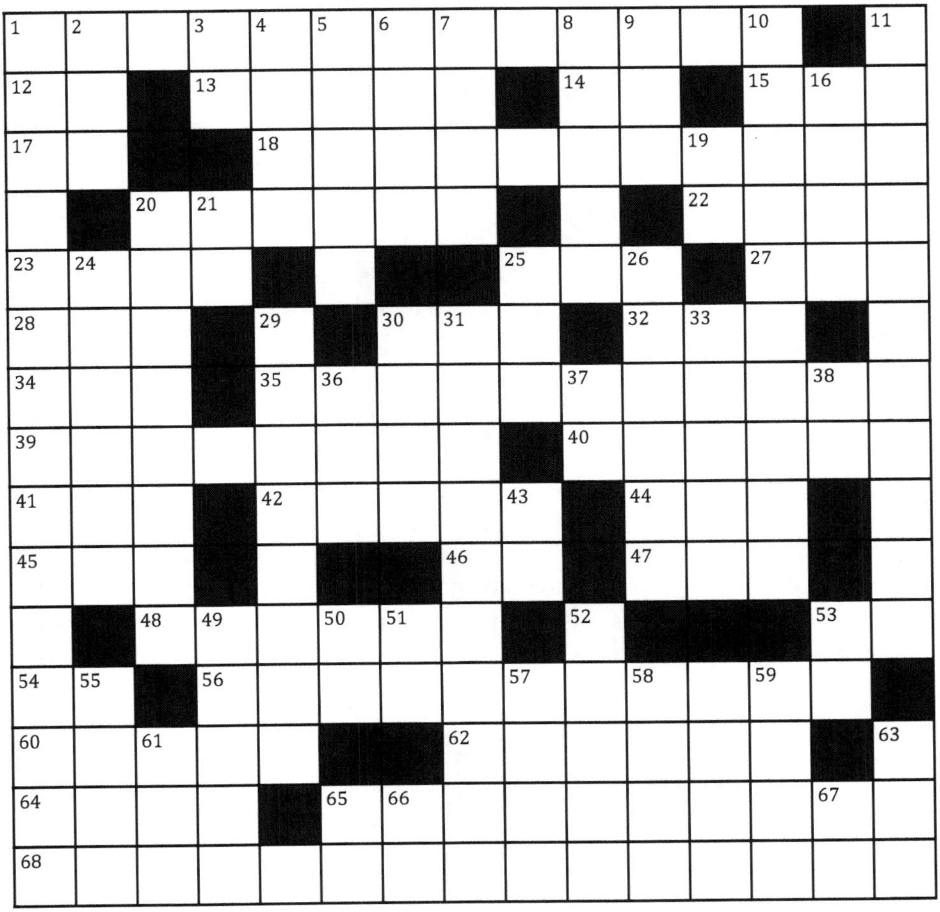
1
2
3
4
5
6
7
8
9
10
11
12
13
14
15
16
17
18
19
20
21
22
23
24
25
26
27
28
29
30
31
32
33
34
35
36
37
38
39
40
41
42
43
44
45
46
47
48
49
50
51
52
53
54
55
56
57
58
59
60
61
62
63
64
65
66
67
68

PETER ZIMMER

At fourteen years old, Zimmer killed his adopted family: father, mother and ten-year-old brother. Law enforcement discovered his father on the porch- (**37A**) five times. Authorities found his mother in a shed on the property (**11D**) numerous times with a rosary lying across her. A (**23A**) stuck out from behind her ear, penetrating the skull. He left his brother's body in the house. Twenty-five stab wounds mutilated his body, defensive wounds indicated he fought for his life. Law enforcement quickly realized one member of the family was missing, and so was the car. They located him quickly and he pled no contest. Due to his age, he served one year for each murder at Ethan Allen School for boys. He refused psychiatric care but struck up a (**3D**) with a (**1D**) volunteer. After his discharge, the couple wed and had a baby girl. Shortly after, his wife received a no-fault divorce. Zimmer met his second wife at a company picnic. They had a son together. Prior to divorce number two, he met a woman in Florida and they quickly developed a romance. Around this time, his (**17D**) located him and they began to get to know each other. He divorced wife number two and continued living with number three. Meanwhile, his birth mother's husband discovered his past and informed number three. She broke off the relationship. But Zimmer refused to let go, (**6D**)her. He mailed her everything from sex toys and flowers to a dead baby pig. (**30A**) received three years in prison. Zimmer changed his name when he left the boy's school with the money he inherited as the only surviving member of his adopted family. Due to his (**1A**), Wisconsin changed their (**24D**) laws, forbidding a killer to benefit from killing his victims.

12A: Very large body of water. **13A**: Strong. **14A**: Rule of society. **15A**: Expression of mild disappointment. **16A**: Coarse wool from the inferior parts of fleece. **19A**:Nilotic ethnic group of Luo people from Northern Uganda and Southern Sudan. **20A**: Phonetic spelling of "s". **21A**: Someone's life story. **22A**: Move dial. _ _ 10 and push the red button. **27A**: Education, Training, Research. **28A**: Not contained. **31A**: Attention-Deficit/Hyperactivity Disorder. **32A**: Atom or molecule with a net electrical charge. **33A**: Staff Sargent. **35A**: Error Correction Code. **36A**: Medical Representative. **39A**: Expressions of ideas through a medium. **40A**: Eye dialect spelling of blue. **42A**: Latin for human. **43A**: Cute simple little restaurant. Order _ go. **44A**: Clothing of the highest quality. **46A**: Home. **47A**: Surmised. **48A**: My parents' sisters. **52A**: Animal Crossing. **53A**: No Evidence of Disease. **54A**: One more. **55A**: Drinks alcohol without stopping. **57A**: Made a decision. **59A**: Upper.

2D: Integrated Circuit. **3D**: California Assertive Community Treatment. **5D**: Not conducive to moral well-being. **7D**: Dragging behind. **8D**: Gold. **9D**: Nasalgastric tube. **10D**: Picked. **18D**: Areas where the governing body of a business meets. **29D**: Out of Office. **34D**: Kept for future use. **38D**: Zeroing in on. **39D**: Times At Bat. **40D**: Son of my father. **41D**: To draw attention to an amazing event. **44D**: A neo-traditional style of Sotho music. **56D**: Above. **58D**: Like. **60D**: Admin Assistants.

JASMINE RICHARDSON

Richardson, Canada's youngest serial killer, planned and carried out murdering her family (**9D**) age twelve with her (**29A**) year-old boyfriend. The couple killed her parents and her eight-year-old brother. When law enforcement found the bodies, they quickly realized Jasmine appeared unaccounted for. Initially, they feared for her safety but found her about eighty miles away along with her boyfriend. The couple was arrested and charged with the murders, along with Jasmine's nineteen-year-old friend for giving them a ride (**46A**) disposing of evidence. Jasmine killed her parents because they disapproved of her relationship with Steinke due to the age disparity. They grounded her for continuing to maintain the relationship. After their arrest, he proposed to her and she accepted. (**59D**) told her at the beginning of their relationship that (**59A**) was a (**6D**)-year-old (**21A**) who liked to drink blood. They met at a (**36A**) (**40**). Reportedly, they watched the movie (**5A**) *Born Killers* just before killing her (**33D**). Steinke commented to friends the movie was the "greatest love story ever" and that the "little brother shouldn't have been spared". The court convicted her of three counts of murder. Under Canadian law, anyone under fourteen can't be sentenced to more than ten years and her name couldn't be publicized. She received ten years followed by four years in a psychiatric facility, then four and a half years of community supervision. Authorities cut her free in 2016. Steinke received three life sentences and will be eligible for parole after twenty-five years, which will suck for a werewolf...

1A: To cook meat at a high temperature on each side. **10A**: Dad. **12A**: Finally. **14A**: Warmth. **15A**: Bend in a circle. **16A**: Pop back up. **18A**: Like a pancake. **20A**: Pick-up. **25A**: The act of enjoying male-female relationship. **31A**: British grandchild. **32A**: Temporary disability insurance touted by a goose. **36A**: Harsh music popular in the late 70s and 80s. **41A**: British English spelling for biased toward. **43A**: Initial Public Offering. **45A**: Suffix. forming nouns denoting linguistic units that are in systemic contrast with one other. **47A**: Latin for sold. **49A**: The use of skill to bring something about. **52A**: One-mast sailboat. **54A**: Romanian for the Lord is my God. **55A**: Power derived from water. **56A**: _ McMahon. Johnny Carson's friend. **57A**: National Standards for National Resources. **58A**: Above. **60A**: Government Treasury Account Symbol. **62A**: Advertises through media.

1D: Hebrew name meaning noble woman, princess. **2D**: Eat, Eat, Eat! **3D**: Spanish for to the. **4D**: A type of coarse snuff. **5D**: Not To Exceed. **7D**: Ultimate Ears. **8D**: Egyptian Sun God. **10D**: Slight breeze through an opening. **11D**: To pretend. **13D**: Reject with contempt. **15D**: Agreeing with someone on something they said. **17D**: Are We Slim Yet. **18D**: Fool, idiot or moron. **22D**: Right Exotropia. **23D**: Electric Unit Hearing. **24D**: At least two sides resort to violence to settle a dispute. **26D**: One dozen. **28D**: Shout of elation. **30D**: Small restaurant. **31D**: Alright. **34D**: Adults Only. **35D**: Credit Union. **36D**: Half quart. **37D**: Velar nasal. **38D**: Opponents. **39D**: Empty slots. **42D**: Past tense. Leaving on foot at high speed. **44D**: Long-term illness. **48D**: Id Est. **49D**: Colonial marine invertebrates ranging in color. **50D**: Organ Procurement Organizations. **51D**: Long strings of plant typically growing up and around obstacles. **52D**: To buy. **53D**: Over-dosed. **59D**: 5G Ultra capacity. **61D**: Equally.

EDMUND KEMPER

Showing indications of a (**19D**) from his early years, Kemper killed his grandparents (**59D**) age fifteen and went on to kill seven women and one girl by age twenty-five. He (**21D**) them, as he was fascinated with necrophilia and (**21A**). As a child he killed a couple of cats—he buried one alive, then dug it up, cut off its head and put on a pike. His mother found remains hidden in his closet. He cut the heads and hands off his sisters' dolls. One of his sister's teased him about kissing his teacher. He told her he'd have to kill her first. His parents divorced and he initially lived with his mother who he described as domineering and abusive and who belittled and humiliated him. He ran away to live with his father, but he had remarried and replaced Kemper with a stepson. His father sent him to live with his grandparents who Kemper believed were senile and abusive. He stated his grandmother belittled and emasculated him and his grandfather frequently. One morning, after arguing with his grandmother, he shot her several times and reportedly stabbed her. When his grandfather returned home he shot him, as well. He then called his mother who told him to call the police. Authorities diagnosed him as (**5D**) (**1A**) and he was committed to a mental (**63A**). Treating psychiatrists disagreed, stating he didn't show signs of auditory or visual hallucinations and seemed highly intelligent, ultimately scoring 145 on an IQ Test. In fact, they allowed him to administer tests to (**1D**) patients which he later reported learning tips from. Upon his release from supervision, his treating (**22D**) (**46A**) him to be a well- adjusted, normal man. Law enforcement rejected his application for employment. He worked for the highway department and began picking up female (**18D**). Kemper felt what he referred to as "little zapples", the internal urge to kill. In his car, he carried handcuffs, plastic bags, knives and blankets. His modus operandi entailed killing the victims by shooting, strangulating, stabbing or smothering. Then, he took their bodies back to his apartment where he decapitated and engaged in sexual activities, including irrumation (a form of oral rape) before dismembering their bodies. His final victims included his mother and her best friend. He treated her body to the same attentions as every other victim. Leaving a note for police, he took off. After not hearing anything on the news, he called the police. They told him to call back. He called again and spoke with an officer he knew. Then he waited for them to pick him up. Due to the detailed confession, he pleaded guilty by reason of insanity. In the course of trial preparations, he attempted suicide twice. He received eight concurrent life sentences even though he requested the death penalty.

11A: German grandpa. **12A**: Islamic law concept of guaranteeing the security of a person. **13A**. Greek for 19. **15A**: Named Entity Recognition. **16A**: Containing two atoms. **17A**: Institute for Health Sciences and Research. **20A**: Original Character. **23D**: Horrible odor. **25A**: Non-qualified Stock Options. **26D**: Institute for the Transformation of Catholic Education. **27A**: Payments required for services. **28A**: A device to play with. **29A**: Flabby. **30A**: New Mexico. **31A**: A specialized category for a specific population. **33A**: Mix of thou and you, phonetically. **34A**: Dressed to the ___. Looking fabulous. **37A**: Dribble Hand-off. **38A**: Original High Protein Wombaroo diet. **39A**: No chance of success. **41A**: Relating to an empire. **44A**: Double crossed. **45A**: Knight Bachelor. **49A**: Hawaiian for lazy, indolent.

51A: A specific classification of novels. **52A**: Better than. **56A**: Expenses related to running a business. **60A**: Catastrophes. **61A**: Adverse Outcome. **62A**: A label.

2D: Witch casts a spell on someone causing bad luck. **3D**: Specific area set under specific rules. **4D**: A business ready to operate for the day. **6D**: AM/FM. **7D**: Give off a sound. **8D**: Not Applicable. **9D**: One who begins. **10D**: A nocturnal bird which appears to have horns. **14D**: Cold beverage filled with shaved ice and fruity sugary juice. **24D**: A religious emperor of Japan believed to be a divine incarnation. **35D**: Investigative Officer. **36D**: Second level of one who seeds. **40D**: Symptom of alcohol withdrawal. **42D**: Permanent Establishment. **43D**: Eating Disorder. **47D**: Office of Economic Opportunity. **48D**: Test Not Performed. **49D**: Heliotropium Steudneri. **50D**: Starting an illegal fire. **52D**: Governmentwide Treasury Account Symbol. **53D**: Prefix for don't agree with. **54D**: National Grid Electricity Transmission. **55D**: Delaware Clinical Research Unit. **57D**: American Society of Nephrology. **58D**: Absolute principle and combines yin and yang.

Chapter Six

HISTORICAL KILLERS

AMELIA DYER

During the Victorian Era, Dyer worked (**22A**) a nurse and took part in baby farming, (**25D**) unwanted (**24A**) for money. After thirty years, authorities wager she killed four hundred babies. Initially, she legitimately cared for the children. At one point, bobbies charged her with neglect and sentenced her to six months hard labor after a doctor raised concern after certifying a (**45A**) number of deaths of (**24A**) within her care. She realized she needed to dispose of the bodies herself and not involve doctors in the deaths. She actively killed the babies, some by (**1A**), others by (**3D**) opiates. During her life, she spent time in a mental (**58A**) or asylum on numerous occasions, deemed mentally unstable. Her bouts of mental illness and suicide attempts appeared to coincide with when she needed to (**12D**) for a little while. Some chalked up her behavior to abuse of alcohol and (**8D**). Afraid of drawing attention to herself, she relocated several times, adopting aliases. Typically, she used dressmaker's tape to wrap around the neck of a baby, strangling her. The last baby she killed, she re-used the tape from the prior murder. Hiding both babies in a carpetbag, she (**9D**) threw them off a bridge into the River Thames. Her crimes came to light when a bargeman fished a sack with the dead babies out of the river. Unfortunately, the wrapping paper in the bag contained her name and address. The information led cops straight to Dyer's door. With the evidence gleaned from the apartment, authorities estimate she killed twenty babies in the last few months. Authorities dredged the Thames, finding six more bodies with the tell-tale white tape around their necks. The (**6D**) and trial proved to be the sensation of the era, culminating in a guilty conviction, and they hung her in 1896. Authorities attributed many murders of babies to her, entering her into the running of most (**17A**) (**1D**). Her case resulted in laws to protect children and (**60A**) to (**48D**).

10A: Prefix meaning early. **11A:** Prefix for side by side. **12A:** Decinewton. **13A:** Affectionate name for people who share quarters. **19A:** Occurrences. **20A:** As well as. **21A:** Yoga term meaning posture. **23A:** Norwegian for wanderer. **27A:** Black female NASA Astronaut currently aboard the International Space Station. **28A:** Form of affection where lips are pressed together. **31A:** Father. **32A:** Commercials. **34A:** Pages. **35A:** Branch of zoology dealing with fish. **37A:** Prince Edward Island. **38A:** variant spelling of -y2. **39A:** On-base plus slugging. **40A:** Base Re-alignment and Closure. **41A:** A person or thing waiting to ambush. **42A:** Utah. **44A:** Japanese for Instigate. **49A:** A rodent from New England who likes to move. 3 words. **51A:** A tool similar to an axe, with an arched blade at right angles to the handle. **55A:** A water hole in the desert. **57A:** Astigmatism. **61A:** Wyoming.

2D: Animated shows for kids. **4D:** Above. **5D:** Lick up. Small man-made streams. **7D:** Only living Native American community designated both a World Heritage Site by UNESCO and a National Historic Landmark. In New Mexico. **14D:** Orthodox Church in America. **15D:** Yoruba for magic. **16D:** Elevator Escalator Safety Foundation. **18D:** Your body rotates 360 degrees. **26D:** Long, on-going story. **29D:** Integrated Circuit. **30D:** Slang for shifty, untrustworthy. **33D:** Symbol for dysprosium. **36D:** Alternative spelling. Youthful not old. **43D:** 11. **46D:** Astrological sign of twins. **47D:** California.

50D: In a church, a semi-circle recess often covered with a hemispheric vault. **53D**: Masters degree in Theology. **54D**: An entity started by the government to operate a commercial enterprise. **56D**: International Alliance of Women. **57D**: Arkansas. **59D**: Tin.

ELIZABETH BATHORY

A Hungarian noble woman, Countess Elizabeth Báthory de Ecsed and four of her servants were arrested and (**13A**) of torturing and killing hundreds of women and girls in a twenty-year span from 1590 to 1610. While Bathory served her sentence locked in the Castle, her (**37D**) faced execution. Some thought the (**2D**) were a witch-hunt, focused on destroying the influence of her family (**11A**) the time. However, over three hundred people testified against them and authorities found mutilated remains, dead and dying females at the time of her arrest. Bathory's family had direct ties to the ruler of (**1A**) and eastern Europe. Historians report Bathory suffered from (**35A**). Treatment at the time entailed placing blood on her lips from a non-sufferer or supplying her with blood and part of the skull from someone without the disease. Rumors developed claiming she bathed in the (**39A**) of victims to maintain her youth and beauty. Lesser gentry sent their daughters to gynaeceum at her castle to learn court etiquette. A Lutheran minister sent investigators to discover the truth. Family members of girls (**43A**) observed injuries on the deceased bodies and a significant amount of young ladies never returned from court. Some people believe Bathory may have served as muse for Braham Stoker's *Dracula* (**28A**) stories. Bathory died as a prisoner in her (**46A**) under suspicious circumstances.

14A: Vietnamese beef broth with rice noodles. **15A**: Not visible, foggy. **16A**: Law Enforcement. **17A**: Canadians end sentences with this exclamation. **18A**: University of Oregon. **19A**: Education. **23A**: Third-person present of have. **25A**: Suffix forming names denoting alcohol and phenols in chemistry. **27A**: In a way that is beneficial. **31A**: An area known for high temperatures, little rain, and sand. **33A**: Old English for small bird. **34A**: Nonconformists in South Wales during the 17the century. **37A**: Southeast. **40A**: Devil. **42A**: Additional Educational Need. **49A**: One. **50A**: Photograph obtained using x-rays. **56A**: The total number of electrons that an atom either gains or loses in order to form a chemical bond with another atom. **59A**: The elements of a situation. **60A**: Having a cautious distrust. **61A**: Donkey.

1D: Accurate story. **3D**: Latin for I do not wish. **4D**: Society for Neuroeconomics. **5D**: Youth VS Apocalypse. **6D**: Italian money. **7D**: Viet-Cong. **8D**: A book of maps. **9D**: Required. **10D**: Identification. **11D**: Ampere-hour. **12D**: Bottom is up, top is down. **14D**: "Lover" of sand. **17D**: Ecosystems MUltiScale modEling. **20D**: Currency. **21D**: Education for Employment. **22D**: Consumers Legal Remedy Act. **24D**: AudioVisual. **25D**: Chose. **26D**: To walk unevenly. **32D**: Relating to oil or fat. **38D**: Emergency Medical Technician. **40D**: To carry out. **41D**: Overextended. **43D**: Related. **44D**: A coastal Bantu tribe from SE Kenya. **45D**: Established the first free public deaf school in 1771 and is known as the "Father of the Deaf." **47D**: Tanzania Digital Inclusion Project. **48D**: Lear's macaw (Anodorhynchus __). **50D**: Shantou Institute of Ultrasonic Instruments. **51D**: French. Ignorant. **52D**: To move chi around the body. **53D**: RoboMaster of North America. **54D**: Alphabet. **55D**: Health and Retirement Study. **57D**: Incident Command Center. **58D**: Transformative Climate Communities.

BLOODY BENDERS

The Bender family settled land along the Osage Trail, the only road headed west. They set up a small (**18A**) and restaurant catering to travelers. About a dozen travelers disappeared within the vicinity. Locals believed the family may have (**19D**) from Germany. Father Bender spoke little English. Ma Bender spoke some but people described her as a "she-devil". Locals described the son as handsome, yet possibly simple. The daughter drew many visitors, advertising herself as a psychic and healer, offering to perform seances. She also advocated for free-love. Her personal writing hinted at a sexual relationship with her brother. Many believed the two weren't siblings, but actually married. The first body floated down a creek sporting a crushed skull and cut throat. A year later, in 1872, two more bodies were discovered. By 1873, travelers began avoiding the area due to the many disappearances. Vigilantes "arrested" a number of people for the (**4D**) but authorities later released them, due to lack of evidence. A man and his infant daughter disappeared in the area. His neighbor, a doctor, searched for him and disappeared as well. He had two brothers, one a military man who brought out fifty soldiers and questioned everyone about the disappearances. The Colonel stayed the night, then returned with soldiers after hearing of a young woman escaping after being threatened with knives. Upon questioning, Ma and Father feigned (**9D**) while the "kids" denied any knowledge of the alleged attack. The Colonel continued questioning the Benders and Ma broke character claiming a witch tried to poison her coffee. Sis suggested the Colonel return at the end of the week and she'd help using her clairvoyant skills. During a town meeting, officials decided to search every (**22D**) in the area. A few days later, a local rancher discovered the Benders' place abandoned and contacted authorities. Due to inclement weather, it took a few days before anyone could respond. They discovered nine bodies in shallow graves, all suffering from severe (**1A**) about the head and sliced throats- except one. A little girl was discovered with no obvious trauma. Authorities thought she had been strangled or buried alive. No one knows what happened (**45D**) the Benders.

12A: Fuel. **15A**: Having mixed feelings. 19th letter of the alphabet. **17A**: Limited Edition. **20A**: Leave. **21A**: Throat clearing to gain attention. **23A**: What fungi grow from. **24A**: Person who used to deliver milk. **28A**: Afternoon. **29A**: Sneaking a look. **30A**: Making smarter, funnier comebacks. **33A**: Plural term for priests in Iranian religions. **34A**: An intersection of two tracts forming the letter x. **35A**: Experimental Allergic Encephalomyelitis. **38A**: Organ responsible for circulation. **40A**: Hawaii News Now. **41A**: Fussing over something unimportant. **43A**: People from Israel. **46A**: Very small piece. **47A**: Montana. **48A**: Across the country. **51A**: New York. **52A**: Compact Disc. **53A**: Monetary unit of Indonesia equal to one hundredth of a dollar. Star Trek character. **55A**: Not you. **56A**: Commander in Chief of the Navy. **59A**: Leavening agent. **62A**: Mythical birds rising from the ashes. **65A**: Gender. **66A**: Staggering clumsily in the water.

1D: Boy scouts learn new skills to earn these. **2D**: Liquid Money. **3D**: User Behavioral Analytics. **5D**: Google Ventures. **6D**: Surname meaning gatekeeper. **7D**: Spanish exclamation. Myself. **8D**: Named Entity Recognition. **10D**: National Cheerleaders Association. **11D**: Men of higher class. **13D**: Everything. **14D**: Observing. **16D**: Street. **25D**: That is. **26D**: Killed, Kidnapped, or Arrested. **27D**: Cuckoo from warmer spots of America. **30D**: Having big breasts. **31D**: Swedish meaning to wait. **32D**: Kilometer. **34D**: The structures that funnel smoke from a fireplace. **36D**: Provided a response to a question. **37D**: A way in which something is done. **39D**: Video game console made by Nintendo. **42D**: District Attorney. **44D**: Lieutenant. **49D**: Ridiculous, stupid. **50D**: Department of Labor and Industry Relations. **54D**: Not closed. **55D**: Most. **57D**: Data Protection Officer. **58D**: Mental Health Unit. **61D**: Task Force. **63D**: Eleven. **64D**: Singapore.

HH HOLMES

American con artist and serial killer Dr. HH Holmes, denied and admitted to killing twenty-seven people, some who still lived at the time. His criminal history appears long and varied, including but not limited to: insurance fraud, bigamy, forgery, swindling, horse theft and (**15A**). Many of his crimes occurred in 1893 in Chicago around the time of the World's Columbian Exposition. (**34A**) built a three-story "Murder Castle" where many of his crimes occurred. Authorities charged him with one murder, his accomplice in many of his schemes. Officials suspected him of murdering his accomplice's (**59A**), several mistresses, some of their children, and a mistress's sister. Actual facts surrounding HH Homes are difficult to find due to the yellow journalism practices of the time and his own (**1D**) lying about … well, everything. The motives surrounding his murders entailed the person being a threat to his livelihood. While attending college, he and an instructor were suspected of graverobbing to obtain cadavers. Later, Homes admitted to using cadavers in (**40A**) scams. He also sold stolen cadavers to medical schools. Holmes stated he preferred to kill using (**49A**), chloroform or gases. He allegedly killed a train conductor and used his identity as he ran from other murder investigations. A mistress and her young daughter went (**30D**). Holmes divulged many stories but people believed her death resulted from a botched abortion and he killed the daughter. A corpse the right size and age of the girl was found (**61D**) his cellar. Holmes had another mistress sign over some property she owned in Texas. Her sister came to visit soon afterward and both women disappeared. Holmes used her name in several scams later on. Most of his victims bore insurance policies naming Holmes as the (**24D**). He killed his accomplice and three of his children solely for the insurance money. The Pinkerton National Detective Agency chased Holmes around the US and into Canada before catching him in Boston as he appeared to be fleeing with his third wife to Europe. The Hearst Newspapers paid Holmes $7500 for his story. After being found guilty, Holmes hung. But his neck didn't break. Instead, his body twitched for fifteen minutes before being (**1A**) dead. Holmes requested his coffin be filled with concrete and buried ten feet deep to deter a (**25A**). You'd have thought he'd donate his body to a medical school…

10A: Expression of grief. **14A**: Ay1. **17A**: Volleyball serve that scores a point without the opposing team touching the ball. **18A**: To unfreeze something. **19A**: Marinated meat. **20A**: Texas. **21A**: Greek Goddess married to Zeus. **22A**: A word for all rabbis. Prefix to show high rank or proficiency. **23A**: Peanut butter. **24A**: Young male. **28A**: Unable to bear weight on a foot. **31A**: 7th letter in the alphabet. Multiple printings of a book. **33A**: Latin: "I hate and I love." **35A**: Forest Service. **36A**: Carnivoran mammal of the Ursidae family. **37A**: Audible inhalation of surprise. **39A**: Reference. **47A**: Portugese: Box of, box that. **48A**: Chemical symbol for Chromium. **54A**: Reasonable, sensible. **57D**: Smallest and least populated island of Japan. **58A**: Revolver or pistol. **60A**: Cooking on a BBQ. **63A**: Chemical symbol for Nickel. **64A**: Youth Rehabilitation Order given to a juvenile after committing a crime. **65D**: Shrimp. **66D**: Latin. Scilicet.

2D: Moriori mythology: Wife of demi-god Maui. **3D**: Norse mythology. Annarr. **4D**: Range of spiritual and religious beliefs that rapidly grew through 1970s. **5D**: Offense or annoyance. **6D**: Modern reinterpretation of classic designs. **7D**: Intensely longed for. **8D**: Electronic Data Interchange. **9D**: Someone in power who acts cruelly. **11D**: Language Arts. **12D**: Thespian. **13D**: One considered visually and sexually appealing. **16D**: Hereditary

Hasidic leaders and spiritual guides, not a Rabbi. **26D**: Long gun for shooting great distances. **27D**: German nickname for bubble. **29D**: Turkish city. The largest city in the Mediterranean Region. **32D**: Military. **35D**: Federal Law Enforcement. **38D**: Personal User Experience. **39D**: Research Object. **41D**: Ruffians, wily jokesters. **42D**: Those living in water. **43D**: Night Ultimate Frisbee League. **44D**: Close-ended Funds. Traded like stocks but money doesn't flow in or out. **45D**: Placing items into a box or suitcase. **46D**: Crying out loudly. **51D**: Stock Market Abbr. Ameren Illinois Company. **52D**: Traditional Neighborhood Development. **53D**: An SI prefix and comes from the Greek word for dwarf. **55D**: Mythological man-eating giant. **56D**: House made of snow. **60D**: Good game. **62D**: Not Rated.

1	2	3	4	5	6	7	8	9	■	10	11	12	13
14			■	15					16	■	17		
18			■	19							■	20	
21			■	22			■	23			■	24	
	■	■	25				26			27		■	■
28	29	30	■	31								■	32
33			■	34		■	35		■	36			
37			38	■				■	39				
40				41	42	43	44		45				46
47							■				48		■
	■			49			50		51	52			53
54	55		56				■	57					
		■	58			■	59						
60		61			62			■	63			64	
65												■	66

JANE TOPPAN

In 1895, **(37A)** Jane began killing people she cared for as a **(43A)**. Twelve known victims, Toppan admitted to killing thirty-one victims using **(22A)** of opiates and **(1D)**. She felt a sexual release watching people as they teetered on the edge of death. Her father suffered from mental illness, at one point, he **(25D)** his own eyes shut. He dropped Jane and her sister at Boston Female Asylum where she stayed until serving as **(47D)** **(38A)** **(50A)** to a family. Her older sister went into an insane asylum. Toppan became a nurse and earned the nickname Jolly Jane due to her sunny disposition. However, she enjoyed mixing, matching and changing up prescribed medications, creating **(5D)** mixes. Fired from two hospitals, she began caring for patients privately in their own homes. Reportedly, she and her foster sister got along well, but that didn't deter her from killing her using strychnine. In 1901, she moved in with a family to care for **(33D)** elderly man, after she killed his wife. She ended up killing him, his sister, and two daughters. Remaining family members ordered a **(68A)** report on one of the daughters which determined she died from poisoning. Arrested and convicted for the murders, authorities deemed her insane. She fought the diagnosis and stated that she knew what she did, she knew **(19A)** was wrong, but still chose to kill. She was committed to a **(1A)** where she stayed until her death at age eighty-four. One of the Hearst **(14A)** printed her alleged confession to thirty-one murders.

12A: Ma. **13A**: Prefix for outer. **15A**: Kitchen tables and chairs. **16A**: Choose. **17A**: Yoctosecond, an SI unit of time equal to 10−24 seconds. **20A**: International Harvester. **21A**: Latin for silken. **26A**: Artificial language for international use that rejects all existing words and is based on an abstract analysis of ideas. **27A**: 100 liters. **28A**: Aircraft End of Life Solutions. **29A**: Emotional Quotient. **30A**: Profitable Growth Operating System. **32A**: Flat surface furniture. used to eat meals. **35A**: A metal tool used for cutting through wood. **37A**: Happy-go-lucky. **40A**: Large feline. **41A**: To visually comprehend the written word. **42A**: Moan, lament. **47A**: Atlanta Public School Technology and Innovation Competition. **49A**: A fiberglass or wooden plank worn on the feet to travel on snow downhill. **54A**: Colorado. **55A**: Phonetic spelling of "c". **56A**: Muslim. **59A**: Use of technology. **65A**: United States. **66A**: Very breakable. **67A**: The color of blood.

2D: Spanish for success. **3D**: Not. **4D**: Against kids age 13-19. **6D**: Surprised admiration. **7D**: Selective Service System. **8D**: Young Person. **9D**: Landlocked Marxist-Lennin State in Southeast Asia. **10D**: Higher. **11D**: Capital city of a state, country or nation. **12D**: In a way that affects the mind. **18D**: Electromechanical device that transmits angular information between two or more remote sites. **23D**: Spicy spinach-like vegetable. **24D**: Problem. **31D**: Shine. **34D**: Board. **44D**: United Kingdom. **45D**: French for rinsed. **46D**: Einsteinium. **48D**: Typeface calligraphy style font. **51D**: Ecological Company. **52D**: De-stress, enjoy one's self. **53D**: Uses pre-defined points in a video to automatically jump to the points. **57D**: Starch extracted from the pith of palm stems. **58D**: Lower Lumbar Instability Group. **59A**: Thick oil used on roofs. **60D**: Tagalog for just kidding. **61D**: Human Resource. **62D**: Small bug associated with lice. **63D**: Global Financial Crisis. **64D**: Independent Review Organization.

GILLES DE RAIS

A companion in arms of (**44A**), Baron Rais served as a knight and lord in the French Army in the early fifteenth century., fighting many a (**36A**). Aside from many military accomplishments, Rais was tried, convicted and condemned for the murder of one hundred forty or more children, heresy and (**27A**). Through inheritance, family connections and (**5D**), Rais owned a significant amount of property. However, the properties weren't necessarily income-producing. Maintaining a complement of 200 soldiers on horse-back ain't cheap. Since (**3D**) measures weren't an option, he sold off some of his properties to continue his lavish lifestyle, angering King Charles VII. He backed out of military life and began pursuing other interests. He sent individuals on quests to find a (**6D**) and a teacher of alchemy. He drew up a contract for the demon. After studying (**37A**) books, Rais began experimenting in his castle. After three tries, no demon appeared. His teacher suggested they needed to include parts of a child to entice the demon. At another evocation, he provided (**18A**) in glass vessels, but no demon. He spent a significant amount of money on his (**42D**) experiments. He decided he wanted some lands he had given to his brother and took them back. The church and the local duke disagreed. Besieging the castle, Rais took officials into custody. While he attempted to work out a compromise with the French monarchy, the church decided to investigate rumors of Rais murdering children. Just prior to the "torture for confession" part of the trial, Rais admitted to the charges. At his execution, the brush at the platform was set afire and he hung. His body was entombed at the Monastery of Notre Dame. Two servants were executed as well, their remains burnt in the fire and scattered in the wind.

1A: Someone who suffered at the hands of another. **11A**: Evil storm god represented as a black bird. **13A**: One. **14A**: The act of being strongly gassy. **17A**: Long Term Support. **19A**: Close by. __ __. **22A**: Egyptian god of fertility. **23A:** No longer. Use scissors. A group of atoms with a positive or negative electrical charge. **24A**: Years old. **25A**: River. **26A**: Overeaters Anonymous. **32A**: Pretending. **34A**: People taking advantage of. **35A**: Text slang. For sure. **39A**: Industrial Training Institute. **40D**: Set of plugins for coders allowing for quicker editing and creating. **41A**: Medium-size sailing ship of late middle ages. **43A**: Segments connecting points. **45A**: Suffix used to make inflected forms. **46A**: A cut-out used to transfer an image using a pencil, paint, etc. **49A**: Thank god. **50A**: The best. **51A**: Greater mouse-deer. **52A**: Us. **54A**: Forming part of a structure. **58A**: To end one's life. **61A**: See. **62A**: Central Standard Time. **63A**: Caught. **64A**: Smells, odors.

1D: Weaker traits, traits making someone more likely to be attacked. **2D**: Feeling of euphoria related to imbibing substances. **4D**: Instagram. **7D**: Forever. **8D**: Traditional standup fighting method from Thailand. **9D**: Optical Signal to Noise Ratio. **10D**: Nantucket. **11D**: Any unknown. **12D**: Unable to perform. **15D**: Southeast. **16D**: A written document on a specific subject for educational or professional purposes. **20D**: Any of various Chinese martial arts. **21D**: -2000 lbs. __ __ __. **28D**: Opportunistic Spectrum Access Medium Access Control. **29D**: Species of cichlid endemic to Lake Victoria. **30D**: Crypto Planets Collection from NFNTYCrypto.

31D: Montana State College. **33D**: Thing identified earlier. **35D**: A short forward pass to a back who is running toward the sidelines. **38D**: Generalized edema. **40D**: Thrown out. **47D**: Sensory input through the tongue. **48A**: Secretary. **52A**: Internet. **53D**: Early Childhood Development. **55D**: United States of America. **56D**: Auto. **57D**: II. **60D**: Utah University.

1	2	3		4	5	█	6	7	8	9	10	█	11	12
13			█	14		15					█	16		
17			█	█	18						█	█		
19		20	21		█	22						█		
23						█	█	█	█	█	24			
25			█	26		█	27	28	29	30	31		█	
32		33			█	34					█	35		
36					█	37				38				█
39			█	40				█	41			42		
43				█	44									
45			█	46	47					█	48			
49		█	█	50				█	█	51				
	█	52	53	█	54			55	56	57				
58	59		60			█	61			█	62			
63						█	64						█	

Chapter Seven

ART THEFTS

ISABELLA STEWART GARDNER MUSEUM

In the early morning hours in 1990, two men posing as (**11D**) gained entry into the museum by informing the guards they were responding to an alarm. They tied up the guards and spent an hour stealing (**1D**) works of art. In almost thirty-five years, none (**45**) the pieces have been recovered and the identities of the robbers is unknown. FBI and art dealers value the stolen works of art at hundreds of (**33D**) of dollars. The Museum is offering a (**1A**)-dollar reward for the safe return of the stolen works, the largest (**46A**) from a private institution. Pieces stolen include works from (**23A**), (**21D**), and (**33A**). A relatively valueless (**47A**) and a Chinese gu were included in the theft. Perplexed authorities question the choices of stolen paintings as many other more valuable works were left behind. The empty frames remain hanging in the gallery as a reminder of the theft and in hopes of the safe return of the pieces. Law enforcement suspected the (**10D**) but made no arrests. They believed the (**64A**) to be "too (**5D**) and foolish" to carry out the deed.

7A: More than one certificate of deposit. **9A**: Safe place. **10A**: Business selling alcoholic beverages. **12A**: Individual Contributor. **13A**: Lazy spud. **19A**: Commune in Loir-et-Cher Central France. **22A**: Lots of people at home. **24A**: Deep red-brown Pacific sea bream, delicacy in Japan. **25A**: Talking Horse, Mr. __. **27A**: Graphic Packaging International. **28A**: Artwork created from tile pieces. **30A**: Text shortened version of they. **31A**: Adult Education Program and Policies. **34A**: Not old – shining in the sky at night. **36A**: International News Media Association. **37A**: Corrections Officer. **38A**: Electronic Toll payment. **39A**: Hold one's self apart emotionally. **40A**: The numbers of. **43A**: What you have when you are alive. **49A**: Running Back. **51A**: Air and Space Forces. **52A**: Produces crude. **56A**: Before the Common Era. **58A**: Alabama. **59A**: Unable to bear weight on a foot. **60A**: British spelling of someone who saves others. **63A**: Last month of the year.

2D: Every. **3D**: Nevada. **4D**: My. **6D**: Basic monetary unit of Romania. **7D**: A food choice. **8D**: Slight breeze blowing through in a house __ the window. **14D**: Atop of. Two. Slab of hamburger. **15D**: Man. **16D**: Honey. **17D**: Pudding male. **18D**: French to kill. **20D**: Either. **26D**: Change the color of fabric or hair. **29D**: Plant growing in body of water. **35D**: Woo University. **40D**: Leaving the nation. **41D**: Cellphone. **42D**: Can't. **48D**: Physical work. **50D**: A large plant with a thick trunk, leaves and can grow for hundreds of years and hundreds of feet high. **53A**: Enterprise Asset Management. **54D**: Average Monthly Balance. **55D**: Placing a rag over one's mouth to hinder speech. **57D**: Cows chew this. **61D**: Vincennes University. **62A**: Latin for among other things.

MONA LISA

Italian (**5D**) painter, (**1A**) painted the Mona Lisa between 1503-1506. Historians believe the model for the painting was a noble woman, (**1D**) and that her husband (**11D**) the painting. No one knows why it was never given to the family. After da Vinci's death in 1519, King Francis I acquired the painting and it traveled to France and now belongs to the Republic of France. It has been displayed at the Louvre since 1797. In 1911, a former (**2D**) of the Louvre stole the painting. Initially, authorities weren't sure if it was stolen or if it was being (**72A**) somewhere else. The Louvre closed for a week while museum officials tried to discover what happened. At one point, Pablo (**35D**) rose to the suspect list. (**9D**), an Italian, walked into the Louvre, hid in a closet and after closing, walked out with the painting. He believed the painting belonged in Italy since da Vinci was Italian. He kept the painting hidden for two years before attempting to sell it to an (**64D**) gallery in Italy. Arrested instantly, Mona Lisa spent a week on exhibit in Italy before returning to the Louvre. She has been the focus of numerous political statement type of attacks which have led to the painting being placed behind bulletproof glass and visitors can only view it for thirty seconds. (**61A**) kept the painting in his bedroom at Tueleries Palace.

13A: I am. **14A**: LxWxH. **15A**: Part of the eye. **16A**: Sound made while meditating. **17A**: Getting a female animal fixed. **19A**: A light source providing UV rays. **21A**: An expression of pity. **22A**: Spanish for water. **23A**: An activity deemed illegal. **24A**: Perform an action. **25A**: Dessert with crust stuffed with fruits. **26A**: Protein-Losing Enteropathy. **28A**: Mother-in-law. **29A**: Organ used for sight. **31A**: Senior. **32A**: Italian pies with tomato sauce, cheese, vegetables and meats. **34A**: Jump. **36A**: Space Systems Integration Office. **38A**: Exclamation to gain someone's attention. **39A**: To the same extent. **41A**: Species of trees in the family Rubiaceae. **42A**: Criminal Investigation. **43A**: Lose control resulting from fear. **45A**: 12pm. **47A**: Text slang expressing surprise. **48A**: Killer whale. **51A**: Commanders in the Roman army. **53A**: Vehicles. **54A**: In addition. **55A**: European Commission. **56A**: Female egg cell. **57A**: Deteriorate. **66A**: Eras. **67A**: Department of General Services. **68A**: Take part in. **71A**: Old English.

3D: Votes in dissent. **4D**: Acute Respiratory Infection. **6D**: Knives. **7D**: Feeling let down. **8D**: American Railway Union. **10D**: Indian Society for Legal Research. **12D**: Urge someone to do something. **18D**: Alcoholics Anonymous. **20D**: Alternative Investment Management Association. **27D**: Lithium. **30D**: European Academy of Neurology. **33D**: Aunt. **37D**: Emblems, avatars. **40D**: Odessa College. **44D**: Now. **46D**: Occupational Exposure Limit. **49D**: To attack viciously. **50D**: Dice game where people bet on the rolls. **52D**: Having a particular kind of scenes. **58D**: European Association for Cancer Research. **59D**: Fabric with a ribbed surface. **60D**: Make. **62D**: Liters per Hour. **63D**: Educational Assistance Organization. **65D**: Not Taken Out. **69D**: Instagram. **70D**: Spanish for tea.

MONTREAL MUSEUM OF FINE ARTS

In 1972, three armed robbers took advantage of a broken (**61A**) and entered the Museum in the early morning hours. They tied up the guards, then stole eighteen paintings and thirty-eight other items. The robbery is the largest heist monetarily in (**12D**) history. It occurred over the Labor Day weekend, making it difficult to reach board members. Other news-worthy ordeals occurred at the same time, reducing media exposure for the theft. A (**23A**) landscape, works by Jan (**1A**) the (**2D**), Corot, Delacroix, Rubens, and Thomas Gainsborough, as well as some figurines and (**19A**) were nicked. The robbers tried (**33D**) (**40A**) the paintings back to the museum, returning one of the Brueghel's paintings to start (**14D**). The negotiations failed (**31A**) progress. At another point, the Museum paid $10,000 but didn't receive any actionable information. In 2017, authorities valued the loss at $11 million. Earlier, in 1933, someone hid in the museum and after hours, passed fourteen paintings through a window in the women's lavatory. A few months later, two halves of a painting were received by media outlets with a note stating the rest of the paintings would be reduced (**30D**) pieces if ¼ of the value wasn't paid. Luckily for the museum, one of the thieves committed a robbery and got caught after shooting an officer. He confessed to the paintings' theft. Fearing prison, he imbibed strychnine while in custody. In 1960, a gang of robbers attempted to steal Van Gogh paintings in a special exhibit. The robbery was thwarted but the gang escaped, unidentified.

5A: 1/12 of a foot. **10A**: Louisiana University. **11A**: A non-concrete concept. **13A**: Coated with a protective oxide layer by an electrolytic process in which the metal forms the anode. **18A**: Australian Tertiary Admission Rank. **20A**: Pennsylvania. **21A**: Plant defined with Sansevieria liberica in various botanical sources. **22A**: Agriculture. **26A**: Argentum. **27A**: Decay. **29A**: Assistance. **30A**: Stock Market Abbv. TransDigm. **32A**: Intelligence. **34A**: National Disability League. **35A**: Petroleum in raw form. **36A**: Body-in-White. **37A**: It was. **39A**: Artificial Intelligence. **43A**: Slice of pie. **44A**: Net Neutrality. **45A**: A thing's person. **46A**: Immigration and Nationality Law Review. **48A**: Cool, wonderful. **50A**: Involving all of the Earth. **52A**: Gums up with an ooze. **53A**: Person in charge of a dojo. **55A**: To soak up gravy using bread. **57A**: Saturday Night Live. **58A**: Something else. **59A**: Prescription. **60A**: Phalange on the foot. **64A**: Second letter of the Greek alphabet. **65A**: In a manner overflowing with anger. **66A**: Second Language.

3D: Sly. **4D**: Boy. **5D**: Someone who lives on a patch of land surrounded by water. **6D**: Contraction of not. **7D**: Specialty. **8D**: Intense dislike. **9D**: Having difficulty. **13D**: Partially open door. **15D**: Ouch. **16D**: Sendzimir rolling mill. **17D**: Effective Year Built. **28D**: People who live in a small city. **38D**: Southeast. **41D**: Groups. **42D**: Male-Female. **43D**: 3.14. **47D**: Sense that uses the tongue. **49A**: Determine the mass of an item. **51A**: Steals. **56D**: A loud reverberating sound of laughter. **62D**: You. **63D**: Tennessee. **64D**: Next to.

LA MAYER INSTITUTE FOR ISLAMIC ART

Housed in Jerusalem, burglars hit the Institute in 1983, stealing two hundred items, including paintings, clocks and watches. The Institute housed a wonderous (**1A**) from David (**30A**). A notable stolen watch, "The Mona Lisa of Watches", named Marie-Antoinette, disappeared as well. French-Swiss watchmaker, Abraham-Louis (**33D**) made the (**46D**) allegedly for Queen (**49A**), with an estimated worth of $30 million. The watch consists of 823 parts made with gold, platinum and sapphires. The guards admitted to sleeping through the robbery as the thief broke the alarm system. Due to the number of items stolen, authorities assumed multiple people were involved. However, the window used to gain entry proved small, difficult for an adult to fit through. The case remained unsolved for over twenty years until an (**16A**) appraiser from Tel Aviv contacted the museum informing them an attorney held many of the stolen pieces. The client inherited the stolen collection after her husband passed away. On his deathbed, he (**4D**) and told her to sell the items. Initially, she attempted to gain the $2 million reward but authorities negotiated it down to $35,000. Investigators found a warehouse, safety-deposit boxes owned by Na'aman Diller in Germany, Israel and the Netherlands. Police identified Diller's wife, Nili Shamrat, an (**12D**) expatriate, living in Los Angeles. A search of her home revealed more of the missing items. Authorities recovered more pieces from French bank safes. Of the 106 stolen (**37A**), investigators found 96. Shamrat received 300 hours of community service and a five-year suspended sentence for harboring stolen property.

14A: The first Hawaiian. **15A**: Purses or bags. **18A**: Greek god of War. **20A**: Morning caffeine beverage. **22A**: Cab. **23A**: One Step From Eden. **24A**: Piers. **28A**: Expanded Polyethylene for waterproofing items. **29A**: Propane. **33A**: Basic Linear Algebra Subprograms. **34A**: Raising up. **36A**: Ghost. **39A**: Police Department. **40A**: Spanish for you. **41A**: Happened before. **48A**: The Millenium Universal College Arab Emirates. **51A**: Short realistic Spanish play about Chicanos. **52A**: Any of several Asian and Pacific trees or shrubs (genus Cordyline) of the agave family with leaves in terminal tuffs. **53A**: Felt sorry for. **54A**: A medieval sovereign of China and ruler over the Turkish, Tatar, and Mongol tribes. **55A**: Latin for singing. **57A**: Near, close-by. **59A**: Unmanned Aircraft. **60A**: Tight, stressed. **63A**: Puke. **64A**: Very unhappy.

1D: Candy made from cocoa plant. **2D**: Louisiana. **3D**: Name meaning ancestor's descendant. **5D**: Will be Queen of England one day. **6D**: Organ Procurement Organization. **7D**: Letter of Undertaking. **8D**: Norwegian for hat. **9D**: Engineering Consulting Service. **10D**: Chaplain. **11D**: What a baby nurses on to obtain milk. **13D**: People prying into things. **21D**: Oil Spill Preparedness Regional Initiative. **24D**: The first dog meme crypto coin. **25D**: Symbol representing a sacred sound. **26A**: Items needed to be solved. **27D**: Kinnikinnick Native Plant Society. **31D**: American Institute of Physics. **32D**: Lakota Nation Invitational. **35D**: Imperative. **38D**: Keep going on. **41D**: An animal whose embryo develops in an amnion and chorion and has an allantois. **42D**: Movements. Steps taken. **43D**: Annoyingly picked at someone. **44D**: A unit of measurement in stating the speed of a moving object in relation to the speed of sound. **45D**: Kinetic Energy. **47D**: Dwarf buffalo. **48D**: Teepee. **49D**: Creator. **50D**: Something to do with ions or charged particles. **58D**: General Hospital. **61D**: Phonetic spelling of "s". **62D**: Southeast.

1	2	3	4	5		6	7	8	9	10	11	12	■	13
14					■	15							■	
	■	16		17						■	18		19	
20	21				■	■	■	■	■	■	22			
23			■			24	25	26	27		■	28		
29	■		30	31	32					■	33			
34		35					■	36						■
37							38			■		■		■
	■	39		■			40		■	41		42		43
■	44		■	45	46	47		■	48					
49			50											
51			■		52			■	53					
54			■		55			56		■		■		
■		57		58		■	59		■	60	61		62	
63					■	64								

BREITWEISER THEFTS

(**51A**) and author, Stephane Breitweiser boasts of stealing two hundred thirty-nine pieces of art from one hundred (**26A**) (**67D**) and galleries from 1995-2001. He traveled around Europe, employed as a (**9D**). About every fifteen days, he stole a piece, typically from smaller (**34D**). He kept the booty in his bedroom at his (**41A**) house in France. As an art connoisseur, he focused on (**1D**) works from the 16th and 17th century masters, calling himself the richest man in Europe. When arrested in Switzerland, Breitweiser's lookout and girlfriend, (**7D**) Kleinklaus, escaped and called his mother. His mother committed perhaps the worst crime of all: she destroyed paintings through fire and kitchen garbage disposal and threw vases, sculptures and jewelry into the (**60A**) Canal. During his trial, Breitweiser interrupted proceedings numerous times to clarify or correct details regarding the items he pilfered. The most expensive painting he stole was Sybille, Princess of Cleves by Lucas Cranach the Elder from a castle in Baden-Baden in 1995, worth approximately $5 million. He nicked it out of it's frame at a Southeby's auction. Authorities recovered one hundred ten items from his "private (**11D**)" with about sixty pieces being unaccounted for. Several items began washing up from the canal and they recovered most of the 107 items she tried to dispose of. In a later search (**50A**) 2011, 40 items were recovered from his home. Authorities found buckets of cash hidden totaling $163,000 in his mother's house, dispelling the belief he never sold any of the works. Typically, he either cut a painting out of a frame or removed the nails. Other objects he hid on his person while his girlfriend kept watch. His mother and girlfriend served about six months. Breitweiser never received more than three years at a time. In 2016, authorities began surveilling him when he tried to sell a stolen paperweight on eBay. Over the years, searches of his home revealed stolen items from numerous galleries.

1A: Loud noise. **7A**: Automobile Association of America. **9A**: Us. **12A**: Crying over. **14A**: Zephyr, the most persistent fixed-wing High Altitude Platform Station (HAPS) on the planet. **16A**: Artificial General Intelligence. **17A**: Having to do with the anus. **19A**: Islamic Studies and Arab Language. **20A**: A small memory card fitting into a camera and computer. **22A**: Alrighty then! **24A**: Old MacDonald had a farm. **25A**: Explain. **28A**: That is. **29A**: Four. **30A**: Air conditioner. **31A**: Reduced Instruction Set Computer. **33A**: Cylinder-like in shape. **39A**: Over-the-top. Streaming tv. **40A**: Spanish for to the. **43A**: Purple flowering bush from olive family, syringa. **46A**. Japan's northernmost main island. **48A**: Norse mythology. Personification of old age. **49A**: Customer Effort Score. What it takes for a customer to complete a task. **56A**: Eastern Oregon Net Inc. **57A**: To infuse or force air into. **58A**: Return on investment. **62A**: To work with. **63A**: Delaware. **64A**. Union of Enterprising Co-Operatives. **65A**: 0. **68A**: Missouri Sioux tribe. **69A**: Be quiet!

2D: Los Angeles. **3D**: Against Medical Advice. **4D**: Oldest of the three furies, responsible for punishing thieves, oath breakers and cheaters. **5D**: A vegetable that makes you cry. **6D**: Right. **8D**: Something happened twice or more. **10D**: Anything more? **13D**: Among other things. **15D**: A person born in the given decade. **21D**: More devily. **23D**: Karat. **27D**: Japanese cute hello. **32D**: Jupiter's volcanic moon. **35D**: Short message service for text messages. **36D**: Irish for post, mail. **37D**: To squeak by, survive. **38D**: Sanskript drg. the process on learning to experience the true Self, separate from the limited physical or ego self. **42D**: To make fun of. **44D**: Aluminum nitride. **45D**: Genus of the legume family. **47D**: Different from. **49D**: Large devices used by pirates during a fight, shooting large heavy balls at the enemy. **51D**: A virtual place online or in a magazine where people can talk. **52D**: Exclamation meaning boredom. **53D**: Deck of cards used by gypsies to tell the future. **54D**: Fake laugh. **55D**: German article a, an. **59D**: Oregon State University. **61D**: Economy. **66D**: Ohio.

MUSEU DE ART DE SAO PAOLO

Using a (**11D**) and a (**43A**) jack, three (**33A**) broke into the (**37A**) in 2007, stealing just two paintings. All told, the robbery occurred in under three minutes while four security guards changed shifts. Their take? Valued at $55-55 million. The museum lacked an actual alarm system, relying on guards and cameras. However, the cameras didn't have infrared capabilities and provided little information. Pablo Picasso's Portrait of Suzanne Bloch and Candido Portinari's (**1A**)(The Coffee Farmer) were the two stolen paintings. (**13D**) financial difficulties, the museum lacked funding for insurance. The thieves attempted to extract a hefty ransom from the museum. Luckily, (**50A**) authorities caught up with two of the thieves a few weeks later, believing an international crime gang to be pulling the strings.

14A: Bulgarian currency. **15A**: Cheekier. **16A**: Oxen. **17A**: Unskilled, dumb. **18A**: Street. **19A**: Regius Professor. **20A**: Victoria's Secret. **21A**: Reconsider a decision. **23A**: European Community. **24A**: Left Hand. **25A**: Votes against. **26A**: Emergency Room. **27A**: Musicians who rap. **31A**: A kingdom in West Asia and the Middle east with coastlines along the Red Sea and the Persian Gulf. **38A**: Morning. **39A**: Adrenomyeloneuropathy. **41A**: To exchange one thing for another. **46A**: Exhausting. **47A**: Natural Logarithm. **48A**: Nickel. **49A**: Uneasy. **54A**: Cream. **55A**: United Nations. **56A**: Home Equity Agreements. **59A**: Fleshy, nutritious fungus that will restore health. **60A**: Center of gravity. **61A**: A blood clot. **63A**: Not probable. **67A**: Stupid, lost. **68A**: Boomerang.

1D: Charles Dickens' book __ Twist. **2D**: Cover for a camera. **3D**: Avenue. **4D**: E-cigarette. **5D**: Equal or similar. **6D**: Hyphen. **7D**: Exit/entrance. **8D**: Remote Control. **9D**: Tiny. **10D**: Emergency Essential. **12D**: Made it happen. **22D**: National Aeronautics and Space Administration. **28D**: Student art society at Pembrook College. **29D**: Overly modest. **30D**: Sturmhaubitze. Rank II German Tank. **31D**: Cushitic ethnic group native to the horn of Africa. **32D**: Tagalog for repeated whispers or chants. **34D**: Region Municipality of York. **35D**: Oil. **36D**: Connected to. **40D**: Old German name meaning love. **44D**: Hardest gem. **45D**: Hexed, cursed. **51D**: A show that's been seen before. **52D**: Great energy in pursuit of a cause. **53D**: Estonian name meaning angel. **57D**: Large, flightless Australian bird. **58D**: Ambulance. **62D**: Obstetrician. **64D**: Slang for I know. **65D**: A Chinese unit of distance equal to .3 miles. **66D**: Nickname for Kanye West.

Chapter Eight

ROBBIN' THE BANK

WILLIE SUTTON

American (**55A**) (**31A**) Sutton spent forty years robbing banks, netting around $2 million. He spent most of his adult life behind bars. His skills transferred to breaking out of prisons, which he did three times. In the joint, the mafioso protected him, liking his stories and non-violent behavior. Sutton dressed up in a (**21D**) and carried non-loaded guns. His disguises included police officer, telegraph delivery, postman, messenger and maintenance man. He showed up just before the banks opened. If a baby cried or a woman screamed, (**19D**) wouldn't rob the bank. He carried either a pistol or a (**26D**) (**1A**) Tommy gun. The first (**42A**) from prison, he used a smuggled (**44A**) and a guard as hostage. While holding the guard, he got a 45' ladder to scale the 30' fence. Free for about 18 months, he was apprehended again for (**3D**) and spent eleven years inside before escaping with eleven other prisoners through a tunnel. Unfortunately, they hit the street at daylight and were instantly spotted. Running in separate directions, law enforcement scooped them all up quickly. Two years later, he and other convicts dressed as guards and carried ladders across the yard at night. When the spotlight hit them, Sutton yelled everything was okay. They escaped. Sutton hit #11 on the FBI's (**24A**) when it first came out. For five years he remained free. Then, an amateur sleuth spotted him on the subway and held him until the cops arrived. The Gambino Crime family deemed the man a "rat" and a contract was put out on him, shooting him in front of his house. Sutton received a compassionate discharge from (**39A**) in 1970 due to poor health and good behavior. He wrote two books about his crimes.

1A: Portable automatic firearm. **12A**: Elder son of Isaac. **13A**: National Endowment for Democracy. **14A**: *Waynes World, Master of Disguise, SNL.* Carvey. **16A**: Physical universe is thus understood as an immanent deity. **17D**: Eighth letter of alphabet. Yes. Layers. **19A**: In Japanese mythology, one of the Shichi-fuku-jin ("Seven Gods of Luck"). **20A**: Discontinued line of motion detective sensors released by Microsoft Xbox game console. **21A**: Create. **22A**: Orienteering Service of Australia. **23A**: Categorize. **27A**: Norwegian for something. **28A**: Round, globe. **29A**: Subtle digs. **34A**: University of Arizona. **35A**: Emotional Abuse. **36A**: Prose. **37A**: To dispute the honesty. **40A**: Eastern Roman patrician and master of soldiers. 400–471 A.D. **50A**: Finnish for oven. **51A**: Numerous accounts of non-sufficient. **54A**: Dad. **56A**: Owwie!. **57A**: To catch a criminal. **58A**: A form of play or support, following rules, using skills and/or luck.

1D: Each part of the calyx of a flower. **2D**: United States of America. **4D**: Traditional South African healing requiring murder to obtain body parts to use in medicine. **5D**: Grated milk product placed on chips for nachos. **6D**: Fixed in place. **7D**: Stock Market. New Mount Mining. **8D**: Education. **9D**: Aralia cordata, of the ginseng family. **10D**: Countries. **11D**: Repairs. **15D**: Black. **17D**: Eighth letter of the alphabet. Yes. Layers. **18D**: Popular, celebrities. **25D**: 2. **32D**: Binding Tariff Information. **33D**: A gold currency unit in pre-Meiji Japan. **38D**: Chemical symbol. U. **41D**: Brown nut similar to a walnut. **43D**: Fragment. **44D**: A multisubunit enzyme that contains both protein-protein as well as protein-DNA interactions. **45D**: Volume Unit. **46D**: A morsel. **47D**: Left Foot. **48D**: Vibration. **49D**: Outer covering of some fruits. **50A**: Finnish for oven. **51D**: International Development Association. **52D**: Kinetic Energy. **53D**: Senior High School.

ALVIN KARPIS

Deemed (**20A**) #1, Karpis proved to be the brains behind the (**21D**) Gang, thought to possess a (**20D**) memory. The public believed that Ma Barker ran the show, but Karpis stated that they sent her (**16A**) the movies while they planned and implemented a (**46A**). Another gang member believed the FBI tagged her as the boss after they killed her in raid, needing to justify killing a sixty-two-year -old mother. The gang "made" their money by kidnapping, robbing banks and committing burglaries. Karpis even robbed a train, netting $27,000. They didn't show any remorse or hesitation when it came to killing those who got in the way of their rewards. In 1936, the Senate railed at J. Edgar Hoover for the Depression Era criminals terrorizing America. Hoover vowed to capture Karpis himself. He didn't need to wait long. The (**7D**) Investigation located Karpis and swarmed his car. Unfortunately, all the agents forgot to bring handcuffs. A wiley agent used a suit tie to bind his hands. Karpis had the distinction of being the (**56A**) held prisoner at (**1A**) Penitentiary, serving twenty-six years. He was the only "public enemy" taken alive, as Dillinger, Pretty Boy Floyd and Baby Face Nelson were all killed in shootouts with the FBI. He resided at Alcatraz since it opened and until it's closure. He worked in the bakery. Upon closure, he transferred to McNeil Island Penitentiary in Washington where he met Charles Manson and taught him how to play guitar. Paroled in 1969, the US deported him to Canada. But after having his fingerprints removed via underworld surgeon, obtaining a Canadian passport proved difficult. He wrote a couple memoirs of his (**62A**) life and later moved to Spain where he died of an accidental overdose of pills and alcohol.

13A: Unemployment. **14A**: Specification. **15A**: More, leftover. **17A**: Slightly acidic. **22A**: Indian. Summer season. **23A**: A slang interjection meaning a comment is stupid. **24A**: 7th note of the scale. **25A**: Continuing education. **26A**: Original Equipment Reproduction. **27A**: Micro olive oil extraction machine. **28A**: Internet-Based Test. **30A**: None. **31A**: Delaware. **32A**: Not Satisfactory. **33A**: Overly tired. _ _. **36A**: Exist. **38A**: Orange County. **39A**: Food produced by bacteria fermentation of milk. **40A**: Killed. **44A**: Stopped a vehicle abruptly. **48A**: Interrogatories. **50A**: Playful skipping movements. **54A**: Optimistically looked toward the future. **56A**: The one stretching or reaching the farthest. **65A**: Form of literary art that uses aesthetic and often rhythmic qualities of language to evoke meanings in addition to, or in place of, literal or surface-level meaning. **66A**: Paying homage to those who came before us. _ _.

1D: Person with control, power. **2D**: Zodiac sign of the Lion. **3D**: Jump to a conclusion. **4D**: Toilet paper. **5D**: Fake. **6D**: An unintentional occurrence. **8D**: Erased on computer. **9D**: To study. **10D**: Radio TeleTYpe. A method of using tones to send digital messages between radios in amateur HF bands. **11D**: Plural of is. **12D**: Implements for climbing higher. **18D**: Water below 32 degrees. **19D**: United Nations. **25D**: Empathy for someone else. **29D**: Breast. **34A**: Biological Use Authorization. **35D**: Past tense for eat. **37D**: Greek god of carnal love. **38D**: Milk's favorite cookie. **41D**: Debit. **42D**: Fifth letter of alphabet. Do too much of something. **43D**: Prefix. Bad, abnormal. **45D**: Disqualification. **47D**: A protein coding gene. Acetyl-CoA Carboxylase Alpha. **49D**: Top. **51D**: Environmental and Occupational Medicine and Epidemiology. **52D**: Past tense of send. **55D**: Decentralization Autonomous Organization. **57D**: Tagalog for yes. **58D**: Neither. **59D**: Cryptocurrency

Ethereum. **60D**: Society for Reproductive Investigation. **61D**: Typical. **63D**: Registered Nurse. **64D**: Listening Reading.

FATHER'S DAY MASSACRE

Father's Day, 1991, someone identified themselves as the vice (**45A**) at the (**1A**) in the early morning hours. The bank recently made the decision to employ (**1D**) to secure the building. A guard allowed the man in. He shot the guard and hid the body. The robber then navigated the maze of the basement levels, heading to the control room where he shot the other three guards. He picked up all of his spent shells, took the VCR security tapes, turned off the alarm system, then headed to the vault room. Early morning tellers counted the Saturday night deposits. He ordered five tellers into the (**24A**) and locked them in. One teller escaped his sight by hiding under her desk. Unfortunately, the woman was frozen in fear. One of the (**3D**) located a broken metal spoon which she used to break out of the vault. The tellers raced up to the main floor and called for help. Other bank employees began to realize something appeared amiss. Law enforcement immediately locked down the fifty-two-story building and began searching. Authorities discovered the hidden teller and transported her to the hospital. On the second search of the building, investigators located the body of the first guard, hidden in the boiler room. An audit revealed approximately $(**9D**) thousand missing. However, the thief left $2 million behind. The (**40D**) Bureau of Investigations recognized the robber had intimate knowledge of the security protocols of the bank. Within two weeks, they charged a previous guard and police officer, James King. A jury found him (**38D**). Police watched him for years and never found the money. He suffered from (**51A**) and resided in a nursing home (**50D**) the end of his life. He maintained his innocence until his death. The (**12D**) has never been solved.

13A: Dissenting answer. **14A**: Adds up to. **15A**: One's opinion of one's self. **16A**: First letter of the alphabet. Your personal beliefs. **18A**: Laparoscopic Adjustable Gastric Banding. **19A**: Came to the understanding of (British spelling). **20A**: Ohio. **21A**: Throw a ball gently but high. **22A**: Melt in your mouth not in your hands. **23A**: Musical track containing more than a single but less than an album. **25A**: German physicist and medical botanist from the 1700s whose reference books are still used today. The plant genus Ebermaiera is named for him. **27A**: Slang for avatar. **29A**: HTTP:/ archive format. **31A**: Thickly populated. **32A**: Coherent. **33A**: Dysporium. **34A**: Government, Risk, Compliance. **35A**: Limited Liability Entity. **36A**: Estonian for crime. **39A**: Automatic Funds Transfer Services. **42A**: A sport played with rackets, balls and a net. Either teams of two or individuals. **43A**: English for ass. **47A**: Woody mouth piece used on clarinet and oboe. **48A**: Radio Guide. **49A**: Leather bottle for wine. **53A**: French built anti-ship missile. **55A**: Epic Nordic Folk Music band. **56A**: Calculated. **58A**: Covered in enamel. **59A**: Alone. **60A**: Seattle. **61A**: People who do things. **62A**: Christianity.

2D: 11th month. **4D**: Items used for a specific purpose. **5D**: Fees associated with membership or subscription. **6D**: America's favorite past-time. **8D**: Nurses Service Organization. **10D**: Accumulated money and assets. **11D**: Letgo my ___. Toaster waffle. **17D**: Basaltic lava. **20D**: Tagalog slang for over-acting. **26D**: Housing, shell. **28D**: At risk. **30D**: In a way that is honestly stating an error. **37D**: How much to use and what to use to make face appear younger? _ _. **41D**: Found, seen. **42D**: Polynesian and Australian woody agave plant. **44D**: Superman who fell off a horse and became paralyzed. **52A**: International Association of Laptop Orchestras. **54D**: Ex-all. **57D**: Unearned run.

ANTHONY HATHAWAY

Previously employed at Boeing (**42D**) a (**15D**) (**50A**), Hathaway received a back injury and developed an (**1A**), evolving into a heroin addiction. After losing his job, he began robbing banks (**47D**) the Seattle area to feed his addictions. Between 2013-2014, Hathaway admitted to robbing as many as (**23A**) banks. Initially, he wore gloves and a (**11D**) metallic fabric over his head. People began referring to him as the (**28A**) (**36A**). Drawing unwanted media attention, he switched things up and pulled a t-shirt over his head and cut out eye holes. Then, he gained the nickname (**54A**), based on the movie. His spree came to (**63D**) end when he robbed a branch bank at a Fred Meyer grocery store. The surveillance cameras caught enough of his vehicle to identify it. His total haul for thirty banks equaled $73,628. He pled guilty to four counts of first-degree robbery and (**32A**) count of felony theft. Convicted, he spent nine years (**12D**) prison, ordered to repay the amount stolen and (**2D**) banned from every bank he robbed. Apple TV+ created a show based on his life and there's also a podcast episode entitled, "Hooked".

16A: For this reason. **17A**: Regarding. **18A**: Woodcock. **20A**: Trademark. **21A**: A mark over a vowel (German, Hungarian) indicating different vowel quality. **25A**: Measure of energy. **26A**: Head-to-head matches. **27A**: Sandu Shui Autonomous County, Qiannan Buyei and Miao Autonomous Prefecture, China. **30A**: French, Latin meaning dark. Greek for Melaina. **33A**: Suffix added to pluralize nouns ending in s. **34A**: Deoxyribonucleic acid. **35A**: A man acts without empathy. **38A**: One who tries. **40A**: A northern constellation representing the lyre of Orpheus or Mercury and containing Vega. **41A**: National Health Care Association. **43A**: Milliliter. **44A**: One's mental make-up. **46A**: An exclamation of surprise. **48A**: Arabic female name meaning miracle. **52A**: Depression in the ground. **62A**: Southeast. **63A**: Books about one's self. **65A**: Not biased. **66A**: A lot of fuss about unimportant matters.

1D: Outtake. **3D**: Me. Mobile phone. _ _. **4D**: Ohio. **5D**: Paid policies covering damages to vehicles, homes, lives and medical. **6D**: Book holding lots of words and their meanings. **7D**: Accountable Care Organizations. **8D**: Diallyltryptamine. Tryptamine derivative. **9D**: Navajo for laughter. **10D**: Type of wine. Fruit that wine comes from. **13D**: Tenth month. **14D**: Personal enemy. **21D**: University California. **22D**: Advanced Organization of Los Angeles. Scientology. **24D**: Surgery to improve vision after cataract surgery. **29D**: Wild pig. **30D**: Medical Doctor. **31D**: Idaho. **33D**: Treated with ether. **37D**: Tattooed. **43D**: Product manufactured by Apple. **45D**: Compact Disc. **49D**: Finnish for wave. **51D**: Effective porosity does not include bound water. **53D**: Mexican form of currency. **54D**: European Union. **55D**: Explanation of Benefits. **56D**: Peanut butter and jelly. **57D**: Alexandria Ocasio-Cortez. **58D**: Nasal gastric tube. **59D**: Triple. Three. **60D**: Micro air vehicle. **61D**: New Hampshire. **64D**: Among other things.

GEORGE LEONIDAS LESLIE

The king of bank robbers, Leslie took part in 80% of the (**17A**) from 1869-1878. Educated as an architect, he opened his own firm in Cincinnati and made his riches providing shovels to the first transcontinental railroad. His father paid $300 for him to be "exempt" from the draft under the Union Conscription Act of 1863. Society frowned heavily on draft dodgers, even more so than deserters. When his parents passed away, Leslie decided to sell everything and move to New York City, hoping for a more anonymous existence. He met up with (**1D**), the biggest fence in New York. Prior to each robbery, he tried to find the (**48A**) of the bank. He studied and built a scale model. Sometimes, he'd obtain a safety deposit box or open a (**63A**) to study the inner workings. Other times, a gang member got a job as a security guard or (**31A**). Leslie gave them a list of questions to learn about the building. He paid off (**21A**) and (**9D**), ensuring he wouldn't be arrested. Marm would spend up to $3k preparing for the robberies. Leslie tried to stop the other (**59A**) of the (**54A**) from hurting people as violence made him uncomfortable. Leslie scored the largest robberies of the time period, $800(**13D**) and $1.6(**1A**). He spent months studying the vault type prior to the robbery. Using a "little joker", a piece of wire inserted into the lock that recorded the combination over time as the vault was opened, he entered the bank at least twice prior to robbing it. Once to place the wire and again to remove it. In 1878, during a robbery, a cashier was killed. Members of the gang worried Leslie might talk to the police. He put off the next robbery hoping to work with another gang. The heat turned up on the gang as law enforcement and the Pinkerton Detective Agency searched for them. One of his gang shot and killed him, ensuring he didn't speak to authorities.

7A: Help someone. **14A**: Emotionally distant. **15A**: Calcium carbonate concretion arising from the cellulose wall of cells of higher plants. **18A**: Laugh out Loud. **19A**: He challenged the Australian legal system, fighting for recognition of the rights of Aboriginal and Torres Strait Islander peoples as the traditional owners of their land. **20A**: Something small, delicate, barely there. **26A**: Australian Company Number. **28A**: Wonder. **29A**: Spanish for comrade, friend. **30A**: Iron deficiency anemia. **33A**: Doctor. **34A**: Doctor of the ear, nose, and throat. Education. **36A**: Liquidation Channel. **37A**: Following to learn from someone. **43A**: Acrid dull-yellow or brown resin, consisting of the concreted milky juice of several species of Euphorbia, cactus-like perennial plants indigenous to Morocco. **45A**: Historical Hindu practice where a widow throws herself on her deceased husband's funeral pyre. **49A**: Move in a circular direction, in whole or part. **50A**: American Association of Retired Persons. **52A**: Operating System. **53A**: Utah Tech. **56A**: To get revenge after someone has hurt someone you care for. **62A**: Male sibling.

2D: International Lunar Observatory Association. **3D**: Gently tossing a ball high in the air. **4A**: Spanish for wolf. **5A**: Nigerian city famous worldwide for its ancient and naturalistic bronze, stone and terracotta sculptures, dating back to between 1200 and 1400 CE. **6D**: Naval Criminal Investigations. **7D**: Spiritual Sensitivity Scale. **8D**: Utah. **10D**: Latin. To strike. **11D**: Type of artistic expression using petroleum colors using brushing. **12D**: Right. **16D**: Abominable snowman. **20D**: Hope for something to happen, out loud. **21D**: Job fixing holes in clothes. _ _. **22D**: Ouch! **23D**: An open area of grassy or arable land. **24D**: Technical. **25D**: North Dakota. **27D**: Moved freely through a closed area. **32D**: Feeling of deep anxiety or dread. **35D**: Female hormone. **37D**: Shepperd. **38D**: Behind on a bill. **39D**: Decibels relative to Isotropic. **40D**: Operator Identification Number. **41D**: Phonetic spelling of what. **42D**: Integrated Management System. **44D**: Archaic spelling of a sound a cat makes. **46D**: Gold. **47D**: Add in. Place into something. **51D**: Emergency Vehicles Operation Course. **54D**: Prefix meaning Earth. **55D**: National Security Information. **56D**: Arch. **57D**: European Theatre of Operations. **58D**: National Hispanic University. **60D**: I. **61D**: Blood Pressure.

1	2	3	4	5		6	■	7	8	9	10	11	12	13
14					■	15	16					■		
17							■	18			■			
19				■		■	20				■			
	■		■	21	22	23		24				25		
26	27	■	28			■	29			■	30			
31										32		■		
33		■		■	■	■	■		34			35		
36		37		38	39	40	41	42			■		■	
43		44							■	45	46		47	
48									■	49				
50			■		■	■	■		51	■		52		
53		■		54		55		■	56		57	58		
59		60	61			■	62							
■	63													

Chapter Nine

HEISTS

SENTRY ARMORED CAR COMPANY

In 1982, a security guard for an (**2D**) company, Sentry, worked with three other men to steal $11(**9D**) from the Warehouse the cash, coins and food stamps were stored. Initially, Christos Potamitis told (**1A**) that robbers entered through the (**39A**) and into the office, (**17D**) him and stole the (**15A**) after tying him up. His story unraveled quickly when investigators found no signs of forced entry. Law enforcement focused on Potamitis as he was the only guard on duty at the time. Eddie Argitakos, an (**52A**) at a travel agency, was identified as the mastermind behind the robbery. Potamitis' (**51A**) helped the (**44A**) hide some of the money. A fourth fugitive, Nicholas Gregory, had not been located. (**64A**) offered deals (**41D**) a return of the funds but the defendants only returned about $1m, with the hopes of living high on the hog at some point. The thieves received fifteen years in prison and $35k in fines. In the course of the investigation, authorities discovered that three corporate (**42A**) and another bean counter misappropriated $29 (**16A**). Through a series of shell games, they appeared to skim from accounts as they transferred and transported funds. Sentry ended up going out of (**36D**).

12A: 17th Greek letter. **13A**: Going. **18A**: Person in charge at work. **19A**: Between. What a young, wingless insect forms. _ _. **22A**: Metric unit of measure equal to 100 sq meters. **23A**: When you go in. **24A**: Infrared. **25A**: Chemotherapy combo of drugs: epirubicin cyclophosphamide. **26A**: Prefix. To reduce, bring down. **27A**: Excited. **28A**: Star of *Casablanca.* **29A**: Landlord. **30A**: Information technology. **31A**: Railroad. **33A**: Northeast. **34A**: French for yew. **36A**: Basic Science Academic Evaluation Board. **45A**: 5th letter of the alphabet. Short for honey. **46A**: Parents' male child. **47A**: Tie to a post. **49A**: Mishbi University. **54A**: LxWxH. **56A**: Illinois. **57A**: Two people physically taking each other down on mats using special holds. **59A**: Diana. **60A**: People covered in sores and body parts falling off. Used to be a major issue with colonies set up to care for patients. **62A**: Informal.

3D: Belonging to which person. **4D**: Forever. **5D**: Using wings to soar in the sky. **6D**: Remote control. **7D**: One who comes. **8D**: Title of Muslim ruler. **10D**: Makes things bigger. **11D**: Stock Market abbrv. Gulf Insurance and Reinsurance. **14D**: Bring into effect. **18D**: To a great degree. **20D**: Not to exceed. **21D**: The physical lay of the land. **27D**: Ike, the 34th President of the US. **32D**: Revenue. **35D**: Exosome complex genes, which encode a multi-protein intracellular complex, mediate the degradation of various types of RNA molecules. **37D**: Dark beers. **38D**: Figuring out if a new computer app works ok. **40D**: Not his one, but that one. **43D**: Like items grouped together. **45D**: Electronic messages. **48D**: World of Warcraft character.. **50D**: Donkey. **53D**: American Type Collection Culture. **55D**: Autoimmune Deficiency Syndrome. **58D**: Regret. **63D**: In computers, the command to list files in a Unix, Unix-like system.

DUNBAR ARMORED ROBBERY

In 1997, Allen Pace III and five childhood friends robbed the Dunbar warehouse of $18.9 million. Pace worked for the Dunbar Armored (**12D**) as a guard. He scoped out the warehouse, noting the (**9D**), patterns of the guards and specifically, how the money remained secure in the vault. Taking pictures of the interior, he (**2D**) the burglary. The day before the heist, Dunbar fired him after employees discovered him messing around with the (**1A**). The next night, the friends went to a house party, (**11D**) an alibi. Providing the group with a shotgun, masks, pistols and radio headsets, Pace led the group inside. On Friday nights, the vault remained open due to the frequency of money coming (**21A**) and out. Using his key, they entered the building and waited in the cafeteria. As the guards came in one by one, the group disabled them, binding them in duct tape. Once they bound all of the roaming guards, they rushed the two protecting the vault, easily (**3D**) them without firing a shot. Due to his employment, Pace knew which bags contained the highest (**6D**) in non-sequential numbers. They quickly loaded up a U-haul van, escaping cleanly. Using an attorney and his paralegal the group laundered a significant amount of the money through real estate and business ventures. Two years later, one of the group made a critical (**55A**): he purchased property, paying in cash— with the bank bands still wrapped around the wad! Concerned, the real estate agent went to the police. He immediately confessed, naming the other culprits. Pace received twenty-five years in prison and the rest received lesser sentences. (**1D**) only located about $5m of the stolen funds.

13A: Descend, dismount. **14A**: Yes. **15A**: British spelling for ass. **16A**: Energy device that disables a person through electrical shock. **18A**: The act of being naked. **19A**: Text slang. Take care. **20A**: Hydroxyoctadecatrienoic acid. **22A**: Progenitor of the Edomites. **23A**: Older Kansas Employment Program. **24A**: Trough. **26A**: Bedroom. **27A**: Wandering. **29A**: Cold garlic and oil sauce. **30A**: Monday-Wednesday. **31A**: Unique, rare. **34A**: Person who fixes computer issues. **35A**: Attempted. **37A**: Alabama. **38A**: Dull, lifeless eyes. **39A**: International Eco Nature Run. **40A**: Stuck with a pointy thing. +ly. **42A**: Honoris causa. For the sake of honor. **43A**: Sticking something into something. Dunking. **45A**: Used in cooking during the 1930s-1970s. Similar to margarine or butter. **46A**: German manufacturer of railway maintenance machines. **48A**: Original Gangsta. **49A**: African antelope. **50A**: New Mexico. **51A**: Sharp or angled side of an item. **53A**: General Practice. **54A**: Associate degree in Arts. **61A**: No charge. **64A**: To add to. **67A**: Use of sound waves to take internal pictures.

4D: Unique, extremely hard to find. **5D**: Phonetic spelling of "l". **8D**: Using a hoe to hoe a row. **10D**: Living room. **17D**: Alrighty. **25D**: Ceodes umbellifera. **28D**: 12th Greek letter. **36D**: Regarding. **44D**: Lyrical writing expressing ideas. **47D**: A gem found in an oyster. **52D**: Local Authority Designated Officer. **56**: It is. **57D**: Skin darkened by the sun. **58D**: Kinetic Development Group. **59D**: Goddess or Valkyrie associated with medical skill. **60D**: Small hard seed in a fruit. **62D**: Eat. **63D**: Emergency Room. **65D**: Teacher's Assistant. **66D**: Ohio.

PIERRE HOTEL

On January 2, 1972, a gang of thieves made up of (**9D**) members and career thieves robbed the vault at the Pierre (**3D**) early in the morning, knowing the vault would be full of jewelry after New Year's festivities. Not only did the (**19A**) make the *Guinness Book of World Records* for the $3(**64A**) booty, but the gang members decided to (**45A**) each other. Samuel Nalo planned and organized the heist. Members of the (**1A**) family and (**7D**) family took part in the robbery. The gang wore disguises and carried guns. (**43D**) the hotel early in the morning, few (**37A**) were on shift and the guests slept. The gang rounded up (**61A**) employees and handcuffed them, unless they looked ill, and referred to the hostages as "sir" and "madam". The entire robbery lasted two and a half hours as the burglars broke into about fifty lock boxes in the (**26D**), only breaking into boxes where they recognized the names. One robber gave each employee a $20 bill, except the guards. Afterwards, Nalo took the stolen baubles to the Lucchese crime family to fence. Demanding a 33% (**11D**), Nalo took the bulk of the haul to Detroit to another fence. Nalo owed a large amount to bookmakers who threatened his life. An informant turned Nalo and another member (**41D**). The Detroit (**49A**) turned over $750k worth of jewels, fearing arrest. Another fence took what he had in his possession and fled (**62D**) Mexico. Two other gang members read about the arrests and relinquishment of goods. Fearing arrest and believing they had been swindled, they fled to (**4D**). Robert Comfort helped plan the heist, took the goods he possessed to the Rochester Crime family to fence. When he went back, they refused to give him the jewels or the money and almost killed him. Another gang member, Donald Frankos, expected to receive $750k but was only paid $50k. Over time, Frankos and two other gang members received $175k. Nalo received whatever jewels hadn't been ripped off by his friends. Frankos threatened to kill Nalo for ripping him off, but someone beat him to it. Frankos let Comfort live, believing he got ripped off too, and was lucky to be alive. But he killed the two who escaped to Europe. When (**39A**) was said and done, Nick "the cat" Sacco received $2m and is the only one alive, living comfortably in witness protection. But that's another story.

12A: Oxford University Press. **13A**: Excitement and mystery associated with love. **14A**: Italian for master. **17A**: Yavapai College. **18A**: To gradually get rid of something. **22A**: Article worn on one's head. **23A**: Local Positioning System. **24A**: Iron. **25A**: Hebrew for spring. **27A**: Genus of flowering plants in the family Araceae. **29A**: Snake-like fish living in oceans. **31A**: Sexual Abuse. **33A**: Massachusetts. **34A**: A specific amount of time. **35A**: Tennessee. **36A**: Marine Expeditionary Unit. **40A**: What gender you are now, you were at birth. **42A**: Randomized neural networks for blood cell classification. **44A**: Tin. **50A**: Specialist in Arabic language and/or culture. **52A**: Covered in spikes, prickly. **54A**: Not Applicable. **56A**: Marrow belongs? **57A**: A portable structure used in camping. **58A**: Research and Information for developing countries. **59A**: Executable file on the hard drive providing machine code. **60A**: A period of time. **63A**: Significant Other. **65A**: The 18th and 7th letters of the alphabet. **66A**: Serial Number.

1D: Organ system made up of lymph nodes, marrow, spleen, etc. **2D**: Animals different from humans. **5D**: Marriage mate. **6D**: When tears fall.**8D**: I am. **10D**: Phonetic spelling of "n". **15D**: Punjabi for engage. **16D**: Steamship. **20D**: Saves. **21D**: The quality of being unaffected by time. **28D**: Something tastes good! **30D**: Always on someone's side. **32D**: Greylag goose. **38D**: Genus Paeonia. **45D**: Crinkle in a car. **46D**: University of California. **47D**: Not malignant. **48D**: Electronic Arts. **49D**: The end. **51D**: Mountain range in Wyoming. **53D**: Prefix. Near, around. **55D**: Remains after a fire burns.

LUFTHANSA HEIST

In 1978, several (**42A**) worked together to plan the biggest heist in America at that time. A guard (**17A**) the (**55A**) terminal at John F. Kennedy Airport told his bookie that large amounts of money arrived regularly at the airport on the Lufthansa airline. James Burke, associated with Lucchese Crime family, planned the robbery with the aide of two employees of the airline. Members of the Bonano family and Gotti family were involved as well. Using a black (**32A**) six men cut off the gate lock and entered the (**1D**) and tower. In the parking lot, a late model Buick with more (**19A**) waited. Eight employees were quickly caught and placed on the (**1A**). Another employee driving by noticed the black van and mask-clad driver. He attempted to call for help but the van driver (**66A**) him and took him to the other hostages. With inside information, the crew opened the two locked doors to the vault, knowing one door needed to be closed prior to opening the second door. The gang absconded with seventy-two fifteen-pound cartons in untraceable money and jewelry. None of the money was ever recovered. But the story doesn't end there! To ensure they weren't caught, the vehicles were to be disposed of in John Gotti's landfill. But one of the men failed to follow through, leaving the van in front of his apartment. Law enforcement and the Federal Bureau of Investigation found it within days. Burke, worried he'd get arrested, ordered hits on nine people involved in the heist. Five others died by (**48A**) means within a few years. One person was convicted in the heist, Louis Werner, the guy who owed $20,000 to a bookie, but he knew better than to name names (**24A**) mention what happened to the booty. Reportedly, Donald Frankos was angry he hadn't been included in the heist.

15A: Caesar's Mushroom. **16A**: Moist and watery. **18A**: District of Columbia. **22A**: Latin for he, she, it. **25A**: Vessels to hold liquids to drink. **26A**: Magic user. **27A**: Passage of minutes and hours. **31A**: Active Living No Limits. **38A**: Perhaps, a possibility. **39A**: Resource to Kill Ratio. **40A**: Hindu queen. **41A**: Zone of the Interior. **45A**: International Gemology Institute. **46A**: Not yet final or absolute. **47A**: Designated hitter. **53A**: Round ball. **62A**: Evenings. **63A**: Permanent professional armies.

2D: Ethiopian Semitic language. **3D**: Norwegian for devil. **4D**: Western Bukidnon Manobo. Path. **5D**: Lassie says, "__ fell down the well!" **6D**: NGAN'GI. Ages, a long time ago. **7D**: Egyptian Sun god. **8D**: Water below freezing. Heat injury. **9D**: Arachidonic acid. **10A**: Unpleasant feelings triggered by real or imagined events. **11D**: Landing ship, tanks. Developed during WWII for amphibious assaults. **12D**: Over-eaters Anonymous. **13D**: A personal traumatic event. **14D**: Identified as someone you've meant before. **20D**: Emcee. **21D**: Extended Play. **23D**: Acting for the concern only for one's self. **26D**: Abaca. **28D**: Lord Voldemort's uncle, __ Gaunt. **29D**: Sumerian god of wisdom, freshwater and mischief. **30D**: Florida. **33D**: Spanish for gold. **34D**: Motivational, size-inclusive, and innovative activewear brand in Denver. **35D**: Delete. **36D**: Contains amino acids and is an intravenous infusion, which is given as a part of intravenous nutritional therapy. **37D**: Black tropical American cuckoos. **43D**: Before the present. **44D**: Foreign Internal Defense. **49D**: A village in Ardahan Province, Turkey. **50D**: Japanese for the way of tea. **51D**: Toilet paper. **52D**: A commune in the French department of Corse-du-Sud, collectivity of Corsica, France. **54D**: Grass plant growing in water or marshy area. **56D**: United States Pharmacopeia. **57D**: Federal Tax Information. **58D**: Helium cryptocurrency. **59A**: No, none. **60D**: Snow. **61D**: Sound of frustration. **64D**: Artificial intelligence. **65D**: Roleplay.

LOOMIS TRUCK TRAILER HEIST

(46A) 1999, an armored Loomis truck with an (3D) trailer left Sacramento traveling to San Francisco. The driver and two guards traveled in the truck. The (1A) had a locking, alarmed door, and no ladder. The truck traveled up (26A) 80, taking just over two hours to make the trip. The truck pulled through a scale and only stopped at lights and signs, as needed. When they opened the truck doors after arriving at the depot, all that remained in the truck was a wet floor. Looking up, the top of the roof had (20A) been cut open and the money was gone. During the trip, the driver and guards noticed nothing amiss. About 270 pounds had been removed, $2.3 million. The (37A) of (10D) looked into the heist and determined the roof was cut from the outside. The FBI cleared the driver and (17A). The only clue left behind was a (58A) military bag from the 1950-60s with the initials "MOV" and a travel tag from the (51A) (30A). Eventually, two witnesses reported seeing someone jump off the truck while it slowed down to stop at the scales near Solano Community College. Dressed in dark clothing, the man didn't appear to be carrying anything. Authorities surmise the robber or robbers jumped on to the trailer from the Loomis depot, then spent the next hour cutting through the roof. They believe the robbers threw the bags out alongside the road for accomplices to pick up, assuming they followed behind the truck.

14A: A warming of the ocean surface, or above-average sea surface temperatures, in the central and eastern tropical Pacific Ocean. **15A**: Morning caffiene beverage made by steeping bags of leaves. **16A**: The finish line for the Ididarod. **18A**: French for want. **19A**: Recreational Equipment, Inc. **23A**: Minimal Detectable Effect. **24A**: People who operate something. **25A**: New. **33A**: International Barcode Of Life. **34A**: Anoint. **36A**: Blood and guts. **40A**: Latin. Folio verso. **41**: Equal Opportunity. **42A**: Slang for too true. **43A**: Electrical engineering. **44A**: Old-fashioned. **47A**: Destruction of tissue by freezing. **49D**: Area of land along a body of water. **53A**: Applied to design, emphasis on function using math and science. **56A**: August. **59A**: Ranger Station. **60A**: Married engineer company. Built the Eames house and Eames lounge chair.

1D: Sea between modern-day Turkey and Greece. **2D**: Loma Linda University. **4D**: Covered in mud. **5D**: Publish music, artwork or a book independently. **6D**: Nitrous Oxide. **7D**: Montana. **8D**: Power inherent in a person in conjunction with Tao. **9D**: Officer in a park. Challenged someone to do something. _ _. **11D**: Lookout Education. **12D**: Imitator. **13D**: Count on someone. **20D**: Germanic tribe around the same time as the Anglos and Saxons. **21D**: Seaward. **22D**: Global Recycled Standard. **26D**: International Law Student Association. **27D**: Not Rated. **28D**: On the subject of. **29D**: Part of something. **31D**: People native to the Aleutian Islands. **32D**: Immigration and Employee Rights. **34D**: Influenced. **35D**: Not going to happen. **38D**: Cow hide. **39D**: Annoys, irritates. **44D**: Month, day, year. **45D**: Icelandic for sand. **46D**: Problem. **48D**: Cambodia's busy capitol. **49D**: A shelter to keep animals that's inescapable. **52D**: Lane. **54D**: 13th Greek letter. **55D**: Grand Tourer. **57D**: General Secretary.

Chapter Ten
JEWELRY THEFTS

ANTWERP DIAMOND HEIST

Over a weekend in 2003, robbers stole loose diamonds, gold, silver and jewelry totaling over $100 (**32D**) in losses. (**45A**) targeted a vault two floors below the main floor, with numerous security measures in place. Security measures included a (**31A**) with (**11D**) million possible (**55A**), an infrared sensor, dopple sensor, magnetic field and seismic sensor. The (**13A**) boasted it's own security force as well (**67D**) being in the heavily patrolled and monitored (**1A**) District. Preparing for the heist took eighteen months. Leonardo Notarbartolo rented a room in the diamond district, portraying a diamond merchant, allowing security to grow accustomed to his presence. The band of thieves placed a camera above the door to the vault, catching the code entered by guards to gain entry. They placed a recording device in a fire extinguisher to record data from the camera. Notarbartolo sprayed hairspray over the infrared detector, a temporary fix until the team disabled the (**70A**). To avoid all the (**63A**), the King of Keys picked the lock of the (**1D**) building next door sharing a balcony and garden. Using a polyester shield, (**54A**) reached the heat sensors and blocked it from picking up the robbers until he deactivated it. The Genius built an aluminum plate to take care of the magnetic field. The King of Keys duplicated the foot-long vault key, then found the original key in a storeroom and stole it. The Monster entered the vault and deactivated the wiring in the ceiling to the alarms and sensors. Styrofoam boxes and light sensors blocked the heat sensors. Using a hand-cranked jack, the King of Keys broke the locks on the boxes and dumped the contents into duffle bags. Unfortunately, law enforcement tracked the team down after Speedy suffered a panic attack while disposing of the evidence. He threw it in a bush in the woods. The perpetrators were caught. They served their time. None of the stolen items were ever recovered.

14A: Short for Leonard. **15A**: Exempli gratia. **17A**: Ampere. **18A**: Plant substance placed on burns. **19A**: The solmization syllable used for the semitone between the fourth and fifth degrees of a scale. **20A**: French military and political leader during the French revolution. Possessive.**25A**: What a tire goes on. **27A**: Someone you look up to. **28A**: Yuck. **30A**: Bone in arm. **34A**: Eww. **35A**: Identification. **36A**: In vitro diagnostics. **37A**: Equal Opportunity. **38A**: Phonetic spelling of "s". **40A**: Legitmate. Physically present. **41A**: Add points for your team. **43A**: Someone who believes god created the earth but walks away after that. **46A**: Landlord. **47A**: Greek bread shaped like a pocket. **49A**: Daily Driven Exotics. **50A**: British spelling for people living next to you. **59A**: A top cellular service provider. **60A**: Items sent back. **62A**: Merit, excellence and intelligence. **66A**: Through. **68A**: District of Columbia. **69A**: South Korea multi-national auto manufacturer.

2D: Non-Uniform Memory Access. **3D**: A kayak in rough water. **4D**: Waiting List. **5D**: Education. **6D**: Rhode Island. **7D**: Promissory note. **8D**: Dollar General. **9D**: Everyone, everything. **10D**: Cat verbalization. **12D**: To protect against an offense. **16D**: Venomous lizard from SW Arizona. **21D**: British spelling for strong smells. **22D**: Necklace that opens up. **23D**: Large four-legged antlered mammal. **24D**: Require. **26D**: Environmental Law Institute. **29D**: Asking about one or another from a defined set. **33D**: Actively stay away from. **39D**: Chosen. **41D**: Those who initially play in the beginning of a game. **42D**: The first woman. **44D**: Stupid, moronic. **47D**: Palm Beach International. **48D**: Blind eel, hag fish. **51D**: General Motors. **52D**: Extra blockers on running plays that can catch throws from quarterback. **53D:** The law of a place where property is situated. **56D:** Opportunistic Underwater Sensor Network. **57D:** Hebrew for no. **58D:** Ship Navigation and Voyage Optimization. **61D:** Term of respect for a man. **64D:** Artificial Intelligence. **65A:** Mother.

1	2	3	4	5	6	7	8	■	9	10	11		12	■
13								■	14			■	15	16
17			■	■	■	■	■	18					19	
20			21	22	23		24	■	■	25		26		
	■	27				■	28	■	29	30				
	■	31			32			■	33					
	■	34		■	35		■	36			■	37		
38	39	■	40			■	41			42	■			
43		44				■	45							
■	46		■		47		48		■	49			■	
50			51	52				53	■	■		54		
■	55							■	56	57	58	■		
59			■		■	■	60					61	■	
62			■	63	64	65				■	66		67	
■	68		■	69			■	70						

AMERICAN MUSEUM OF NATURAL HISTORY

'(**62A**)', Jack Roland Murphy, targeted the JP Morgan jewelry collection at the Museum stealing 24 precious gems in the biggest (**23A**) (**43A**) in 1964. He stole the (**6D**), (**2D**) and (**1A**). After casing the joint, Murph realized that security was severely lacking to non-existent. The burglar (**17A**) failed to work and nineteen (**56A**) remained open two inches at night for ventilation. The thieves crawled through a window and discovered the (**45D**) on the display case was non-operational. The stolen jewels valued at over $400,000. Authorities arrested Murph and his accomplices after the hotel they stayed at reported them for throwing lavish parties. Police found (**11D**) and charged the men. They were released and fled to Florida. Law enforcement arrested Murph and his accomplice later for robbing and assaulting Eva Gabor. The accomplice told police where the gems were stored in exchange for a lighter sentence. Authorities found all the gems except for the Eagle Diamond which they believe the robbers cut down into pieces. The burglars served three years.

13A: Hard covering on the end of finger and toe. **14A**: Japanese for sun. **15A**: Two. **16A**: How many years old. **18A**: A woven floor covering. **20A**: Nickname for sargeant. **21A**: Needing to eat. **24A**: Open Educational Resource. **26A**: Language Server Protocol. **27A**: Clinical Fraction Full-Time Equivalent. **28A**: Deep-Learning Auto-Encoders. **30A**: Japanese grill. **34A**: Spear-like. **36A**: Person in charge of a ship. **37A**: Energy Efficiency Ratio. **38A**: International car registration for Venezuela. **39A**: Placing a vehicle in police custody. **41A**: Non-living thing. **44A**: Made a decision. **45A**: Small tiny insects that can lift very heavy items. **48A**: Sexual Assault. **49A**: Milwaukee Symphony Orchestra. **51A**: Land Development Information History. **52A**: To fix wounds. **53A**: 6th note of a major scale. **54A**: Chic. **58A**: Make disappear. **60A**: Thursday. **61A**: Advertisement. **63A**: Similarly.

1D: Made up of a double-stranded helix held together by weak hydrogen bonds between purine-pyrimidine nucleotide base pairs. **3D**: Untruth. **4D**: Old. **5D**: Fiesta. **7D**: Aim at something. **8D**: Upper extremity. **9D**: Hurry. **10D**: University of Delaware. **12D**: Used to refer to the persons being addressed as the object of a verb or preposition when they are also the subject of the clause. **19D**: A person who travels around without a home. **22D**: Below. **29D**: Louisiana. **25D**: Bitter indignation about being treated unfairly. **27D**: From China. **30D**: Human-Computer Interaction. **31D**: Biophysical Profile. **32D**: Alpha Tau Omega. **33D**: Chung-Ang University Hospital. **35D**: A short cylindrical wood piece to put in a hole to hold something. **42A**: The steps or ways to complete a project. **46D**: Large striped wild feline. **47D**: Cutting edge. **50D**: Holy man. **55D**: A Singlish term used for emphasis or reassurance. **56D**: German. Sore. **57D**: Weather Researching and Forecasting. **59D**: Saint. **61A**: Alcoholics Anonymous.

SCHIPHOL AIRPORT DIAMOND HEIST

In 2005, two men disguised as KLM workers, driving a stolen KLM vehicle, entered the (2D) (28A) (1A). The two men intercepted a truck carrying (26D) of dollars' worth of (15A) headed for a (13D) Airplane flying to (8D). Armed with guns, the two forced the driver and guard onto the ground and drove off with over $70m in diamonds. Authorities recovered part of the diamonds in one of two getaway cars. More than half (19A) the loot was never located. After a twelve-year investigation, including undercover operations, authorities arrested seven people in France and (41A). Two years later, a Dutch court convicted four of the perpetrators, released two and one died while (62D) custody. The mastermind of the heist received seven years, the most of the thieves. Those convicted appealed their sentences. The court released them while their appeals worked their way through the system. The mastermind disappeared. (29A) located him in Ibiza in February 2024. The (55A) didn't go the way they thought. The court ordered the criminals to pay millions in (23D) for the unrecovered jewels. While they claim to possess no knowledge of what happened to the booty and are destitute, the court didn't believe them.

14A: Each. **16A**: Research Experiences for Undergraduates. **17A**: Special rewards, food typically. **18A**: Transthoracic Echocardiogram. **20A**: Starred in the *Dark Knight Rises* and *Les Miserables*. **22A** Friday. **24A**: No contest. **25A**: Common Semetic root for god. **27A**: Extended Play. **33A**: The intention behind words or actions. **35A**: Postscript. A planet that no longer is. **37A**: Triple. **40A**: Cut of meat. **45A**: A pleasing view. **46A**: Rhode Island. **47A**: Scandinavian name meaning eternal ruler. **49A**: Ultraviolet. **50A**: No empathy. **56A**: North Indian tree producing timber and damar resin. **57A**: Prefix. Variant spelling of in. **58A**: Underwriters Laboratories. **59A**: Just coming in. **61A**: A feathery scarf. **63A**: To drag someone along providing a little bit of what they want without giving them everything for as long as possible. **65A**: The Sabbath. **66A**: General Secretary. **67A**: Hatchet.

1D: A group. **3D**: Someone from Idaho. **4D**: Greek pocket bread. **5D**: Present of have. 20th letter of the alphabet. **6D**: Meditation vocalization. **7D**: Indian small, rounded spouted vessel. **9D**: One who holds ideal beliefs. **10D**: Resource support. **11D**: Family of musical instruments. Resonator bells, chime bars, glockenspiels, metallophones, xylophones, bass bars, and timpani. **12D**: Real Estate. **21D**: Starred in TV drama *Crossing Jordan*. **30D**: Utah. **31D**: Toilet paper. **32D**: Examinations Under Oath. **36D**: What is typical. _ _. **38D**: Junior. **39D**: Businesses serving alcoholic beverages. **42D**: Common literary elements. **43D**: Salesmen. **44D**: Lost. **48D**: Tibetan wild ass, khyang and gorkhar. **51D**: Cerebral palsy. **52D**: Oldest and largest high IQ society. **53D**: Circular meat chunk between a bun. **54D**: Female Slavic name similar to Helga meaning prosperous. **58D**: United Parcel Service. **60D**: Refractive Index. **64D**: City of angels.

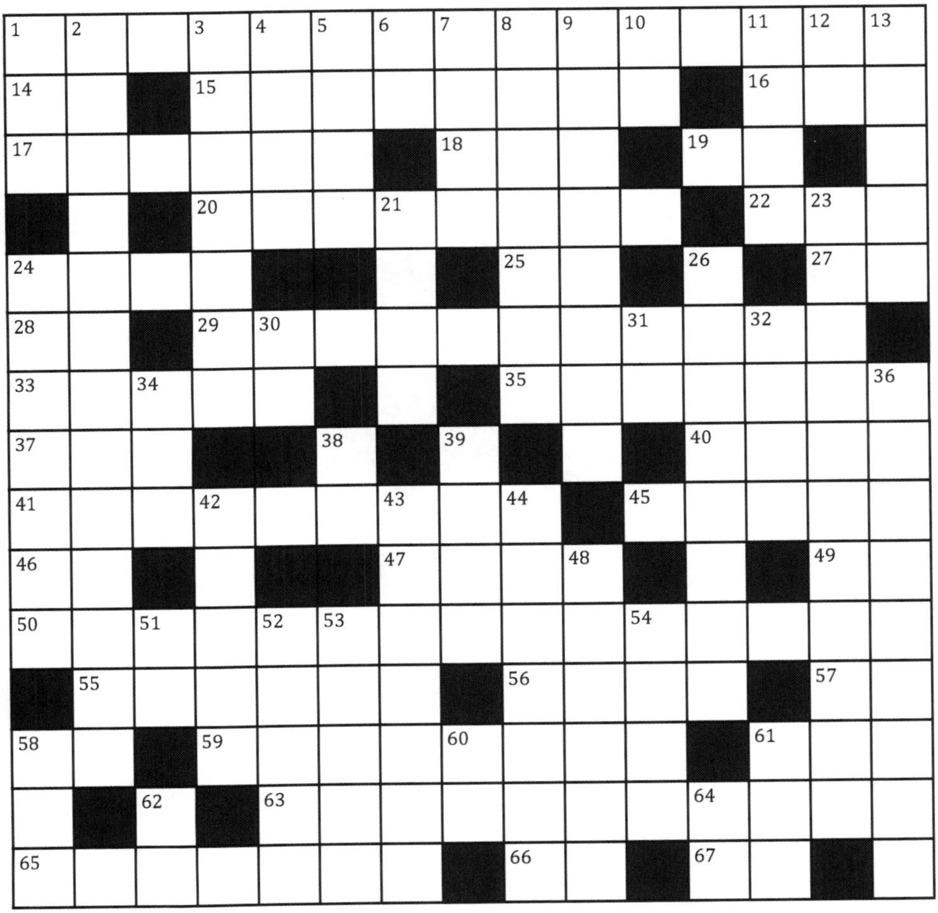

GRAFF DIAMONDS

In 2009, two people posing as customers entered Graff Diamonds in London and robbed the store of over $65 m in (**24D**) and jewelry by stealing forty-three pieces. One necklace alone was valued at over $4 m. Using the services of (**10D**) (**32A**), the robbers spent four hours perfecting their disguises, using (**18D**) latex and wigs. The men arrived by taxi and staff allowed entry into the store. Brandishing guns, the duo (**17D**) staff and cleaned out the display cases. Using an employee as a hostage, the men made their getaway in a blue BMW, after firing a shot (**20A**) the air, causing mass confusion. A few streets over, they switched to another car, after firing a shot into the ground, again causing confusion. Several streets later, they switched to a third car. Laser inscribed with the Graff logo, the diamonds also sported a Gemological (**1A**) of America number. Officials from the Barnes (**65A**,) an elite team with the London's Metropolitan Police Officials tracked the duo down after one of their getaways vehicles crashed into another vehicle. In the ensuing chaos, a throwaway phone was abandoned in the car, which police found and traced numbers on the phones, leading to the perpetrators. All in all, law enforcement arrested ten perpetrators. The mastermind behind the crime received a sentence of (**5D**) years. His co-conspirators were sentenced to sixteen years. None of the (**45A**) pieces were ever recovered.

8A: Fish, Wildlife and Parks. **11A**: Broth with veggies and/or meat. **12A**: Water gauge. **13A**: 12th Greek letter. **14A**: To float as you fly. **15A**: American profession basketball team from Arizona. **16A**: Opinion of yourself. **18A**: Doomsday. Last day of judgement. **19A**: United Nations. **21A**: German for four. **23A**: Mythical being with pointy ears. **24A**: Mixed-color psychedelic shirt (scrambled). **26A**: Multinational Enterprise. **27A**: Defense Industry Initiative. **29A**: Time long past. **30A**: Chinese for longevity. **34A**: Afternoon. **35A**: Street. **36A**: Three. **37A**: Exclamation meant to scare. **38A**: Bathed by sprinkling water on the head. **42A**: Employment Opportunity. **43A**: Suffix forming adjectives. **44A**: One of the great lakes. Also a city in Pennsylvania. **47A**: Limited. **48A**: Moves closer to. **49A**: Integral Ad Science. **50A**: Spanish tea. **51A**: Place kids go to be educated. **54A**: A unit of measurement equal to half an em and approximately the average width of typeset characters, used especially for estimating the total amount of space a text will require. **55A**: Spanish for yes. **56A**: Bondage Sadomasochism. **58A**: 1. **59A**: Viet-Cong. **60A**: Para-aminobenzoic acid. **62A**: Funny, humorous. **64A**: Equal Employment.

1D: Supplied or distributed. **2D**: Person, place, or thing. **3D**: Supplies solar power. **4D**: Toilet papers. **6D**: Australian fuzzy unisex boots. **7D**: Phonetic spelling of "m". **8D**: First in place, order, rank. **9D**: Three words: Side of a building. Hard-shelled dried fruit. To sift. **20D**: To provide further clarification. **22D**: A plan of action. **25D**: Not me. **28D**: Very necessary. **31D**: Hello. **33D**: Necessity. **39D**: Office of International Affairs. **40D**: Received Standard. **41D**: To act. **46D**: Genus of flowering plants in the family Ericaceae. **51D**: Signally Maintenance Management Systems. **52D**: Korean for lake. **53D**: Opioid Overdose Education & Naloxone Distribution. **63D**: University of Queensland.

CARLTON INTERNATIONAL HOTEL

In 2013, an armed (**46D**) walked into a poorly guarded private salon at the Carlton Hotel, in (**10D**), on the (**3D**). Wearing a baseball cap and a scarf, the (**8D**) stole $136m worth of gems and (**29D**) from the private (**11D**) of Lev Avnerovich Leviev, the (**7D**) (**47A**). Law enforcement suspect a member of the (**66A**), an organized crime gang, who escaped from prison days prior to the heist. They also believe more than one (**18A**) took part in the robbery. The heist is the biggest ever in France, and possibly of all time. The theft occurred at the hotel where (**1A**)'s 1955 film *To Catch a Thief* was set. Lloyds of London through SW Associates offered a $1.3m reward.

13A: Unentertained. **14A**: Follicle Stimulating Hormone. **15A**: Mother. **16A**: Surprise in Text slang. **17A**: Adapted Physical Education National Standards. **20A**: Zero. **22A**: Account Executive. **23A**: Next Generation Learning Challenges. **25A**: Cut into small squares. **26A**: Main cook. **28A**: Catalan for to lead. **29A**: Short-term prison. **30A**: The fundamentals. **31A**: Named Entity Recognition. **33A**: Education Play. **34A**: Fe. **36A**: A Soviet military automatic pistol designed by Fedor Tokarev. **37A**: Electronic Data Interchange. **38A**: Wednesday. **40A**: Autonomic dysreflexia. **41A**: A highly spiced stew of various meats and vegetables originating from Spain and Portugal. **43A**: Division. **44A**: Country singer: 'Before He Cheats', 'Jesus Take the Wheel'. **50A**: New York. **51A**: To mock. 25th letter of the alphabet. **53A**: The fabric a bathrobe is made out of. **54A**: Chapter. **56A**: To disagree with. **60A**: Alcoholics Anonymous. **61A**: Tiny bumps along your skin when cold. **63A**: Morning. **65A**: Thinking about.

1D: Left someone without notice or making arrangements for their care. **2D**: Future Maasai Leader. **4D**: Starred in *Bridget Jones' Diary*, *Jerry McGuire*. Married to Kenny Chesney briefly. **5D**: Ehlers-Danlos Syndrome. **6D**: Henry Ford College. **9D**: Human Machine Interface. **12D**: Knock out. **19D**: Fire god of Hinduism. **21D**: A a long, leafless flower stalk coming directly from a root. **24D**: Have control of where someone is. **27D**: Hawaii. **32D**: Something that can be eaten. **35D**: CAD CAM solution for sheet metal cutting, providing applications for punching, profiling and bending. **39D**: A couple. **42D**: Used to draw attention to something. **45D**: Net neutrality. **48D**: Law Enforcement Review Agency. **49D**: Including you. **51D**: A strip of leather to fasten or carry something. **52D**: Tractor-trailer. **54D**: Connecticut. **55D**:The person in charge of an event at their house. **56D**: Office of Economic Development Engagement. **57D**: Latin for swear. **58D**: Credit Privacy Number. **59D**: Territorial Support Group. **64D**: Spanish for my.

Chapter Eleven

PONZI SCHEMES

CHARLES PONZI

An Italian conman, Ponzi operated in Canada and the US in the early 1920s selling postal reply coupons, promising 50% return in 45 days and 100% in 90 days. In reality, he repaid older investors with money from new investors. Unfortunately, it caught up with him about a year afterward, costing investors $20m. In theory, the invester purchased (**1A**) in different countries at a cheaper rate, afterward (**6D**) them for US postage stamps. The US stamp would be sold at the going rate, so the investor pocketed the difference in cost. In 1920, Ponzi started his Securities Exchange Company. The first month, February, 18 people invested, for $1850. The second month he paid them with the proceeds from newer investors. It grew from there. Within four months, he received $420k. The next month, $2.5m. By July, he raked in $1m PER DAY. Ponzi deposited the money in a small local bank. He hoped to deposit enough to basically take over the bank. Many of his investors didn't withdraw their funds, instead allowing the funds to roll-over and re-invest. With the amount of deposits daily, the investment appeared to be doing very well. However, an analysis would reveal that the fund was in terrible shape. He hadn't (**1D**) postage stamps. In fact, he did nothing to legitimately grow the fund. When he considered the logistics, he'd end up filling whole (**4D**) with postage stamps to sail from Europe to the US. But since people tended to leave their interest to re-invest, it didn't pose an issue. Until it did. One analyst questioned how he realized the returns he boasted. Ponzi sued him and won a $500k libel suit. People stopped questioning him openly, for a little while. But then, investigative journalists began to doubt his legitimacy. To dissuade investigators, he quit taking new investors. A journalist did the math and discovered Ponzi couldn't be trading stamps. The post office agreed there wasn't the kind of activity required if Ponzi's scheme worked. The article caused investors to start pulling their money. Ponzi paid out $2m in three days, often mingling with the crowd outside his door, passing out coffee and donuts. The State's attorney's interest became piqued, and he hired an auditor to examine Ponzi's books. However, his accounting system consisted of index cards bearing investors names and amounts. To circumvent the investigations, Ponzi hired a publicist. But the publicist quickly realized Ponzi was full of hot air. He sold his story to a newspaper causing another run. Ponzi paid off the investors in one day. Banking personnel realized Ponzi obtained large loans from the bank. They worried that if Ponzi went under, the entire local banking business would drown with him. Banking officials froze withdrawals from the main account (**33D**) they believed it to be overdrawn. The auditor's preview indicated Ponzi's investment fund was at least $7m in the red. The banking commission seized the bank due to numerous irregularities, foiling Ponzi's plan to raid the vault to cover his losses. Bank officials reduced his $1.5m certificate of deposit by $500k to cover overdrafts. Ponzi surrendered to the State (**17D**) avoiding a public arrest. The news toppled five banks. Investors received about thirty cents on the dollar, totaling $20m in losses. He received a 5-year sentence, serving 3.5 years. Upon his release, the state charged him, which he fought all the way to the Supreme Court. The court ruled the federal charges differed from state charges and didn't result in double jeopardy. His first trial resulted in acquittal, the second deadlocked, the third found him guilty. After he finished his sentence, he was deported to Italy.

13A: A minor figure in the Hebrew Bible, mentioned in Books of Samuel, an elite soldier in the army of David, king of Israel and Judah, and the husband of Bathsheba, the daughter of Eliam. **14A**: Xenon. **15A**: Evaporating water from something wet. **16A**: A ditch. **17A**: Building financially, whether positive or negative. **19A**: Stopper on a wine bottle. **20A:** Cold airstreams meeting hot airstreams. **22A:** Began again. **23A:** Not. **24A:** A ways away. **26A:** Optical Network Terminal. **27A:** Center. **28A:** South America. **29A:** Rushing with a quick great force. **34A:** Electroconvulsive therapy. **36A:** Taking steps to get ahead of everyone else. **40A:** A bill owed. **42A:** Vibrant, charismatic personality. **43A:** Couple. **44A:** Young Gentlemen Education Health Exams. **45A:** Institutional Student Learning Outcomes. **47A:** Egyptian sun god. **49A:** Very precise parameters. **50A:** One-eye piece. **55D:** Missouri. **56A:** International Atomic Energy Agency. **57A:** Very small, tiny. **59A:** Office of Strategic Services. **60A:** Male hormone. **62A:** 13th Greek letter. **63A:** Not black and white tv.

2D: Milk's favorite cookie. **3D:** Mountain range between California and Nevada. **5D:** Exclamation of understanding. **7D:** Abbrev, for second. Upper Respiratory Tract Infection. Garments worn by men around the neck.___ **8D:** A man. __ __. **9D:** Having received an MRI in the past. **10D:** Pioneer. **11D:** Intelligence derived from electronic systems used by foreign targets. **12D:** Full of excitement. **18D:** Reactive Neuromuscular Training. **21D:** And not. **25D:** Addressed directly. **27D:** Points out someone's flaws (British spelling). **30D:** Unemployment Insurance. **31D:** Scary dream. **32D:** People who enjoy playing games. **35D:** Taking Care of Business. **46D:** Absolute leader of a Yakuza clan. **48D:** Someone who pretends to be someone else in a play or tv show. **50D:** Midstate Technical College. **51D:** Office of Chief Executive Officer. **52D:** National Institute for School Leadership. **53D:** Written reminders of a number of items. **54D:** Eötvös Loránd University. **61D:** Off-road Vehicle.

LOU PEARLMAN

From flying high in (**67A**) to creating a couple of the most popular boy bands of all time, to (**13D**) investors of over $1b in a Ponzi scheme, Pearlman kept his fingers in a whole lotta pies, until it crashed down, like his blimp. Thought to be the longest-running scheme, Pearlman enticed (**30D**) for over twenty years to invest in his three companies: Transcontinental Airlines, (**1A**) and the parent company, Transcontinental International Inc. Unfortunately, these (**10D**) only existed on paper, until he created the boy bands 'NSYNC and the Backstreet Boys. He used the success of the bands to expand his investors. Using falsified documents from AIG, Lloyds of London and the Federal Deposit Insurance Corporation, he convinced investors of the legitimacy of his investment plan entitled Employees Investment Savings Account. He furthered his con by obtaining bank loans using (**54A**) financial statements created by his fake (**3D**) firm. In February 2007, Florida announced that the investment company was a fraud and ordered Pearlman to turn over any and all assets in foreign accounts. Most of the $95m collected from investors disappeared. Pearl took off, appearing in Germany, Russia, Belarus, Israel, Spain, Panama and Brazil. Eventually, authorities caught up to him in Bali. The United States charged him with conspiracy, money laundering and false bankruptcy. Sentenced to twenty-five years, the judge provided Pearlman with an early out. For every million dollars Pearlman helped to re-coop, his sentence would be reduced by a month. The judge prioritized investors over financial institutions. (**1D**) and lenders discovered that many of Pearlman's personal belongings, artwork and easy-to-sell items were fakes. They sold what they could on eBay. Pearlman died in 2016 in prison from health issues.

15A: To scout an area. **16A**: Not sanctioned by Jewish law. **17A**: Not heated up prior to eating. **19A**: Energetic Materials Production, Obsolescence and Formulation. **20A**: Polish for centipede. **21A**: The snake that killed Cleopatra. **22A**: Egyptian sun god. **24A**: 19th Greek letter. **25A**: In front of you. **28A**: Equity Linked Note. **29A**: Fabric that is glossy on top and dull on the back. **31A**: Central link. **32A**: Tuberculosis. **34A**: Hacker News. **35A**: Part of a plant divided by a cleft. **36A**: Facial indications of happiness. **40A**: Orange capitol of Spain. **43A**: Eskimo. **44A**: In existence at the time under consideration. **45A**: (Plural) A kind of math. 1a*2b(2a+3b)=. **47A**: Georgia. **48A**: Elevated Railroad. **49A**: Caused a device to operate. **57A**: The least important chess piece. **60A**: Endpoint Detection and Response. **61A**: French for weapons. **62A**: University New Mexico. **63A**: Prejudice based on age. **65A**: Destroy. **66A**: Psychology.

2D: Something you pay to use. **4D**: 12pm. **5D**: Pokes around another's space. **6D**: Disney World: The happiest place __ __. **7D**: Move head up and down. **8D**: Registered nurse. **9D**: Survives by barely getting by. **11D**: Outside plant. **12D**: 17th Greek letter. **14D**: Senior. **18D**: Kilogram. **23D**: Published business commercials. **26D**: Norse for avenged. **27D**: Exclusivity. **33D**: Depressed color. **37D**: 1,000,000+. **38D**: Endowment Investment Board. **39D**: Plan to accomplish something. **41D**: Hatchet. **42D**: Negative reaction to a situation. **46D**: Having ph below 7. **50D**: Utah University. **51D**: For comparison. **52D**: Memory chip that retains its data when its power supply is switched off. **53D**: Obstruct a stream or river. **55D**: Customer Relations Management. **56D**: Touch down. **58D**: Water, Environment, and Sanitation Society. **59D**: A wire that runs from a device to the electrical plug. **64D**: Mercedes-Benz.

REED SLATKIN

(2D) of (4D) and a (1A), Slatkin ran a (34D) scheme for about five years, (60A) $593 million from 800 investors, many Scientology members. Using funds from later (48A), Slatkin paid earlier investors $279m on a $128m, without making most of the investments he proclaimed. SEC closed down the scam in 2001 and froze his accounts. On the same day, the FBI executed search (57A) related to Slatkin. He funneled (37D) to the Church of Scientology and associated entities and victimized members of the church. Convicted for his crimes, Slatkin received fourteen years in prison. During his trial, his attorney cast aspersions toward Scientology. Attorneys for Scientology described Slatkin's excuses as shameful (47D) replied that Slatkin "sold the psychiatrists a bill of goods". Released to a halfway house in 2013, he died two years later.

12A: Town and municipality in the Sugamuxi Province, part of the Colombian department of Boyacá. **13A**: Information Technology. **14A**: North Carolina. **15A**: Phonetic spelling of the letter "n". **16A**: Open for Antiracism. **17A**: Symptom of internal bleeding _ _. **21A**: Even more costly. **23A**: Romanian for rings. **24A**: Dark-skinned person of African descent according to the Hebrew Bible. **25A**: Housing and Accommodation Support Initiative. **26A**: High Definition. **27A**: Serial Number. **28A**: United Parcel Service. **30A**: The liquid form of myrrh. **32A**: Meat juices and __ used for making gravy. **36A**: Online School Payments. **37A**: Town in Saskatchewan, Canada. 42km from Saskatoon. **38A**: Tennessee. **39A**: Integrated Research. **40A**: Information. 19th letter of the alphabet. **44A**: Sudden Cardiac Arrest. Not more. **46A**: Room where experiments take place. **52A**: Instruction. **54A**: American Association of Teachers Italian. **55A**: More than enough. **56A**: Overdraft. **59A**: Indefinite article placed in front of words starting with a vowel. **61A**: Past tense of keep. **63A**: Subject. **64A**: Short of temper. **65A**: Rhythm and ___. 19th letter of the alphabet.

3D: Illinois toll road. **5D**: Nasal Gastric Tube. **6D**: Traditional Japanese footwear. **7D**: Someone who tells untruths. **8D**: Over-the-counter. **9D**: Deposit money, hoping to make more. **10D**: Volcanic rock. **11D**: Medications to aid in improving mood. **15D**: More than 1 #8. **18D**: San Pedro, Oaxaca, Mexico. **19D**: Fermented cereal-based low-alcoholic beverage of cloudy appearance and sweet-sour taste. **20D**: Spanish for my. **22D**: Lithium. **28D**: Bottom. Yes. **29D**: Atomic #50. **31D**: Give permission. **33D**: Registered Nurse. **35D**: Figuring out an answer with little information. **41D**: Dual clutch transmission. **42D**: Competitive activities of enjoyment. **43D**: Pounds. **45D**: Leather pieces with buckles used to carry or contain items. **49D**: British word for someone who informs in criminal matters. **50D**: Finnish for hot weather. **51D**: Effective Transit New York. **53D**: Idiot. **58D**: Beer. **62D**: Extended essay.

SCOTT ROTHSTEIN

Once the managing (**12D**), chairman and Chief Executive (**1D**) of a major law firm, Rothstein lost everything as the Ponzi scheme he started, toppled. Facing (**16A**) Influenced and (**23A**) (**1A**) Act (RICO) charges, Rothstein turned himself in to authorities. He implemented one of the largest (**54A**) schemes in history, using the $1.2b to fund his over-the-top lifestyle. His investment scheme involved his law firm. He told investors that investment funds purchased structured settlements. Allegedly, his plan bought out long-term settlements, for a lump sum payment to the recipient. Because he was an (**7D**), he wrote shady wording in the fine print regarding the actual definition of "(**52A**) settlement". Laws protect structured settlements, requiring court oversight to make any changes. Of course he didn't want anyone looking (**49D**) what he was doing and he stated that falsifying all the legal paperwork required too much work. He guaranteed investors 20% returns in three months. He spun stories of cashing in on settlements prior to court involvement in cases of sexual harassment, (**67A**) and pharmaceutical companies. Using (**8D**) funds from the law firm's account, he re-paid earlier investors. Just prior to the indictments, he instructed underlings to research countries that wouldn't extradite to America or Israel. The answer he received: (**29D**). He wired $16m from the company account to (**43A**) and skipped out, leaving just $117k. The firm employed 70 lawyers, 150 employees in 7 cities and two countries. He emailed a suicide note to his partners from Morocco. They talked him off the ledge and enticed him to return to the US. When his private chartered flight landed, authorities arrested him and his firm slapped him with a lawsuit. He received a fifty-year prison sentence, is held in an undisclosed facility, and his prison number is not published.

14A: Flowers. **15A**: Despite the fact. **18A**: Annual Percentage Rate. **20A**: A thought. **21A**: University of Oregon. **22A**: Rowed. **27A**: Thoughts of one's self. **28A**: Give off. **32A**: An old-fashioned hat worn by women. **33A**: Process of notarizing a document remotely. **34A**: Extrusion-grade version of the base resin PET. **35A**: Open Government Partnership. **37A**: Road. **38A**: Farewell. Belongs to you. **40A**: Open area of grassy land. **41A**: French for me. **42A**: Smell emanating off. **50A**: Education Department of Alabama. **51A**: University of California. **57A**: Spanish for yes. **58A**: A unit of geological time. **60A**: French for French. **64A**: Country where the Olympics started. **66A**: Bad feelings, evil intent.

2D: Real Life. **3D**: Blood and guts. **4D**: Muslim girl name meaning collection of opinion. **5D**: Used to treat acetaminophen overdose. **6D**: A type of people or thing already referred to. **9D**: International Organization of Employers. **10D**: An otter belonging to us. **11D**: Nasal gastro. **13D**: Genus Strelitzia. **17D**: The continent housing Italy, France, England. **19D**: A pointed piece of wood that fits in a hole. **24D**: Follow orders. **25D**: Archaic form of to. **26D**: Physical Education. **30D**: The country the original Indians came from. **31D**: Typescript. **38D**: Bank of America. **39D**: University North Carolina Charlotte. **44D**: Those who size. **45D**: Bullsh*t. **46D**: Light. **47D**: Arkansas. **48D**: Nebraska University. **53D**: Parent's brother. **54D**: Down. Ribbon. **55D**: Japanese for calm. **56D**: Institute of Engineering and Technology. **59D**: Greek nickname for Helen, meaning bright shiny one. **60D**: February. **61D**: Spanish for love. **62D**: Chew on a bone. **63**: What we inhale. **65D**: Continuing Education.

GREATER MINISTRIES INTERNATIONAL

By the time the Evangelical (**1A**) was shut down, they had defrauded 18,000 people of almost $500m, mostly from (**12D**). (**23A**) (**51A**) bribed church officials to recruit new members. Citing (**37D**) (**4D**), the scam promised double the investment in seventeen months or less. But all the money disappeared. They published a newsletter selling herbal remedies, cancer treatments, a (**31A**) to survive "end-times plagues" and plans for "Greater Lands", an Ecclesiastical Domain ... similar to the Vatican, a power unto themselves. Church leaders received seventeen to twenty-five year sentences.

13A: Member of Buddhist people living in Laos. **14A**: Awesome. **15A**: What you attach a trailer to. **16A**: A student learning on the job without pay. **18A**: Not capable. **20A**: Top. **21A**: Touchdown. **22A**: An article of clothing worn around the neck. **25A**: Old. **26A**: Garment worn while cooking. **28A**: Sexual inappropriateness. **30A**: Reservation. **32A**: Similar to. **33A**: Kansas Health Institute. **34A**: University of Music. **38A**: Oinkers. **39A**: Dreams. **42A**: Syrup. **43A**: Electronic Bill of Laden. **44A**: Community of buildings occupied by monks or nuns. **48A**: The component attached to both wheels on a car. **49A**: Those who deliver. **52A**: International Business Machines. **54A**: Present tense ofwas. **55A**: Children. **56A**: Blood pressure. **58A**: Beer. **59A**: Use of tiles in art work to form a picture. **60A**: Irish Gaelic name for Ireland. **62A**: Not. **63A**: Yuck **64A**: Lane. **65A**: You get 23 of these from each parent. **66A**: What you do, decisions you make. **67A**: Gunk, goop. **68A**: App that tells you where to go.

1D: Atlantic pigeonwings. **2D**: Something to grasp to open, turn, push, pull, or close. **3D**: Decay. **5D**: Substance put into a laser printer. **6D**: Zeus' lover turned into a cow because Hera was jealous. **7D**: Arrange in a straight line. **8D**: Rah! **9D**: Health Insurance Portability and Accountability Act. **10D**: Goddess of Weaving with an extra T. **11D**: Remote control. **24D**: Sumerian god of water. **27D**: Song. Those 13–19. **29D**: Possessive of he. **32D**: Doing away with. **35D**: 1760 yards. **40D**: Saxophone. **41D**: Serious Adverse Event Review. **45D**: One who receives a bribe. **46D**: Car door open noise. **47D**: Mythical city on the coast of Brittany. **50D**: Vermont. **53D**: A combination of people united by a treaty. **57D**: More. **61D**: Representative.

Chapter Twelve

CYBER CRIME

COLONIAL PIPELINE RANSOMWARE ATTACK

In 2021, **(59A)** Pipeline suffered a hack to their computer system, losing 100 **(69A)** of information. The next day, the company received a ransom **(18A)**, presumably from the same **(24D**.) Immediately, Colonial shut down the **(51A) (73A)** oil from Texas to the Southeastern states, affecting 17 states and Washington, D.C. With FBI supervision, Colonial paid the 75 **(46D)** ($4.4m) within hours. However, it took a significant amount of time to reboot the computer system running the pipeline. **(1A)** suspected a hacker group known as **(41A)** for the attack. A month later, the Federal Bureau of Investigations recovered 63.7 of the bitcoins. But due to a market drop, the value of the coins equaled $2.3m. **(2D)** believe the attack originated from a breached employee's password obtained on the dark web. President Biden declared a state of emergency. Darkside released a statement saying their goal is to make money, not jeopardize society. They didn't take responsibility for the attack. The company restarted the pipeline six days later. All operations returned to normal within three days. Authorities revealed that Darkside appears to be based in Russia. Through the magic of computers, they discovered that Darkside had ransomed a significant amount of entities, earning $90m. According to a **(25D)** Release, 99 suffered Darkside **(33A)** attacks, leaving approximately 47% of victims paying the ransom to avoid attack.

13A: Large tree-dwelling bird of American tropical rainforests. **14A**: Japanese for red demon. **15A**: Et cetera. **17A**: Vermont. **20A**: Slalom. **22A**: Institute for Law Enforcement and Protective Services Excellence. **23A**: Packed like sardines. **25A**: Below. **27A**: Two terminal electronic components conducting electricity in one direction. **28A**: Honorable Artillery Company. **29A**: To enrage. **31A**: American Society of Clinical Hypnosis. **32A**: Assemble equipment of a sailboat to make it ready for operation. **38A**: Kentucky. **39A**: Knowledge Transfer. **40A**: Note in the fixed-do system. **44A**: Titanium. **45A**: Money Services Business. **47A**: Recuperation. **49A**: Referee. **53A**: American Shoulder and Elbow Surgeons. **55A**: Translation. **56A**: Appendage on an animal attached to the butt. **63A**: Speaker inserted into the ear. **66A**: Phonetic spelling of "s." **67A**: Northeast.

1D: Ulcerative disease of the genital area. Lymphogranuloma venereum. **3D**: Washington. **4D**: Drawing to a close. **5D**: Famous past tense. **6D**: Forest giraffe and zebra giraffe. **7D**: Malware placed on a computer system which won't be removed until someone pays an exorbitant fee to the person who placed it on there. **8D**: Locked with a secret message requiring a cypher to understand. **9D**: In, into, on. Prefix. **10D**: Visible in twilight hours, usually near bodies of water due to high humidity. **11D**: Horse's vocalizations. **12D**: Teletype. **16D**: Pleasing to the ear, addictive to listen to. **19D**: A high-elevation train. **26D**: What a dog does with his tail. **34D**: Landlord. **35D**: The Association Real Estate License Law Officials. **36D**: Raba Kistner Corporation Inc. **37D**: *Guardians Of the Galaxy* character who monitors planets, creates new life, and experiments upon countless species. **42D**: Slavic name meaning of the yew tree. **43D**: Delaware. **48D**: Vocalized loudly. **50D**: A small, domesticated form of the European polecat. **52D**: The parts of a plug that go into the plugin. **54D**: Liquid from a tree. **57D**: Alabama. **60D**: Jump. **61D**: New England Youth Retreat. **62D**: International Society for Transgenic Technologies. **64D**: Gold. **65D**: Human granulocytic anaplasmosis. **68A**: Regret. **70D**: Body Odor. **71D**: Emotional Intelligence. **72D**: Tin.

NASA CYBER ATTACK

In 1999, a fifteen-year-old did the unthinkable: He hacked NASA and the Department of (**7D**), specifically, the Defense (**1A**) Agency. Not realizing his "playing around" entailed criminal behavior, Johnathon James (**29A**) $1.7m (**48A**) proprietary software from NASA pertaining to (**51A**) controls aboard the (**11D**) Space Station. NASA closed down for three weeks, purging their system. After installing a backdoor to DRTA, he downloaded over (**1D**) thousand emails and obtained usernames and passwords for nineteen employees. DTRA deals with assessing threats from nuclear, (**49A**), special, conventional, and chemical weapons. Convicted, James served his time on house arrest until he flunked a UA whereby he finished his time in a prison, earning the badge as the (**19D**) hacker to be sent to prison. (**54D**) father, a computer analyst, proudly released his name after sentencing, noting he couldn't do what his son accomplished. Tragically, James committed suicide nine years later when law enforcement accused him of taking part in the (**38A**) of TJX. He denied any involvement.

13A: Covered in hair. **14A**: Perennial and renewable. **15A**: Latin for to infinity. **17A**: Energy Efficiency Ratio. 25th letter of the alphabet. **20A**: Overdrawn. **21A**: Internet story. **22A**: The act of threatening someone unless they pay. **24A**: Company began with a little bicycle workshop in the village of Mollet near Barcelona, founded in 1922 by Simeó Rabasa i Singla. **26A**: Utah University. **27A**: Statistic. Not. **34A**: Past tense of sing. **35A**: Fleabane. **37A**: At the minimum. **43A**: Every Student Succeeds Act. **44A**: A spot for a chopper to land. **45A**: Unless. **47A**: Groups of military troops. **55A**: Appropriate. **56A**: Appendage to aid in hearing. **57A**: Spanish for my. **58A**: The most tight. **59A**: Someone's hopes for the future.

2D: Exclamation of sarcasm. **3D**: UK clothing manufacturer Rires__. **4D**: Emergency Room. **5D**: Female Arabic name meaning wonderful. **6D**: French. Feminine stiffen. **8D**: An individual thing that is complete on it's own but can be part of a whole. **9D**: The country north of the US. **10D**: Invented by Crapper. **12D**: Taking the pain away. **16D**: Period. **18D**: Send products to another country for sale. **23D**: Edict. Similar to. __ __. **25D**: Japanese Buddhist festival held annually in August to honor the dead. **28D**: Touchdown. **29D**: Killed the most. **30D**: Positive attributes used for the owners' benefit. **31D**: Town located in the northern part of lake Siljan, in Sweden. **32D**: Assisted Out-patient Treatment. **33D**: Digital number. **36D**: Curved sword. **38D**: Heated Exhaust Gas Oxygen Element. **39D**: When items are in a row. **40D**: Kidney Paired Exchange. After treatment. **41D**: Nationally Recognized Testing Lab. **42D**: Go to sleep. **46D**: Boredom of the rich. **49D**: Obnoxious child. **50D**: Input/output. "To __ or not to be." **52D**: Vigorish. **53D**: Math. Occurring at position "I" in a sequence. **57D**: Millimeters.

WANNACRY RANSOMWARE

The (**1A**) stole and leaked an exploit developed by the National (**1D**). Shortly thereafter, a (**21A**) cryptoworm wiggled across the globe, infecting computers using the Microsoft (**20A**) Operating System. (**38A**) developed a (**30D**), but older machines and people who couldn't take their computers down to install the fix became infected. Over 300k computers in 150 countries contracted the virus until a kill switch stopped the spread. Damages ranged from hundreds of millions to billions of dollars. Security experts believed the attack originated in North Korea, but they denied the allegations. The worm locks up the computer. Owners must pay a ransom in (**14A**) to receive the key to unlock the computer. Hackers require bitcoin payments through encrypted wallets. The NSA failed to report the exploit, intending to use it offensively, themselves. Microsoft discovered later on, but by that time it had been stolen from NSA. After the (**20D**) (**55A**) attack, 327 payments totaling over $130k were received by the wallets. Linguistic analysis of the ransom notes indicated the culprits were fluent in Chinese and proficient in English. The metadata attached to the notes used the time stamp of North Korea.

11A: Slang for no. **12A**: Organ used for sight. **13A**: I would. **16A**: Try to ensure something doesn't occur. **18A**: Unobservable. **19A**: Employment Insurance. **23A**: Female Latin name meaning gladly. **25A**: I am. **26A**: Uno. State of disorderly retreat. _ _. **27A**: Crunching with one's teeth. **29A**: Using a keyboard to write. **31A**: Young Chef Olympiad. **33A**: Dad. **34A**: Artificial Intelligence. **35A**: Allen and Wright rootbeer. **36A**: Alumni. **42A**: The name of a higher class in Victorian times. **44A**: A clear coating on top of a table. Frozen water. _ _. **46A**: Engineering Validation Test. **47A**: Youth Camp. **48A**: Timid. **49A**: Unsure, easily agitated. **53A**: Traditional Japanese masked drama with singing and dancing. **58A**: Tiny. **59A**: You. **60A**: Also. At that time. **62A**: Processing again.

2D: Used to refer to one or some of a thing or number of things. **3D**: Administers medications to an unsuspecting person. **4D**: Sold an option on something. **5D**: World Economic Outlook. **6D**: Restraining order. **7D**: White grape used in making wine. **8D**: Observed. **9D**: War to make social change within a nation. **10D**: Terminal Deoxynucleotidyl Transferase. **13D**: Out. Street. **15D** Wander. **17D**: Yuck! Forms nouns denoting quality or condition. **22D**: Welding Outlook Inc. **24D**: A small number. **27D**: Nation. **28D**: World Assembly of Muslim Youth. **32D**: More clever. **34D**: From Asia. **39D**: Vinyl discs music use to be recorded on. **40D**: Operating System. **41D**: Using a rod to catch aquatic animals. **43D**: One who protests violently. **45D**: Watching. **50D**: Vice President. **51D**: University of Oklahoma. **52D**: Southwestern Atheletic Club. **54D**: A sign of what is to come. **56D**: 1. **57D**: Metropolitan Transit System. **61D**: Hello.

HEARTLAND PAYMENT SYSTEMS

In 2008, two (**8D**) (**5D**) (**36D**) malware on Heartland Payment Systems, stealing 100m (**68A**) cards. After that, they ramped up their cybersecurity and offered a data (**1A**) which they later came to regret. Someone broke into their office and stole (**7D**) password protected (**20D**). Before long, the private information of payroll customers hit the dark web, including social security numbers and banking information. Authorities hit Heartland with $140m (**24A**) fines and penalties. The second breach involved only one man and he was sentenced to twenty years in prison. Heartland's experiences served as a warning to other companies, resulting in significant (**4D**) upgrades for all types of (**1D**).

14A: United Parcel Service. **15A**: String used for crocheting and knitting. **16A**: The organ in which a woman carries a fetus. **17A**: Before Christ. **18A**: The use of humor to expose one's shortcoming. **19A**: Iceland. **21A**: Barely scraping by. 19th letter of the alphabet. **25A**: Over the counter. **30A**: Exponential Moving Average. **31A**: Senior. **32A**: Spanish for earrings. **33A**: Inner supports on a bicycle wheel. **35A**: Turkish for again. **37A**: Flowering plants in the cashew family. **38A**: United Paramount Network. **39A**: Congressional Quarterly. **41A**: Equally. **43A**: Education Technology. **44A**: Should. 19th letter of the alphabet. **46A**: Indiana University. **47A**: Fair Practice. **48A**: Southeast. **49A**: Very typical of a certain type of person. **52A**: Residential Assistance. **54A**: Australian bitter peas. **55A**: Large homes and properties. **57A**: The characters making up the alphabet. **58A**: Flaxseeds, sunflower seeds and almond meal. **59A**: Child. **60A**: An atom or group of atoms with an electrical charge. **63A**: Sharp and angled. **65A**: Present day.

2D: Roleplay. **3D**: Esquire. **6D**: Gram. **9D**: Actual time of arrival. **10D**: Theodoxus fluviatilis. **11D**: Father, son and holy spirit. **12D**: Europe. **13D**: Used to address a man in Spanish countries. **21P**: Extended play. **22D**: Indicative mood of be. **23D**: Grade. **26D**: North American Open Masters. **27D**: What happened prior? **28D**: Over-extended. **29D**: New style. **34D**: Coral rock in the lagoon. **40D**: Silent. **41D**: An unbiased feline. __ __ __. **42D**: Very showy. **45D**: Google Classroom. **50D**: French for yew. **51D**: Computational Science and Engineering. **53D**: Make amends. **55D**: A long poem. **56D**: Pop. **61D**: Oregon. **62D**: South Dakota. **63D**: Eat. **64D**: Goodnight. **66D**: Obstetrician. **67D**: Nickname for Diana.

EQUIFAX

The People's (**1A**), China's military, backed a team of hackers who successfully stole the personal (**2D**) of 145 million (**6D**) from Equifax's website by introducing (**12D**). The FBI stated aside from the economic value of the information, the information stolen will also provide China with knowledge toward developing (**10D**) intelligence and the creation of (**7D**) -gathering packages. State-sponsored intrusion by China includes (**24D**) (**47A**), trade secrets and private business information. Six weeks after the US attack, the United Kingdom discovered that 13 million English customers were also involved in the attack affecting America. Not to be left out, 8,000 Canadians also were caught up in the breach. Employees updated the SSL Certificate which appeared to be nine months overdue. Immediately, they received alerts regarding intrusions. The SEC fined Equifax $100m, then ordered them to set up $300m to compensate victims and$175m to compensate states. (**4D**) fined them over $12m. Equifax received heavy criticism for their lax security and their failure to immediately notify those impacted.

14A: A person whose name isn't given. **15A**: Not the Fareast. Closer. **16A**: Travaux forcs. **17A**: Meets someone and makes them feel comfortable at their home. **18A**: Organ used for sight. **19A**: Employment Opportunities. **20A**: Grain used in whiskey. **21A**: 6. **22A**: In insurance, provides protection against uncertainties. **23A**: Exclamation to gain someone's attention. **25A**: Not rated. **26A**: Gotten off topic. **28A**: Pomp and pizzazz. **30A**: Trademark. **31A**: Marked with lines or wrinkles. **32A**: Before indoor plumbing, people washed up using this. **36A**: To walk quietly, without attracting attention. **38A**: Relating to the ears. **39A**: Reflecting the moral of the unconscious. **41A**: Left rear. **42A**: Burns the hair. **44A**: Osteoarthritis. **45A**: Middle East Institute. **46A**: Works hard. **50A**: Money paid to a policy covering medical, home, car, etc assurances. **52A**: Young thing. **53A**: South Carolina. **54A**: Homes of honey makers. **58A**: University of Ohio. **59A**: University of England. **60A**: Someone over 60. **62A**: Educational paper required for earning a degree. **64A**: Armed forces. **66A**: Popular form of spoken theater during the Edo period. **67A**: Promotes religious unity.

1D: Aggressive thoughts exist in hidden form, making aggression more likely. **3D**: Box Office. **5D**: Ryanodine receptor. **8D**: Office of Emergency Services. **9D**: Non-applicable. **11D**: Regarding. **13D**: Mythical city on the coast of Brittany. **27D**: Dinosaur. **29D**: Labor Education and Research Center. **33D**: Things that are not important. **34D**: Two component regulatory systems for efflux proteins in Gram-negative bacteria. **35D**: South America. **37D**: A poem of serious reflection. **40D**: God Of War. **43D**: Blood sugar. **45D**: Medical doctor. **47D**: Joint allowing the leg to bend. **48D**: Office of Environment and Heritage. **49D**: Italian for events. **51D**: To cause harm to another. **55D**: Island. **56D**: Canal in the body that blood flows through. **57D**: Security Intelligence and Analysis System. **61D**: Object Relational Mapping. **63D**: Santa's catch phrase. **64D**: 12th Greek Letter. **65D**: I am.

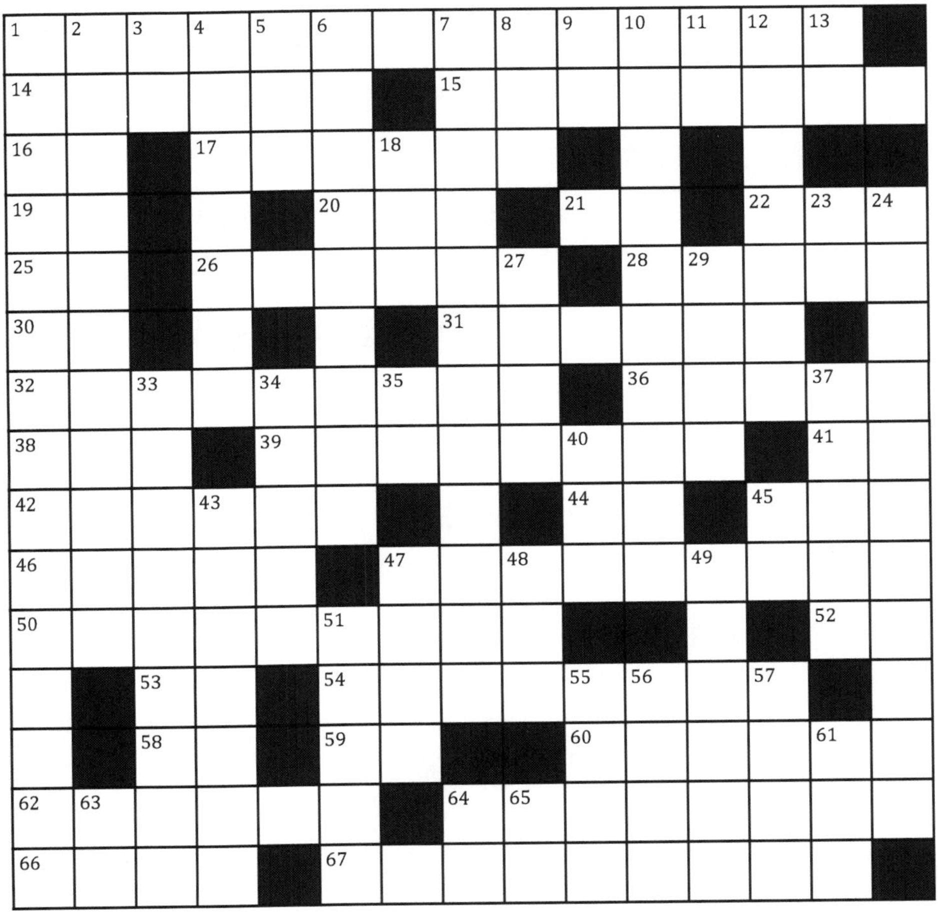

Chapter Thirteen

KIDNAPPED!

A BUSLOAD OF KIDS

Outside a little town in California, three armed men kidnapped a school bus with twenty-six children and a driver. They were driven about two hours away to a rock (**21D**) where the (**35A**) led them to a buried (**1A**). The kids climbed down a (**10D**) to an area with a couple mattresses, a little food and water and a pit bathroom. The kids ranged from 5-14 years old. The kidnappers wrote their names and ages on wrappers of (**24D**). They intended to ransom the children for enough money to remodel the (**31D**) (**56A**) House in Mountain View, California. Even though the three men came from wealthy families, they were deeply in debt. They attempted to call the police station regarding the (**6D**) but were unable to get through as the parents and media kept calling to get information. The bus (**36D**) and the older (**3D**) stacked the (**64A**) up and wedged the trap door open. They all climbed out of the prison and hiked to a guard's shack at the quarry. One of the kidnapper's family owned the quarry and law enforcement arrested them a few days later. The men received life in prison without parole but on appeal, their sentences were changed to chance of parole. The turning factor was that they didn't actually physically harm anyone. After this case, California re-vamped their laws regarding physical harm and emotional distress. Long-term psychological studies of the children revealed most developed phobias and PTSD. Twenty-five years after the incident, many still suffered symptomology and a significant had been charged with controlling behavior toward another. Chowchilla renamed the park after the bus driver and has an annual holiday commemorating the bus driver's birthday. The kids sued the kidnappers and received enough of a pay off to afford really good therapy but not enough to buy a house, according to one victim.

13A: Rhode Island. **14A**: Homo sapien. **15A**: Incapable. **17A**: An unintentional event. **19A**: Multiple High Definition televisions. **20A**: Those who are easy to deceive. **21A**: All-terrain vehicle. **22A**: Fake meat food. **23A**: Hindi for wave. **27A**: Straw at the end of a stick used to sweep a floor. **29A**: Normal. **30A**: Curriculum Vitae. **32A**: Emirates through Karachi. **33A**: Mister. **34A**: Plural of man. **40A**: Kilobyte. **41A**: Institute for Creation Research. **42A**: As a sailboat. Agile. **43A**: Years of Service. **45A**: Nuclear Threat Initiative. **46A**: Charged atom. **47A**: People protecting others or things. **51A**: When a person takes charge politically over others. **55A**: Trumpet. **58A**: Held together with wire. **59A**: How long someone has lived. **60A**: Relating to or denoting a branch of the Finno-Ugric language family. **63A**: Emotional Abuse. **67A**: Irish National Liberation Army. **68A**: Walk in again. **69A**: One billionth gram.

1D: Selling illegal items, such as drugs. **2D**: Federal laws used to indict organized crime gangs, Mafia, etc. **4D**: Timed Up and Down Stairs. **5D**: Denoting a mass or part of a specified kind. **7D**: Dynamite. **8D**: Gold. **9D**: Took a deep breath. **11D**: Electronic Benefit Transfer. **12D**: Reusable launch vehicle. **16D**: Phonetic spelling of "s". **18D**: Carbon Oxygen. **25D**: How long someone has been alive. **26D**: Paying to live somewhere temporarily. **28D**: Okey Dokey. **37D**: Aches. **38D**: Creates semen in men. **39D**: Speed Over Ground. **44D**: To splash with mud. **48D**: Astronomical Unit. **49D**: Down Low. **50D**: Southeast. **52D**: What is used to clean out the anal cavity. **53D**: Romanian Game Developers Association.

54D: The color of grass. 57D: Man-eating beast. 61D: Gastroesophageal reflux. 62D: Gear. 65D: Theodore Roosevelt. 66D: Street.

JAYCEE DUGARD

In 1991, (**24A**)-year-old Jaycee walked to the bus stop. A car pulled up alongside her. The passenger jumped out, (**12D**) her and threw her in the back seat. Her (**1D**) witnessed the abduction and chased after them on a bicycle, failing to catch the vehicle. Numerous people around the (**55A**) witnessed the abduction but no one could provide meaningful information. After being released from prison for a prior kidnapping, Phillip Garrido and his (**21A**) chose to kidnap Jaycee in hopes of curing his (**1A**) (**10D**). Local, state and federal authorities failed Jaycee in horrific fashion, leaving her chained in a (**42**) for eighteen years. Jaycee bore two (**34A**) during the time. Garrido visited the (**3D**) of California-Berkley with the two girls, ages 11 and 15. He wanted to put on a religious event. The staff at the university were concerned for the girls and felt the situation appeared questionable. A woman asked Garrido to return the next day after getting his information. Campus police performed a background check and noticed that Garrido was a registered sex offender and shouldn't be around children. He returned the next day and law enforcement arrested him. Probation released him but told him to come to the office with his entire family. The probation officer separated the girls from Garrido and discovered Jaycee had been (**17A**) eighteen years prior. Garrido received a prison sentence over 400 years and his wife will never be getting out either. Jaycee sued the state and feds, receiving a $20m settlement. California was pleased with the out-of-court settlement saying that a lawsuit would have been "greater invasion of privacy and greater publicity for the state".

13A: Treatment. **14A**: Small bite. **15A**: American Expedition Vehicles. **16A**: Plan. **18A**: Provide evidence in support. **20A**: A writing implement. **23A**: For example. **26A**: Maintained a steady rate walking or running. **27A**: Loud noise warning of something. **29A**: Combines numbers to get a new total. **31A**: Repetitive thumping of the fingers. **32A**: Phonetic spelling of "l". **33A**: Adding soap to water creating bubbles. **38A**: Hadden Township Equity Initiative. **39A**: Improvised Explosive Device. **40A**: Provisional release from prison. **41A**: Employment Income. **43A**: Didn't reciprocate a lover's feelings. **44A**: Flushed cheeks. **46A**: Major motorcycle rally in North Dakota. **48A**: Native American. **49A**: Identification. **50A**: Off-shore Industrial Environmental Habitat. **51A**: Gigabytes. **53A**: Suffix. Spasm. **57A**: Gulps down beer. **58A**: Academy of Computer Science and Software Engineering. **59A**: Petroleum. **61A**: Interactive Electrode Localization Utility. **62A**: Unhappy. No reason to celebrate. **63A**: Archaic form of apply. **64A**: Sheep ticks with an extra "s". **65A**: Large extinct flightless bird resembling the emu.

2D: No longer. **4D**: Assist. Ulmus. _ _. **5D**: Licensed Practical Nurse. **6D**: Sound the little dog made. **7D**: Adult diapers. **8D**: Equal. **9D**: 2. **11D**: Northeast. **17D**: Knockout. **19D**: A bond between two people. **21D**: Washington. **22D**: Iron. **25D**: Workers who park cars at posh hotels and restaurants. **28D**: Gorilla. **30D**: Holds down, doesn't acknowledge. **35D**: Synthetic Risk and Reward Indicator. **36D**: National Latin Exam. **37D**: General Education Diploma. **43D**: Switzerland in French. 4th letter of the alphabet **45D**: A venerated prophet in Judaism, Christianity, and Islam. **47D**:

Point in your opponent's favor. **52D**: Softest wood. **54D**: Not appealing to look at. **55D**: Not the front. **56D**: Lyrical expression of ideas. **60D**: International Organization for Standardization.

JOHN PAUL GETTY III

Part of one of the richest families in 1973, Getty lived in (**42D**). He toyed with the idea of (**1A**) his own (**25A**) to receive money from his (**41A**.) He decided against the plot after gaining employment as a model at age seventeen. But the (**11D**), a criminal organization, kidnapped him and sent a (**45D**) note to his father for $17m. His (**18A**) begged his grandfather for the funds, but granddad refused to pay, citing concerns his other grandchildren would become targets. The kidnappers sent another ransom demand but due to a strike by the postal company, the letter was delayed. The gang grew tired of the prolonged (**65A**) and Getty's treatment became rougher. They routinely played (**2D**) with a pistol at his head. When grandad continued to hold out, the Ndrangheta sent a lock of his hair and his ear to the (**39D**), stating he would be returned in bits. Getty's health rapidly deteriorated. His ear became infected and he developed (**33A**). His captors fed him large amounts of penicillin to fight the infection, resulting in an allergic reaction. Granddad negotiated the new ransom demand from $3.2m to $2.2m, the tax-deductible allowed amount. The gang held Getty for five months. Authorities captured nine of the perpetrators and convicted two. Most of the money failed to be recovered. Getty suffered an overdose later and became permanently disabled.

14A: Largest city in Switzerland. **15A**: Moving fast in a straight line as if driven by wind. **17A**: Out of the way. **19A**: Female version of Joe. **20A**: Red Seal Endorsement. **21A**: Internet domain for the Russian Federation. **23A**: In Abrahamic religions, Jewish prophet, a high priest, and the elder brother of Moses. **30A**: Dried edible seaweed. **31A**: Color slightly. **32A**: The powerful beings in charge of everything. **35A**: Doctorate degree. **36A**: One of the Oromo clans in the Horn of Africa. **37A**: Egypt's main river. **40A**: Criminal organization, term typically associated with the Mafia. **46A**: Living structure of Southwestern Native Americans. **48A**: Sumerian city-state in ancient Mesopotamia. **49A**: International Ancient Art Dealers Association. **50A**: Virginia's nickname coined by King Charles II after their loyalty during the English Civil War. **51A**: To come out in first place. **52A**: Medical. **53A**: Old English. **54A**: Associated Press. **55A**: American Astronomical Society. **56A**: Technology Integrated Health Management. **58A**: Bacterial Vaginosis. **59A**: Minnesota Multiphasic Personality Inventory. **61A**: Stratovolcano in Italy. **62A**: Writing news stories.

1D: Highlands in the US. **3D**: Expressed grief. **4D**: Obstructed the view of something or someone. **5D**: Early Childhood Education Research Alliance. **6D**: To quiet someone. **7D**: Republic of South Africa. **8D**: Thespian & tear. _ _ _. **9D**: Temple University Hospital. **10D**: Thought. **12D**: Refering to a soldier in the army. **13D**: A contracting muscle moves part of the body. **16D**: Norse god of wind and sea. **22D**: Top. 2. **26D**: Thai for waterfall beef. **27D**: One of Columbus' ships. **28D**: Rastafarian concept relating to oneness of humanity and God within everyone. **29D**: General Electric. **34D**: Putting code within a document. **35D**: An undercover cop dresses as a__. **38D**: A possibility. **41D**: Dreariness. **43D**: Canadian Territory forming the Arctic Archipelago. **44D**: A tropical US state made up of islands. **47D**: Bondage. **59D**: Mobile Network Operator. **64D**: Sadomasochism.

CHARLEY AND WALTER ROSS

Considered the first kidnapping for ransom in the US (if you leave out Native Americans' history), in 1874, Charley and Walter Ross played outside their (**1A**) in a well-to-do section of Philadelphia. A (**8D**) (**25A**) pulled up to the boys and offered them candy and (**16D**) to climb in the carriage. The two men in the carriage sent five-year-old Walter into a store with a (**17A**) to purchase (**21D**). When he came out, the carriage and his four-year-old brother disappeared. Their father, Christian Ross, received ransom demands mailed from all over Philadelphia. The letters appeared to be written by someone barely literate. While the Ross's lived (**57D**) a large house and owned a small store, the family lost most of their money in the stock (**51A**) crash in 1873. They were incapable of paying the $20,000 ransom. Ross approached the (**41D**) regarding the kidnapping, turning the situation into a national story. Locals enlisted the Pinkerton National (**35D**) Agency and attempted to pay the ransom several times but the kidnappers failed to show. Six months later, two burglars chose the wrong house. The owner, a judge, lived next door (**6D**) his brother, who heard the commotion and responded with weapons. One burglar was killed and the other mortally wounded. Joe Douglas admitted to kidnapping Charley. Those present weren't clear if the boy still lived (**13A**) not. Douglas didn't disclose the whereabouts of the child. Authorities brought Walter to identify the two men. He agreed they kidnapped him and his brother. One of the men had a (**58A**) nose, making him easily recognizable. Charley was never found.

12A: Shame. **13A**: Oregon. **14A**: Afrikaans for parents. **15A**: Tighten a muscle. **20A**: Spanish for police. **23A**: Place to catch a bus. **26A**: School Resource Officer. **27A**: An officer above a lieutenant colonel and below a brigadier general. **29A**: A hormone that is responsible for water, osmolar, and blood pressure homeostasis. **31A**: Phonetic spelling of "n". **32A**: Diminutive in size compared to what's typical. **34A**: A reddish complexion. **36A**: A joke. **38A**: An exercise that also relaxes. **39A**: Arrived. **40A**: To quickly rub thumb against middle finger creating a sound. **42A**: Rapids in a river. **45A**: Scottish. To gulp. **47A**: Salt. Daughter of my sibling. **48A**: Drinks. Alone. **49A**: Customer Managed Keys. **50A**: Haitian Creole. Surprised with an extra i. **53A**: Robotics Education and Competition Foundation. **55A**: Latin for conquer. **62A**: Equal. **63A**: Nevada. **64A**: Potassium Nitrate.

1D: Government Operations and Fiscal Policy. **2D**: In. Symbol representing a company. **3D**: Thing on a fishing pole that holds the line. **4D**: Country south of the US. **5D**: Arkansas. **9D**: In baseball, after 3 of these, the other team gets their turn at bat. **10D**: Competitive events. **11D**: Made a mistake. **18D**: United Bank for Africa. **19D**: Lithuanian company. One of the largest vertically-integrated organic food companies in Europe. **24D**: Small horse. Hiking. **28D**: Made legal. **30D**: Relating to a bird of happy omen in Hindi. **33D**: Norwegian for generous. Hindu mantra. **37D**: Response to a question. **39D**: An essential electrolyte located in all bodily fluids. **43D**: Party, festivities of a higher class. **44D**: Electronic Control Module. **46D**: Peaks above a body of water. **52D**: At any time. **54D**: Uniform Resource Locator. **56D**: Common Era. **59D**: Over Active. **60D**: Montana. **61D**: Environmental Policy.

NELL DONNELLY

(**46D**) American (**26D**) and businesswoman, Donnelly and her (**44A**) were victims of a (**1A**) in 1931. The kidnappers sent a (**50A**) demand for $75,000 to her husband by mail and called her (**28A**) to inform him of where they abandoned her car. The attorney's wife assumed the call was a hoax and didn't pass on the message. As soon as Donnelly's husband received the (**14D**), he called the attorney. Realizing she had been kidnapped, her attorney called his partner. About to testify (**7D**) front of the state legislature, he begged off announcing why. Her kidnapping became a media sensation. Local authorities contacted the (**1D**) boss. He denied any knowledge of the abduction but immediately sent people out to find her. Law (**62A**) later received a call informing them where Donnelly could be found. (**22A**) found her and her chauffeur in a candy shop, surrounded by people. Donnelly disclosed that a group of armed men stormed the empty house they'd been kept in and rescued them. Police apprehended four men. Three were convicted and sentenced to life in prison and thirty-five years. The fourth lucked out and drew a bonehead jury who acquitted him. He admitted to taking part in the kidnapping but thought the victim was married to an oil tycoon.

12A: An accumulation of earth and stones carried and finally deposited by a glacier. **13A**: Device that makes a car go faster or stop if depressed with the foot. **15A**: Closest. **17A**: Transcendentalist who wrote *Walden*. **18A**: Square. **19A**: To make something no longer frozen. **21A**: Greek for small one. **25A**: Forming nouns denoting an action that is completed. **27A**: Student Affairs in Higher Education. **29A**: Maid service. **31A**: Department of State Education. **32A**: Secret Service. **33A**: Secretary. **34A**: Atom that has an electrical charge. **35A**: Identification. **36A**: Items used to chew food. **37A**: Teacher's aide. **38A**: Ohio University. **39A**: Gross. **49A**: One of the first leaders of the early Christian Church. **51A**: French pastries stuffed with cream or chocolate. **53A**: To extrapolate. **56A**: Merit Excellence Intelligence. **59A**: Necessary. **63A**: Negatory.

2D: Dallas Museum of Art. **3D**: NE. **4D**: Plural present of "be". **5D**: Light desserts. Danish, eclairs. **6D**: Hindi dumplings made of whole wheat or fresh rice flour. **8D**: Dummy. **9D**: South American country where the Inca came from. **10D**: Federal Aviation Association. **11D**: Most blondes tend to be __-__. **13D**: Water hemlock and giant hogweed are examples. **16D**: =. **20D**: Assessment of Teaching Assistant Skills. A Latin phrase that means in case: in __. **23D**: Plural of this. **24D**: Eat. **30D**: Tie again. **39D**: Design For Manufacturing and Assembly. **40D**: Flight of stairs. **41D**: Tourism, Economic Affairs, Transport, and Telecommunication. **42D**: Me. Loop a shoe lace. Me. **43D**: Global Response Staff. **45D**: Exclamation of disbelief. **47D**: Operate something. **48D**: A worker who foxes shoes. **52D**: Mineral spring. **54D**: Phonetic spelling of "g". **55D**: Global System for Mobile Communications. **57D**: English. **58D**: Possibly. **60D**: Article in front of a noun that starts with a vowel. **61D**: Low.

CONCLUSION

Whew! I hope you found this entertaining and learned a little something along the way. Sometimes, true life can be crazier than fiction. Within the serial killers chapters, it's interesting to see the similarities in early childhood that led to the resulting pathology.

I found it extremely thought-provoking learning how different countries sentence the perpetrators of crimes, whether it be killing babies, stealing millions in art or jewels, or holding companies' computer networks hostage.

It's also fascinating to see how crime has evolved with the times, such as art thefts and diamond heists overcoming modern technology. And modern technology leading to the new cyber-crimes. But murder doesn't appear to change much.

The true crime stories featured in this book were just enough to whet the appetite. You now have a research/reading list if you want to learn more about these fascinating true-to-life tales. Keep a watch out for other books in this combined genre.

SOLUTIONS

Aileen Wuornos

```
K I L L E D █ O N E █ A S █ B
E R I O █ A B █ F A M I L Y
G U L A G █ R A P E D █ X O E
█ █ █ U █ O █ I █ █ I █ V █
P R O S T I T U T I O N █ E M
I █ I E █ H █ I █ O J O █ O
T A L L █ R E B E L █ E C H O
T █ F L O R I D A █ C █ O R
M O O D █ U █ D █ B I T E █ E
A █ L E A T H A L █ N I C K █
N █ F A █ █ O █ T O █ I F
█ M O E █ A B A N D O N E D █
P A W N █ L A D █ R █ O N A
U L █ S U I C I D E █ F L A X
S E V E N █ M A I D █ O P I
```

Juana Barraza

```
B O W I N G █ P A █ B O Y █ B
I █ R █ O █ K I L L E R █ A L
█ M E X I C O █ C U E █ B U
M A S K █ H █ S O █ R A P E D
█ G T █ I F █ H █ S I R █ G
S I L E N C E █ O M █ R E N E
I C E █ U █ M A L E █ G █ O
X █ R E D █ A C I D S █ N A N
T O █ F E E L █ C I █ K A L E
Y O U █ V E █ O P I N E D
█ D R E S S E S █ N C █
E L E V E N █ I L █ G Y M
C O X █ T A C O S █ O A
H A I R █ S █ P I █ H O L D
O █ T R A N S V E S T I T E
```

Miyuki Ishikawa

■	S	E	E	D	■	■	O	B	E	Y	S	■	■
M	I	D	W	I	F	E	■	R	■	■	S	O	A	P
I	N	■	N	■	I	■	O	F	F	■	A	B	A
N	G	■	J	■	G	E	T	■	I	■	A	I
G	L	E	A	M	■	H	■	H	U	S	B	A	N	D
■	E	X	P	O	R	T	■	■	H	A	N	D	■
■	■	A	L	A	Y	■	H	A	■	D	O	T
T	W	E	N	T	Y	-	S	E	V	E	N	■	N	A
I	■	■	■	■	F	A	A	■	U	B	E	R
S	T	I	F	F	■	O	R	P	H	A	N	E	D	■
■	E	M	A	I	■	■	A	P	■	E	■	V
I	M	P	O	V	E	R	I	S	H	E	D	■	H	E
E	P	■	L	E	M	■	E	■	I	D	A	T
■	L	E	■	M	■	N	E	G	L	E	C	T	■
L	E	G	A	L	I	Z	A	T	I	O	N	■	C	A
E	■	O	B	I	T	■	P	H	■	G	■	H	B
A	H	■	O	K	■	■	D	O	W	N	■	A
T	■	C	R	E	M	A	T	I	O	N	■	E	■	N
H	A	R	T	■	O	L	■	T	C	■	O	W	E	D
A	R	A	I	■	R	O	B	O	T	■	B	I	O
L	■	T	O	U	T	E	R	■	O	R	E	O	■	N
■	T	E	N	■	I	■	A	■	R	O	A	R	■	I
P	I	■	A	C	■	K	I	■	O	T	N	■	N
■	C	E	R	T	I	F	I	C	A	T	E	S	■	G
D	■	S	A	■	A	■	N	E	■	S	R	■	W
O	R	P	H	A	N	A	G	E	S	■	S	P	A	N

Joanna Dennehy

A	B	S	E	N	T	■	C	E	L	L	M	A	T	E
T	■	T	W	O	■	C	O	P	■	O	■	G	A	L
T	I	A	■	O	A	■	L	A	U	G	H	E	D	■
A	■	B	O	N	N	I	E	■	R	■	U	N	■	U
C	A	B	■	■	A	R	■	L	I	S	T	E	N	■
K	■	E	N	G	L	A	N	D	■	L	K	■	O	W
S	A	D	■	U	■	Q	U	I	L	L	■	F	■	I
■	N	■	C	A	R	■	T	■	S	O	R	E	L	■
E	T	A	R	■	P	A	C	T	■	D	I	L	L	■
L	I	V	E	D	■	I	■	H	■	G	■	E	F	I
■	-	■	Y	■	S	E	Q	U	I	N	■	■	N	■
E	S	C	A	P	E	■	S	■	I	■	D	O	G	■
B	O	O	T	H	S	■	R	■	L	A	■	■	L	■
■	C	U	T	■	R	I	G	H	T	S	■	E	Y	■
■	I	R	A	■	P	E	N	■	O	Y	■	I	P	■
W	A	T	C	H	■	G	E	M	■	■	B	I	D	■
E	L	■	K	■	B	I	O	M	E	T	R	I	C	■

Beverley Allitt

■	B	I	■	A	V	■	■	I	N	S	U	L	I	N
M	U	N	C	H	A	U	S	E	N	■	G	A	R	E
U	S	S	R	■	M	■	P	■	■	T	H	R	E	E
R	■	T	U	■	P	A	R	O	L	E	■	G	■	D
D	A	I	S	■	I	R	E	D	■	N	O	E	L	■
E	■	T	H	I	R	T	E	E	N	■	■	■	I	S
R	I	U	■	T	E	■	■	■	A	F	■	■	M	U
■	■	T	W	O	■	G	R	I	E	V	I	O	U	S
U	N	I	T	■	E	R	A	■	E	A	R	■	■	P
■	E	O	■	■	E	N	G	L	I	S	H	■	■	I
C	O	N	V	I	C	T	E	D	■	L	■	O	R	C
O	■	■	I	P	A	■	■	H	■	■	O	■	■	I
C	H	A	R	A	C	T	E	R	I	Z	E	D	■	O
O	A	R	■	■	T	I	M	E	■	E	N	■	D	U
A	D	M	I	N	I	S	T	E	R	E	D	■	I	S

Dorothea Puente

```
M U R D E R E D . . T R O O P
E . O I L . T I S S U E . A R
N O M A D . A S S E T . E T O
T . A L E S . A . G . S A S S
A S . . R A . B R A I N S . T
L E D . L U L L . . . E F I
. X . B Y . E I G H T . R T
J U R Y . A . D R U G S . E U
. A I . O L D . A . A B E T
. L . O P E R A N D I . R . I
P L Y . E . E R . R . C A M O
A Y . P R E S C R I P T I O N
C . P R A T S . . N . A N D
. B R O T H E L . K I . S U N
C O O . E . D O R S A L . S O
```

Pedro Alonzo Lopez

```
T R I N K E T . L . F . . . L
R . S . P R O L I F I C . F E
A F L . . O . H U N D R E D
F L A S H F L O O D S . . M
F U N K . E . D . . T R A P
I N D I G E N O U S . E . L
C K . L . U R N I . A R E A
K I L L I N G . I S M . A S H
I E . S R . G O . T O . P . A
N . . I C E . V E L V E T .
G I R L S . T . I R E . R
. . A . I . K . S . L Y E
B . P R O S T I T U T E . I N
R U E . R . D U N . G A N G
A B D U C T . S T I N G . G
```

Bruno Ludke

E	X	A	M	■	V	■	F	O	S	S	I	E	■	A
X	■	M	E	D	I	C	I	N	E	■	■	V	A	L
P	I	E	D	■	E	■	F	■	R	A	D	A	■	L
E	■	N	O	■	N	O	T	H	I	N	■	D	I	E
R	E	D	■	C	N	■	E	■	A	D	■	E	N	G
I	T	S	■	O	A	■	E	E	L	■	■	D	T	E
M	A	■	N	■	A	N	Y	■	G	I	■	■	E	D
E	■	F	I	F	T	Y	-	O	N	E	■	■	L	■
N	O	O	N	E	■	■	Y	■	R	E	A	L	■	■
T	M	■	S	S	■	H	E	Y	■	M	A	K	E	R
S	A	G	A	S	■	A	E	■	A	T	■	C	A	■
■	N	■	■	I	R	A	■	N	E	X	T	■	■	■
W	O	M	E	N	■	N	■	R	O	■	N	■	U	P
■	U	O	■	P	A	T	E	■	R	E	■	L	A	I
C	R	I	M	I	N	O	L	O	G	I	C	A	L	■

Dennis Rader

K	I	L	L	E	R	■	C	■	A	R	A	Y	■	Z
I	■	A	U	T	O	E	R	O	T	I	C	■	T	O
L	O	B	■	■	O	Y	O	■	■	■	E	U	R	O
L	■	■	F	E	T	I	S	H	E	S	■	N	O	S
■	P	■	E	U	■	■	S	■	Y	E	■	I	P	A
■	E	L	E	V	E	N	-	Y	E	A	R	■	H	D
S	P	A	■	■	A	■	D	■	■	M	■	V	I	I
E	■	T	O	R	T	U	R	E	■	■	L	I	E	S
R	O	T	■	O	■	T	E	L	L	S	■	■	S	M
V	O	Y	E	U	R	I	S	M	■	A	M	B	■	■
E	■	■	■	G	■	■	S	■	A	D	■	I	M	B
■	A	S	P	H	Y	X	I	A	T	I	O	N	■	O
A	■	U	E	■	■	U	N	I	T	S	■	D	O	U
S	E	M	E	N	■	■	G	R	A	T	E	■	■	N
S	M	O	T	H	E	R	■	■	I	N	■	D	E	A	D

Javed Iqbal

A		S	T	R	A	N	G	L	I	N	G		H	D
P	H	I		B	O	L	A			A	C	A	I	
S	I	X		R	U	N	A	W	A	Y	S		D	S
	S	T	O		S	E	X	U	A	L	L	Y		S
V	E	F		I		O		A		I			N	O
A	P	E		A	N	D					T	O	O	L
T	A	N	D		G		O		C	D		P	O	V
	K		U			O	R	P	H	A	N	S		I
D	I	S	M	E	M	B	E	R	I	N	G		A	N
	S		P	R	I	O	R			G	O	I	N	G
	T	O					O		L			D		
L	A	W		P	A	M	P	H	L	E	T	S		
E	N	A		C	R	I	M	E	S		C	R	Y	
F	I	N	D		I		N		A		T	A	O	
T			H	Y	D	R	O	C	H	L	O	R	I	C

Harold Shipman

F	I	F	T	Y		I	M		A	D	D	I	C	T
I		R	Y	E		M	E	A	D		I		E	O
F		O	P	E	R	A	N	D	I		A	P	E	X
T	O	M	E		A	N		M		O	M	I		I
E				V	P		M	I	C	R	O	N	I	C
E	N	G	L	I	S	H		N	O		R	E	P	O
N		R		C		U	P	I	N		P	D		L
	D	E	S	T	O	N	E	S		C	H		H	O
P	E	A		I		D		T	I	H	I		E	G
R	A	T		M	U	R	D	E	R	I	N	G		Y
O	N	E		S	T	E	E	R		E	R	A		
B		S	O		D	I	E	D		A	N	D		
L	E	T	H	A	L		D	I	E		N		I	
E	M		R	E	A	P		M	O	D	U	S		
M	E	D	I	C	A	T	I	O	N	S		P	C	

William Bonin

	T	H	E	M		F	O	R	M	A	T	I	V	E
A	W	E			A	A	A		A	S	O		A	M
L	E	T	H	A	L			A	L			F	N	A
I	N		E	X	E	C	U	T	E	D		O		S
E	T	N	A		S	U	E		S	O		U	P	C
	Y		T	V		L		S		O	U	R		U
T	-	S	H	I	R	T		E	A	R		T		L
	O	N		C		S	E	X		S		E	T	A
O	N	O		T	O		K				B	E	E	T
F	E	W		I	N	J	E	C	T	I	O	N		I
	I	M		U		L	R		Y		I	N
	C	O	N	S	E	N	S	U	A	L		A		G
T	U	N			M	O	L	E	S	T	I	N	G
	R	A	P	E	D		E	S	H		B	O	A	R
M	U	R	D	E	R	E	D		Y	O	U	N	G

Joseph James DeAngelo

B		B	C		K	I	D	N	A	P	P	I	N	G
L		U	L	A	E			P	L	A	I	N		E
E	C	R	U		P	D			O	N	E		O	N
U	R	G	E		T	A	U	N	T	E	D		F	E
	I	L		A		T		I		D		P		A
	M	A	L	L	E	A	B	L	E		O	H	L
E	E	R	I	E		B	A		L		A	L	O	O
	S	I	X		R	A	N	S	A	C	K	I	N	G
T		E		H	A	S		P		R		C	E	Y
O	B	S	C	E	N	E		R	A	I	N	E	D
M	E		O			H	E	L	M
	A	T		T	H	R	E	E		E	X		H
M	U	R	D	E	R		M	S	O		L	O	K	I
O		I	M	P		H	I		P	I		H	I	M
I	M	P	L	E	M	E	N	T	A	T	I	O	N

184   Solutions

Karla Homolka and Paul Bernardo

D	E	V	E	L	O	P	E	D		T			A	N
O	X	A			A	N		V	O	M	I	T		
M	I	N	O	R	S			M	E		O	O		
E	T		M	E	D	I	C	A	T	I	O	N		
S	S		A	S		N		E	R	N		I	V	
T		C		U	S		D	U	R	E	S	S		I
I	T	O		S	P	U	R		I	N			A	D
C	O	N	S	C	I	O	U	S	N	E	S	S		E
		C	H	I	N		G		A		I	N	T	O
F	O	R		T			G	A	R		S	O	O	T
O	N	E		A	S		E	X	I	S	T		N	A
		T	I	T	H	E	D		A		E	N		P
S	C	E	N	E				H	N		R	A	P	E
A	H				L	I	F	E		A		T	I	S
D	I	S	M	E	M	B	E	R	E	D			O	N

Gwendolyn Graham and Cathy Wood

S	E	A		I	N	F	I	R	M	I	T	I	E	S
M	I	C	H	I	G	A	N		A		A	N	A	L
O	T	H	E	R		B		A	D	D	I	C	T	
T				S	E	E		A	S	I				
H	O	M	I	C	I	D	E	S		A	I	R		M
E	N	F	O	R	C	E	M	E	N	T		C	O	P
R	E	S	I	D	E	N	T	S		H		E	R	R
E				S		I	S		R	E	I			
D	I	S	E	A	S	E		A	M		L	A	G	S
	L	A	M	B		X		R	P	I		T	O	O
A	I	D	E	S		H	U	M	A	N		E	N	N
S		S		F	U	B	O	S		A	D		M	
A	L	Z	H	E	I	M	E	R	S		L		H	E
B	O	O		E	V	E	R	Y		W	O	M	E	N
	B	O	N	D	E	D			M	O	U	N	T	

Fred and Rosemary West

A	M	H	E	R	S	T		T	O	R	T	U	R	E
S	U	M	M	I	T		S	E	X	U	A	L		L
P	T		I		E	B	E		I		B	U	T	E
H	I		R	A	P	E	D		S		L		O	C
Y	L		A		D	A	U	G	H	T	E	R		T
X	A	C	T		A	U	C	A		E		A	I	R
I	T		E		U	T	E	M		R	E	P		O
A	I	M	S		G	I		M	U	R	D	E	R	S
T	O	O		T	H	E	R	A	P	Y				H
E	N	L	I	S	T	S		P		H	A	L	O	
D		E		E		O	N	E		E	P	I	C	
	E	S		P	R	O	P	E	R	T	Y		K	K
C	A	T	A	E		O	O		E		R	E		
	R	E	M	A	I	N	S		C	A	R	E	D	
	D	I	S	A	P	P	E	A	R	E	D			

Juan Carlos Hernandez and Patricia Martinez

C	A	N	N	I	B	A	L	I	Z	E	D		
A	S		O	N	E		U	T	E	R	U	S	
R		M	O	T	H	E	R		N		S	T	O
N	A	E		E	E	R	E		I		A	R	
E	E	X		L	A		D	O	T		S	O	A
A	F	I	E	L	D		C	H		T	L		E
S		C	R	E	E	K		T		E	E	L	
A	G	O		C	D		C	O	N	C	R	E	T
D	O		A	T		S	H		O		R	A	N
A			U		O	I	L			D			
	D	I	S	A	B	I	L	I	T	Y		A	L
L	O	C	A	L		L	D		I	O		U	D
	N	O			R		C	U	T	E	R		
C	O	N	F	E	S	S	E	D		N	O	D	E
	R		A	R	S	O	N		G	E	O	D	E

Gerald and Charlene Gallegos

S	E	X	U	A	L	L	Y	■	E	L	E	V	E	N
A	■	M	E	D	I	A	■	■	O	A	■	■	■	Y
D	I	S	T	A	N	C	E	■	M	O	R	T	E	M
O	■	■	G	E	N	E	■	O	■	I	■	A	■	P
M	U	R	D	E	R	E	D	■	L	E	N	G	T	H
A	■	E	■	■	D	A	T	E	■	G	A	■	■	O
S	L	A	V	E	S	■	■	A	S	K	■	M	O	M
O	I	L	■	■	F	■	B	T	K	■	■	I	■	A
C	O	M	P	A	T	I	B	L	E	■	K	I	L	N
H	■	■	M	A	R	R	I	E	D	■	■	L	■	I
I	B	M	■	I	■	O	D	■	A	I	L	■	■	A
S	E	■	I	R	A	N	■	■	A	C	A	I	■	C
T	E	E	N	A	G	E	R	S	■	■	C	A	■	■
I	C	Y	■	G	E	T	■	E	X	O	T	I	C	■
C	H	O	R	E	S	■	E	X	E	C	U	T	E	D

Carol Bundy and Doug Clark

P	R	O	S	T	I	T	U	T	E	S	■	A	B	S
D	U	N	■	H	■	O	■	A	■	T	■	T	E	A
■	N	E	C	R	O	P	H	I	L	I	A	■	■	D
M	A	■	E	L	S	E	■	U	■	L	I	M	O	
A	W	A	K	E	N	■	A	I	R	■	C	L	A	M
K	A	Y	■	S	O	U	L	■	I	■	O	R	C	A
E	Y	■	T	O	■	T	E	N	T	H	■	■	■	S
■	S	T	O	M	A	C	H	■	G	L	O	M	■	O
H	■	E	P	E	B	■	A	■	L	O	A	C		
E	T	A	■	S	U	■	A	M	A	■	I	O	T	H
A	R	T	S	■	S	H	E	A	R	■	C	C	T	I
D	O	■	A	B	I	■	S	M	A	S	H	E	S	
S	O	U	V	E	N	I	R	S	■	S	■	I	S	T
■	P	I	E	■	G	R	E	E	N	■	I	N	T	I
A	S	I	D	E	■	U	N	D	O	I	N	G	■	C

Faye and Ray Copeland

▪	M	O	D	U	S	▪	▪	S	C	A	M	▪	▪	B
E	E	▪	R	▪	▪	C	H	E	C	K	▪	A	H	I
P	▪	F	I	V	E	▪	O	V	▪	▪	▪	M	U	G
I	▪	I	F	▪	B	O	N	E	S	▪	H	I	M	▪
C	A	T	T	L	E	▪	▪	N	E	N	E	▪	A	S
▪	B	E	E	T	▪	▪	P	T	A	▪	▪	O	N	E
▪	I	▪	R	▪	E	B	A	Y	▪	R	▪	P	▪	N
A	L	▪	S	I	X	T	Y	-	N	I	N	E	▪	T
H	I	S	▪	▪	E	▪	▪	S	▪	F	▪	R	U	E
E	T	▪	P	▪	C	H	A	I	▪	L	E	A	R	N
M	Y	▪	A	▪	U	▪	▪	X	▪	E	O	N	▪	C
▪	▪	C	R	O	T	C	H	▪	▪	▪	D	▪	▪	E
H	O	B	O	▪	I	H	I	O	▪	▪	D	I	E	D
O	▪	▪	L	▪	O	O	▪	H	O	B	O	▪	I	▪
G	O	V	E	R	N	O	R	▪	N	O	T	I	N	G

Philadelphia Poison Ring

S	U	P	E	R	S	T	I	T	I	O	U	S	▪	C
U	N	▪	X	▪	A	I	N	▪	N	O	N	E	▪	O
P	▪	S	E	A	T	E	D	▪	S	I	G	N	▪	U
P	O	A	C	H	▪	▪	E	M	U	▪	A	T	T	N
O	▪	M	U	▪	S	▪	M	I	R	A	G	E	▪	T
S	O	▪	T	A	K	E	N	▪	A	D	▪	N	A	E
E	X	P	E	D	I	T	I	O	N	▪	▪	C	A	R
D	I	O	D	E	S	▪	▪	T	▪	C	O	M	E	F
▪	▪	T	▪	▪	▪	Y	▪	E	▪	▪	O	D	I	E
P	O	I	S	O	N	S	▪	E	▪	B	O	▪	▪	I
L	▪	O	U	R	▪	P	E	R	M	A	N	E	N	T
E	▪	N	R	A	▪	I	M	P	A	S	S	▪	O	I
A	R	S	E	N	I	C	▪	▪	V	I	▪	D	O	N
▪	▪	▪	▪	G	▪	E	X	P	E	C	T	I	N	G
D	E	P	R	E	S	S	I	O	N	▪	O	D	E	▪

Delfina and Maria de Jesus Gonzalez

I	N	V	E	S	T	I	G	A	T	E	D	■	A	P
N	O	E	L	L	■	C	H	U	R	N	■	P	D	R
C	T	R	■	E	G	L	O	T	■	F	O	R	D	O
A	E	T	H	E	R	■	S	H	O	O	T	E	R	S
R	B	I	■	P	I	N	T	O	■	R	■	D	E	T
C	O	C	A	I	N	E	■	R	O	C	■	I	S	I
E	O	A	■	N	E	N	■	I	R	E	■	C	S	T
R	K	L	■	G	R	E	A	T	■	M	E	T	■	U
A	■	■	F	■	■	■	W	I	S	E	■	A	R	T
T	H	E	R	M	A	L	■	E	N	N	O	B	L	E
E	E	R	I	E	■	A	■	S	A	T	■	I	T	S
D	R	U	G	G	E	D	■	■	P	■	■	L	■	■
■	O	P	H	A	N	I	M	■	P	E	N	I	L	E
L	I	T	T	L	E	S	T	■	E	D	I	T	O	R
I	N	■	S	O	■	H	A	I	R	S	T	Y	L	E

Ivanova and Olga Tamarin

A	D	V	E	R	T	I	S	E	■	■	T	O	G	A
P	E	A	R	L	■	G	E	N	D	A	R	M	E	S
P	F	T	■	■	R	A	V	I	O	L	I	■	A	S
E	O	I	E	■	■	E	■	B	■	■	A	E	R	U
A	R	C	■	C	A	N	N	I	B	A	L	I	S	M
L	M	A	■	H	O	S	T	I	L	E	■	C	H	P
■	E	N	F	O	R	C	E	M	E	N	T	■	I	T
A	D	I	O	S	■	■	E	A	S	E	■	M	F	I
S	■	■	R	E	■	C	N	■	■	■	■	E	T	O
■	T	W	E	N	T	Y	-	S	E	V	E	N	■	N
A	Y	E	■	■	P	S	Y	C	H	O	T	I	C	S
S	L	A	U	G	H	T	E	R	H	O	U	S	E	■
O	E	■	■	O	■	■	A	M	E	R	I	C	A	N
T	R	A	P	D	O	O	R	■	■	■	■	U	S	O
A	S	S	I	S	T	S	■	B	L	E	S	S	E	D

Gang of Amazons

S	C	H	O	O	L	T	E	A	C	H	E	R	█	B
H	E	A	L	T	H	I	E	R	█	E	M	O	C	Y
O	█	W	O	M	A	N	█	M	█	A	B	B	O	T
O	D	A	R	█	█	█	S	O	L	V	A	B	L	E
T	E	I	I	D	█	M	U	R	D	E	R	E	D	█
O	N	I	█	M	E	A	N	Y	█	N	K	R	B	A
U	T	A	H	█	A	T	N	█	H	█	█	S	L	F
T	I	N	█	I	R	R	I	T	A	T	E	█	O	F
█	S	█	P	O	L	I	C	E	M	A	N	█	O	O
S	T	A	R	█	I	A	█	█	█	T	█	█	D	R
I	█	M	O	D	E	R	A	T	E	S	I	Z	E	D
█	E	N	F	O	R	C	E	M	E	N	T	█	D	A
A	M	B	E	R	█	H	E	A	R	T	Y	█	█	B
G	U	N	S	█	K	█	█	█	█	█	█	N	I	L
E	S	█	S	C	O	O	T	E	R	█	V	O	T	E

Briley Brothers

R	E	F	O	R	M	A	T	O	R	Y	█	U	S	E
O	X	I	D	E	█	C	A	T	H	O	L	I	C	S
B	E	N	E	F	I	C	I	A	L	L	Y	█	A	C
B	C	█	T	█	█	O	L	█	█	█	█	E	R	A
E	U	A	S	C	O	M	Y	C	E	T	E	S	█	P
R	T	█	█	R	I	P	█	A	N	Y	M	O	R	E
I	I	█	K	I	L	L	I	N	G	█	█	P	A	D
E	O	P	I	M	█	I	T	A	L	A	I	█	P	█
S	N	R	L	E	█	C	E	█	G	R	A	D	E	D
█	E	L	S	█	E	M	B	A	R	K	E	D	█	█
A	M	G	E	█	G	█	█	█	█	A	█	A	█	L
M	A	N	D	I	B	U	L	A	R	N	O	T	C	H
E	Y	A	█	S	█	█	F	L	A	G	S	H	I	P
N	O	N	C	I	V	I	L	I	Z	E	D	█	T	█
D	█	T	E	S	T	I	F	I	E	D	█	D	Y	E

Hernandez Brothers' Sect

P	R	I	E	S	T	E	S	S	■	C	H	E	F	■
R	O	A	C	H	■	W	A	T	C	H	■	F	O	R
O	M	N	I	R	A	N	G	E	■	A	D	O	R	E
S	A	C	R	I	F	I	C	E	■	R	A	B	B	I
T	I	■	M	E	■	P	E	A	R	■	■	■	I	N
I	N	D	E	P	E	N	D	E	N	C	E	■	D	C
T	■	■	P	■	D	E	■	D	■	T	■	S	D	A
U	N	B	I	A	S	E	D	■	B	E	A	T	E	R
T	O	E	S	■	■	I	P	A	R	■	A	N	N	■
I	N	V	E	S	T	I	G	A	T	I	O	N	■	A
O	N	Y	X	■	W	R	I	T	E	S	■	D	A	T
N	■	■	S	E	I	T	E	■	T	■	A	B	I	
■	A	C	T	O	R	S	■	L	X	I	■	R	O	O
■	P	A	R	A	P	H	I	L	I	C	■	D	U	N
S	E	R	A	P	S	■	B	A	S	S	I	S	T	■

Elmer Wayne Henley

S	T	R	A	N	G	U	L	A	T	I	O	N	■	■
E	X	■	C	O	N	T	R	O	V	E	R	S	Y	■
X	■	E	Q	U	A	T	E	S	■	■	E	■	A	M
U	■	O	U	T	R	A	G	E	O	U	S	■	■	A
A	B	■	A	■	L	■	■	■	S	■	O	B	■	S
L	O	K	I	■	Y	O	U	R	S	E	L	V	E	S
A	U	■	N	D	■	A	T	■	E	■	V	E	N	I
S	T	■	T	O	R	T	U	R	E	D	■	R	E	V
S	O	N	A	T	A	S	■	E	K	E	S	■	F	E
A	N	■	N	■	P	■	A	C	■	L	■	K	I	L
U	N	A	C	C	E	P	T	A	B	I	L	I	T	Y
L	I	M	E	A	D	E	■	L	O	C	A	L	I	■
T	E	R	S	E	■	T	O	L	■	A	D	L	N	■
S	R	■	■	C	H	A	F	E	■	T	I	E	G	■
■	E	■	G	I	R	L	F	R	I	E	N	D	■	■

Craig Price

W	O	M	A	N	■	I	S	S	■	■	■	M	A	S
■	S	O	M	E	T	H	I	N	G	■	N	I	X	T
M	A	T	E	■	W	■	X	E	A	R	E	D	■	A
A	K	I	N	■	■	E	■	T	E	S	E	I	A	B
R	A	F	■	■	N	A	Y	■	S	■	G	R	A	B
I	■	F	I	F	T	Y	■	E	I	G	H	T	■	E
J	O	■	C	O	Y	A	S	■	E	B	B	■	A	D
U	■	T	E	N	■	Y	E	A	R	■	O	L	D	■
A	R	E	■	T	O	■	V	I	■	D	R	I	V	E
N	A	N	O	■	N	I	E	C	E	■	H	E	E	D
A	N	D	■	A	E	O	N	■	M	O	O	■	R	G
■	G	E	A	R	■	■	■	M	E	N	O	T	T	I
P	E	R	■	M	U	R	D	E	R	E	D	■	I	E
H	■	E	M	■	Z	O	N	E	S	■	■	A	S	S
I	N	D	E	F	I	N	I	T	E	L	Y	■	E	T

Mason Sisk

I	N	V	E	S	T	I	G	A	T	O	R	S	■	P
N	E	■	S	T	A	I	R	■	A	B	■	T	C	S
S	W	■	E	X	T	E	N	S	I	V	E	L	Y	Y
T	■	F	A	M	I	L	Y	■	E	■	E	P	I	C
I	R	A	N	■	S	■	■	B	R	A	■	M	O	H
T	E	L	■	B	■	E	V	E	■	R	F	O	■	E
U	G	L	■	U	N	M	I	T	I	G	A	T	E	D
T	R	O	U	B	L	E	D	■	E	U	C	H	R	E
I	E	U	■	B	L	E	E	D	■	E	E	E	■	L
O	T	T	■	L	■	■	O	J	■	D	D	R	■	I
N	■	S	E	E	I	N	G	■	P	■	■	■	B	C
A	C	■	C	U	L	P	A	B	I	L	I	T	Y	■
L	E	T	U	P	■	■	M	A	N	A	R	E	■	O
L	U	N	A	■	Q	U	E	S	T	I	O	N	E	D
Y	E	L	L	O	W	I	S	H	O	R	A	N	G	E

Peter Zimmer

C	I	R	C	U	M	S	T	A	N	C	E	S		
O	C	E	A	N		T	O	U	G	H		T		
U		L	A	W		A	W			O		A	B	B
N		A	C	H	O	L	I		E	S		B	I	O
S	E	T	T	O		K	N	I	F	E		B	R	A
E		I		L		I	G	N	F	N		E	T	R
L	O	O	S	E		N		H	E		A	D	H	D
I	O	N		S	S	G		E	C	C		M		R
N		S	H	O	T		A	R	T		B	L	O	O
G		H	O	M	O		B	I	S	T	R	O	T	O
	F	I	N	E	R	Y		T			O		H	M
	O	P	I	N	E	D		A	U	N	T	I	E	S
A	C		N	E	D		A	N	O	T	H	E	R	
C	H	U	G	S		D	E	C	I	D	E	D		A
T	O	P		S	E	C	R	E	T	A	R	I	E	S

Jasmine Richardson

S	E	A	R		N	A	T	U	R	A	L		D	A
A	T	L	A	S	T		H	E	A	T		A	R	C
R	E	A	P	P	E	A	R			F	L	A	T	
A	T		P	U		W	E	R	E	W	O	L	F	
H	E	T	E	R	O	S	E	X	U	A	L	I	T	Y
	T	W	E	N	T	Y	-	T	H	R	E	E		A
C		E		C		H						O	Y	
A	F	L	A	C		P	U	N	K	R	O	C	K	
F	A	V	O	U	R	I	N	G		I	P	O		D
E	M	E		A	N	D		V	E	N	I	I		
	I		C	O	N	T	R	I	V	A	N	C	E	S
S	L	O	O	P		E		I	L	I	E		E	
H	Y	D	R	O		E	D		N	S	N	R	A	
O		A		U	P		H	E		G	T	A	S	
P	U	B	L	I	C	I	Z	E	S		S		S	E

Edmund Kemper

S	C	H	I	Z	O	P	H	R	E	N	I	C	■	H
E	■	E	■	O	P	A	■	A	M	A	N	■	■	O
X	I	X	■	N	E	R	■	D	I	■	I	H	S	R
O	C	■	D	E	C	A	P	I	T	A	T	I	O	N
F	E	T	I	D	■	N	S	O	■	I	T	C	E	■
F	E	E	S	■	T	O	Y	■	F	L	A	C	I	D
E	■	N	M	■	N	I	C	H	E	■	T	H	O	O
N	I	N	E	S	■	D	H	O	■	O	H	P	W	■
D	O	O	M	E	D	■	I	M	P	E	R	I	A	L
I	■	B	E	T	R	A	Y	E	D	■	K	T	■	■
N	O	T	E	D	■	T	■	H	E	H	A	■	■	■
G	E	N	R	E	■	G	R	A	N	D	E	R	■	R
■	O	P	E	R	A	T	I	N	G	C	O	S	T	S
A	■	D	I	S	A	S	T	E	R	S	■	A	O	■
T	A	G	■	I	N	S	T	I	T	U	T	I	O	N

Amelia Dyer

S	T	R	A	N	G	U	L	A	T	I	O	N	■	I
E	O	■	D	■	P	A	R	A	■	P	■	D	N	■
R	O	O	M	I	E	■	P	R	O	F	I	L	I	C
I	N	C	I	D	E	N	C	E	S	■	A	L	S	O
A	S	A	N	A	S	■	A	S	■	S	T	I	A	N
L	■	I	N	F	A	N	T	S	■	E	P	P	S	■
K	I	S	S	■	D	A	■	A	D	S	■	P	P	■
I	C	H	T	H	Y	O	L	O	G	Y	■	P	E	I
L	■	I	E	■	O	P	S	■	A	■	B	R	A	C
L	I	E	R	■	U	T	■	X	■	A	O	R	U	■
E	■	S	I	G	N	I	F	I	C	A	N	T	■	O
R	A	T	N	E	G	O	■	A	D	Z	E	■	U	■
■	P	Y	G	M	E	N	T	S	■	O	A	S	I	S
A	S	■	N	■	H	O	S	P	I	T	A	L	■	■
R	E	Q	U	I	R	E	M	E	N	T	S	■	W	Y

Elizabeth Bathory

T	R	A	N	S	Y	L	V	A	N	I	A	■	A	T
R	■	C	O	N	V	I	C	T	E	D	■	P	H	O
U	N	C	L	E	A	R	■	L	E	■	E	H	■	P
T	■	U	O	■	A	C	A	D	E	M	I	C	S	■
H	A	S	■	O	L	■	U	S	E	F	U	L	L	Y
■	V	A	M	P	I	R	E	■	D	E	S	E	R	T
S	■	T	I	T	M	I	C	E	■	E	S	A	U	
E	P	I	L	E	P	S	Y	■	S	E	■	A	■	R
B	L	O	O	D	■	■	D	E	M	O	N	■	V	
A	E	N	■	R	E	P	O	R	T	E	D	L	Y	
C	A	S	T	L	E	■	O	■	V	■	■	E	■	
E	■	A	E	■	S	K	I	A	G	R	A	P	H	
O	X	I	D	A	T	I	O	N	N	U	M	B	E	R
U	■	C	I	R	C	U	M	S	T	A	N	C	E	S
S	U	S	P	I	C	I	O	U	S	■	A	S	S	■

Bloody Benders

B	L	U	D	G	E	O	N	I	N	G	■	G	A	S
A	M	B	I	V	A	L	E	N	C	E	S	■	L	E
D	■	A	S	■	M	E	R	C	A	N	T	I	L	E
G	O	■	A	H	E	M	■	O	■	T	■	M	■	I
E	■	S	P	O	R	E	■	M	I	L	K	M	A	N
S	■	■	P	M	■	■	P	E	E	K	I	N	G	■
■	C	H	E	E	K	I	E	R	■	M	A	G	I	■
C	H	I	A	S	M	■	E	A	E	■	R	■	M	
H	E	A	R	T	■	W	■	H	N	N	■	A	D	O
I	S	R	A	E	L	I	T	E	S	■	■	T	A	D
M	T	■	N	A	T	I	O	N	W	I	D	E	■	E
N	Y	■	C	D	■	■	S	E	N	O	D	O		
E	■	M	E	■	A	D	M	I	R	A	L	■	P	■
Y	E	A	S	T	■	P	H	O	E	N	I	X	E	S
S	E	X	■	F	L	O	U	N	D	E	R	I	N	G

HH Holmes

P	R	O	N	O	U	N	C	E	D	■	A	L	A	S
A	O	N	E	■	M	U	R	D	E	R	■	A	C	E
T	H	A	W	■	B	R	A	I	S	E	D	■	T	X
H	E	R	A	■	R	A	V	■	P	B	■	B	O	Y
O	■	■	G	R	A	V	E	R	O	B	B	E	R	■
L	A	M	E	■	G	E	D	I	T	I	O	N	■	A
O	D	I	■	H	E	■	F	S	■	B	E	A	R	
G	A	S	P	■	■	L	■	R	E	F	■	M		
I	N	S	U	R	A	N	C	E	P	O	L	I	C	Y
C	A	I	X	A	Q	U	E	■	A	■	C	R		
A	■	N	■	S	U	F	F	O	C	A	T	I	O	N
L	O	G	I	C	A	L	■	O	K	I	N	A	W	A
■	G	■	G	A	T	■	C	H	I	L	D	R	E	N
G	R	I	L	L	I	N	G	■	N	I	■	Y	R	O
G	E	N	U	S	C	R	A	N	G	O	N	■	S	S

Jane Toppan

M	E	N	T	A	L	A	S	Y	L	U	M	■	P	A
E	X	O	■	N	E	W	S	P	A	P	E	R	S	■
D	I	N	E	T	T	E	S	■	O	P	T	■	Y	S
I	T	■	I	H	■	S	E	R	I	C	E			
C	O	C	K	T	A	I	L	S	■	R	O	■	H	L
A	■	A	E	L	S	■	E	Q	■	P	G	O	S	
T	A	B	L	E	■	S	A	W	■	J	O	L	L	Y
I	N	D	E	N	T	U	R	E	D	■	L	I	O	N
O	■	R	E	A	D	■	O	I	N	G	■			
N	U	R	S	E	■	A	P	S	T	I	C			
S	K	I	■	S	E	R	V	A	N	T	■	C	O	
■	N	■	C	E	E	■	I	S	L	A	M			
T	E	C	H	N	O	L	O	G	I	C	A	L	L	Y
A	M	E	R	I	C	A	■	F	R	A	G	I	L	E
R	E	D	■	T	O	X	I	C	O	L	O	G	Y	■

Gilles de Rais

V	I	C	T	I	M	■	D	E	M	O	N	■	Z	U
U	N	O	■	G	A	S	E	O	U	S	N	E	S	S
L	T	S	■	R	E	M	N	A	N	T	S	■	■	E
N	O	T	F	A	R	■	O	S	I	R	U	S	■	L
E	X	C	U	T	I	O	N	■	■	■	A	G	E	
R	I	U	■	O	A	■	S	O	D	O	M	Y	■	S
A	C	T	I	N	G	■	U	S	E	R	S	■	F	S
B	A	T	T	L	E	■	M	A	G	I	C	A	L	■
I	T	I	■	E	■	E	M	M	E	T	■	N	A	O
L	I	N	E	S	■	J	O	A	N	O	F	A	R	C
I	N	G	■	S	T	E	N	C	I	L	■	S	E	C
T	G	■	■	A	C	E	■	■	N	A	P	U		
I	■	W	E	■	S	T	R	U	C	T	U	R	A	L
E	X	E	C	U	T	E	■	S	A	W	■	C	S	T
S	U	B	D	U	E	D	■	A	R	O	M	A	S	■

Isabella Stewart Gardner Museum

T	E	N	M	I	L	L	I	O	N	■	C	D	S	■
H	A	V	E	N	■	E	■	■	B	A	R	■	■	P
I	C	■	■	C	O	U	C	H	P	O	T	A	T	O
R	H	O	D	O	N	■	H	O	U	S	E	F	U	L
T	■	R	E	M	B	R	A	N	D	T	■	T	A	I
E	D	■	G	P	I	■	P	■	M	O	S	A	I	C
E	Y	■	A	E	P	P	■	M	A	N	E	T	■	E
N	E	W	S	T	A	R	■	I	N	M	A	■	C	O
■	O	■	E	T	O	L	L	■	A	L	O	O	F	
A	M	O	U	N	T	S	■	L	I	F	E	■	O	F
B	O	U	N	T	Y	■	F	I	N	I	A	L	■	I
R	B	■	A	■	T	■	O	■	A	F	A	■	C	
O	I	L	B	E	A	R	I	N	G	■	B	C	E	
A	L	■	L	A	M	E	■	S	A	V	I	O	U	R
D	E	C	E	M	B	E	R	■	G	U	A	R	D	S

Mona Lisa

```
L E O N A R D O D A V I N C I
I M █ A R E A █ I R I S █ █ O M
S P A Y I N G █ S U N L A M P
A L A S █ A G U A █ C R I M E
D O █ █ P I E █ P L E █ M I L
E Y E █ █ S R █ P I Z Z A S █
L E A P █ S S I O █ O I █ S O
G E N I P A █ C I █ P A N I C
I █ █ C █ N O O N █ E █ O O █
O R C A █ C E N T U R I O N S
C A R S █ E L S E █ U █ E C
O V A S █ █ █ D E G R A D E
N A P O L E A N █ A G E S █ N
D G S █ P A R T I C I P A T E
O E █ P H O T O G R A P H E D
```

Montreal Museum of Fine Arts

```
B R U E G H E L █ I N C H █ S
█ █ L U █ A B S T R A C T
A N O D I Z E D █ L █ A T A R
J E W E L R Y █ P A █ F E N U
A G █ R E M B R A N D T █ A G
R O T █ █ A I D E █ T D G
█ T O █ W I T █ N D L █ O I L
B I W █ O █ O █ T W A S █ A I
R A N S O M █ P I E C E █ N N
I T S E L F █ I N L R █ T █ G
N I F T Y █ W █ G L O B A L
G O O S █ S E N S E I █ S O P
S N L █ A L I O █ R X █ T O E
█ S K Y L I G H T █ B E T A
█ S E E T H I N G L Y █ S L
```

LA Mayer Institute for Islamic Art

```
C L O C K C O L L E C T I O N
H A L O A ■ P O U C H E S ■ O
O ■ A N T I Q U E S ■ A R E S
C O F F E E ■ ■ ■ ■ ■ T A X I
O S F E ■ ■ D O C K S ■ E P E
L P ■ S A L O M A N ■ B L A S
A R I S I N G ■ S P I R I T ■
T I M E P I E C E S ■ E ■ R ■
E ■ P D ■ ■ O S ■ ■ A G A I N
■ M O ■ K W A N ■ T M U C A E
M A R I E A N T O I N E T T E
A C T O ■ T O I ■ P I T I E D
K H A N ■ C A N T I O ■ O ■ L
E ■ N I G H ■ U A ■ T E N S E
R E T C H ■ D E P R E S S E D
```

Breitweiser Thefts

```
C L A M O R ■ A A A ■ W E ■ C
L A M E N T I N G ■ A A L T O
A ■ A G I ■ A N A L ■ I S A L
S D ■ A O K ■ E I O ■ T E L L
S E V E N T Y - N I N E ■ I E
I V ■ R ■ A C ■ ■ ■ ■ R I S C
C I G A R S H A P E D ■ Q T T
A L A ■ ■ M O T H E R S ■ ■ I
L I L A C S ■ H O K K A I D O
■ E L L I ■ C E S ■ T ■ ■ I N
F R E N C H A R T T H I E F ■
O ■ R ■ E O N I ■ A E R I F Y
R O I ■ R H O N E R H I N E
U S E D ■ U N E C O ■ Z E R O
M U S E U M S ■ O T O E ■ S H
```

Museu de Art de Sao Paolo

O	L	A	V	R	A	D	O	R	D	E	C	A	F	E
L	E	V	A	■	S	A	U	C	I	E	R	■	O	X
I	N	E	P	T	■	S	T	■	N	■	O	■	R	P
V	S	■	E	■	T	H	I	N	K	T	W	I	C	E
E	C	■	■	L	H	■	N	A	Y	■	B	■	E	R
R	A	P	P	E	R	S	■	S	■	S	A	U	D	I
■	P	E	R	P	E	T	R	A	T	O	R	S	■	E
A	■	M	U	S	E	U	M	■	A	M	■	A	M	N
T	R	A	D	E	■	H	Y	D	R	A	U	L	I	C
T	I	R	I	N	G	■	I	■	L	N	■	N	I	
A	N	T	S	Y	■	B	R	A	Z	I	L	I	A	N
C	■	■	H	■	C	R	E	M	E	■	U	N	■	G
H	E	A	■	F	L	O	R	O	A	■	C	G	■	
E	M	B	O	L	I	■	U	N	L	I	K	E	L	Y
D	U	M	B	F	O	U	N	D	■	K	Y	L	I	E

Willie Sutton

S	U	B	M	A	C	H	I	N	E	G	U	N	■	M
E	S	A	U	■	H	■	N	E	D	■	D	A	N	A
P	A	N	T	H	E	I	S	M	■	H	O	T	E	I
A	■	K	I	N	E	C	T	■	D	E	S	I	G	N
L	■	R	■	O	S	O	A	■	I	■	S	O	R	T
■	T	O	P	T	E	N	L	I	S	T	■	N	O	E
O	R	B	■	I	■	S	L	I	G	H	T	S	■	N
R	O	B	B	E	R	■	E	■	U	O	A	■	E	A
P	O	E	T	R	Y	■	D	■	I	M	P	U	G	N
■	P	R	I	S	O	N	■	A	S	P	A	R	■	C
■	■	I	■	■	■	P	■	E	S	C	A	P	E	
■	R	E	V	O	L	V	E	R	■	O	O	N	I	■
I	N	S	U	F	F	I	C	I	E	N	C	I	E	S
D	A	■	F	■	B	A	N	K	■	O	U	C	H	
A	P	P	R	E	H	E	N	D	■	G	A	M	E	S

Alvin Karpis

A	L	C	A	T	R	A	Z	F	E	D	E	R	A	L
U	E	▓	S	P	E	C	▓	E	▓	E	X	T	R	A
T	O	▓	S	▓	A	C	I	D	U	L	A	T	E	D
H	▓	P	U	B	L	I	C	E	N	E	M	Y	▓	D
O	S	H	M	A	▓	D	E	R	▓	T	I	▓	C	E
R	▓	O	E	R	▓	E	▓	A	B	E	N	C	O	R
I	B	T	▓	K	▓	N	I	L	▓	D	E	▓	N	S
T	O	O	B	E	A	T	▓	B	E	▓	▓	O	C	▓
Y	O	G	U	R	T	▓	M	U	R	D	E	R	E	D
▓	B	R	A	K	E	D	▓	R	O	B	B	E	R	Y
A	▓	A	▓	A	▓	Q	U	E	S	T	I	O	N	S
C	A	P	E	R	S	▓	P	A	▓	▓	N	▓	▓	▓
A	▓	H	O	P	E	D	▓	L	O	N	G	E	S	T
C	R	I	M	I	N	A	L	▓	P	O	E	T	R	Y
A	N	C	E	S	T	O	R	W	O	R	S	H	I	P

Father's Day Massacre

U	N	I	T	E	D	B	A	N	K	T	O	W	E	R
N	O	▓	E	Q	U	A	L	S	▓	W	▓	E	G	O
A	V	A	L	U	E	S	▓	O	▓	O	▓	A	G	B
R	E	A	L	I	S	E	D	▓	O	H	▓	L	O	B
M	M	▓	E	P	▓	B	▓	V	A	U	L	T	▓	E
E	B	E	R	M	▓	A	V	I	▓	N	▓	H	A	R
D	E	N	S	E	▓	L	U	C	I	D	▓	▓	D	Y
G	R	C	▓	N	▓	L	L	E	▓	R	O	I	M	▓
U	▓	A	F	T	S	▓	N	▓	T	E	N	N	I	S
A	R	S	E	▓	P	R	E	S	I	D	E	N	T	▓
R	E	E	D	▓	O	▓	R	G	▓	▓	B	O	T	A
D	E	M	E	N	T	I	A	▓	E	X	O	C	E	T
S	V	E	R	▓	T	A	B	U	L	A	T	E	D	▓
▓	E	N	A	M	E	L	L	E	D	▓	O	N	L	Y
▓	S	T	L	▓	D	O	E	R	S	▓	X	T	Y	▓

Anthony Hathaway

O	P	I	O	I	D	A	D	D	I	C	T	I	O	N
T	E	C	H	N	I	C	A	L	█	H	E	N	C	E
█	R	E	█	S	C	O	L	O	P	A	X	█	T	M
U	M	L	A	U	T	█	T	H	I	R	T	Y	█	E
C	A	L	O	R	I	E	█	█	D	U	A	L	S	S
█	N	U	L	A	O	█	C	Y	B	O	R	G	█	I
M	E	L	A	N	N	I	E	█	O	N	E	█	E	S
D	N	A	█	C	A	D	█	B	A	N	D	I	T	█
█	T	R	Y	E	R	█	L	Y	R	A	█	N	H	A
M	L	█	P	S	Y	C	H	E	█	Y	I	K	E	S
A	Y	A	█	█	D	E	S	I	G	N	E	R	█	█
C	█	A	█	P	█	█	█	█	R	█	D	I	P	█
█	E	L	E	P	H	A	N	T	M	A	N	█	S	E
A	U	T	O	B	I	O	G	R	A	P	H	I	E	S
N	█	O	B	J	E	C	T	I	V	E	█	A	D	O

George Leonidas Leslie

M	I	L	L	I	O	N	█	S	U	P	P	O	R	T
A	L	O	O	F	█	C	Y	S	T	O	L	I	T	H
R	O	B	B	E	R	I	E	S	█	L	O	L	█	O
M	A	B	O	█	█	█	T	█	W	I	S	P	█	U
M	█	I	█	P	O	L	I	T	I	C	I	A	N	S
A	C	N	█	A	W	E	█	E	S	E	█	I	D	A
N	I	G	H	T	W	A	T	C	H	M	A	N	█	N
D	R	█	C	█	█	█	█	█	█	E	N	T	E	D
L	C	█	S	H	A	D	O	W	I	N	G	█	S	█
E	U	P	H	O	R	B	I	U	M	█	S	A	T	I
B	L	U	E	P	R	I	N	T	S	█	T	U	R	N
A	A	R	P	█	E	█	█	█	E	█	█	█	O	S
U	T	█	G	A	N	G	█	█	A	V	E	N	G	E
M	E	M	B	E	R	S	█	B	R	O	T	H	E	R
█	D	E	P	O	S	I	T	A	C	C	O	U	N	T

Sentry Armored Car Company

L	A	W	E	N	F	O	R	C	E	M	E	N	T	■
■	R	H	O	■	L	■	C	O	M	I	N	G	■	E
■	M	O	N	E	Y	■	■	M	I	L	L	I	O	N
B	O	S	S	■	I	N	T	E	R	L	A	R	V	A
A	R	E	■	E	N	T	E	R	■	I	R	■	E	C
D	E	■	E	A	G	E	R	■	B	O	G	A	R	T
L	D	■	I	T	■	■	R	R	■	N	E	■	P	■
Y	V	E	S	■	B	S	A	E	B	■	R	O	O	F
■	E	X	E	C	U	T	I	V	E	S	■	T	W	O
E	H	O	N	■	S	O	N	■	T	E	T	H	E	R
M	I	S	H	B	I	U	■	F	A	T	H	E	R	■
A	C	C	O	U	N	T	A	N	T	■	A	R	E	A
I	L	■	W	R	E	S	T	L	E	R	S	■	D	I
L	E	P	E	R	S	■	C	A	S	U	A	L	■	D
S	■	P	R	O	S	E	C	U	T	E	R	S	■	S

Dunbar Armored Robbery

A	R	M	O	R	E	D	V	E	H	I	C	L	E	S
U	■	A	V	A	L	E	■	N	O	■	A	R	S	E
T	A	S	E	R	■	N	U	D	I	S	M	■	T	C
H	O	T	R	E	■	O	■	I	N	■	E	S	A	U
O	K	E	P	■	■	M	A	N	G	E	R	■	B	R
R	■	R	O	A	M	I	N	G	■	■	A	O	L	I
I	■	M	W	■	U	N	U	S	U	A	L	■	I	T
T	R	I	E	D	■	A	L	■	G	L	A	S	S	Y
I	E	N	R	■	S	T	I	N	G	L	Y	■	H	C
E	■	D	I	P	P	I	N	G	■	■	O	L	I	O
S	P	E	N	O	■	O	G	■	G	N	U	■	N	M
■	E	D	G	E	■	N	■	L	■	■	T	■	G	P
A	A	■	■	M	I	S	T	A	K	E	■	P	■	A
F	R	E	E	■	T	■	A	D	D	I	T	I	O	N
U	L	T	R	A	S	O	N	O	G	R	A	P	H	Y

Pierre Hotel

L	U	C	C	H	E	S	E	C	R	I	M	E	■	F
Y	■	R	■	O	U	P	■	R	O	M	A	N	C	E
M	A	E	S	T	R	O	■	Y	C	■	F	■	■	E
P	H	A	S	E	O	U	T	■	H	E	I	S	T	■
H	A	T	■	L	P	S	■	F	E	■	A	V	I	V
A	R	U	M	■	E	E	L	■	S	A	■	■	M	A
T	E	R	M	■	■	O	■	T	N	■	■	M	E	U
I	■	E	M	P	L	O	Y	E	E	S	■	A	L	L
C	I	S	■	E	■	A	■	■	R	E	R	N	E	T
S	N	■	D	O	U	B	L	E	C	R	O	S	S	■
Y	■	F	E	N	C	E	■	A	R	A	B	I	S	T
S	P	I	N	Y	■	N	A	■	I	N	B	O	N	E
T	E	N	T	■	R	I	S	■	M	S	I	N	E	T
E	R	A	■	E	I	G	H	T	E	E	N	■	S	O
M	I	L	L	I	O	N	■	O	■	R	G	■	S	N

Lufthansa Heist

C	A	F	E	T	E	R	I	A	F	L	O	O	R	■
A	M	A	N	I	T	A	C	A	E	S	A	R	E	A
R	H	E	U	M	Y	■	E	■	A	T	■	D	C	■
G	A	N	G	M	E	M	B	E	R	S	■	E	O	S
O	R	■	Y	■	C	U	P	S	■	■	M	A	G	E
T	I	M	E	■	F	■	R	■	■	■	A	L	N	L
E	C	O	N	O	L	I	N	E	V	A	N	■	I	F
R	■	R	K	R	■	C	■	R	A	N	I	■	Z	I
M	A	F	I	O	S	O	F	A	M	I	L	I	E	S
I	G	I	■	■	N	I	S	I	■	L	■	■	D	H
N	O	N	A	C	C	I	D	E	N	T	A	L	■	N
A	■	■	L	■	H	■	■	■	S	P	H	E	R	E
L	U	F	T	H	A	N	S	A	■	■	E	V	E	S
■	S	T	A	N	D	I	N	G	A	R	M	I	E	S
■	P	I	S	T	O	L	W	H	I	P	P	E	D	■

Loomis Truck Trailer Heist

A	L	U	M	I	N	U	M	T	R	A	I	L	E	R
E	L	N	I	N	O	■	T	E	A	■	N	O	M	E
G	U	A	R	D	S	■	■	N	■	V	E	U	L	
E	■	R	E	I	■	J	A	G	G	E	D	L	Y	
A	■	M	D	E	■	U	S	E	R	S	■	A	■	
N	E	O	■	I	N	T	E	R	S	T	A	T	E	
■	■	R	A	I	L	R	O	A	D	■	I	B	O	L
A	N	E	L	E	S	■	■	A	■	G	O	R	E	
F	E	D	E	R	A	L	B	U	R	E	A	U	■	M
F	V	■	U	■	E	O	■	E	■	T	T	■	E	
E	E	■	R	■	D	A	T	E	D	■	I	■	I	N
C	R	Y	O	P	A	T	H	Y	■	C	O	A	S	T
T	■	■	N	E	T	H	E	R	L	A	N	D	S	■
E	N	G	I	N	E	E	R	I	N	G	■	A	U	G
D	U	T	C	H	■	R	S	■	E	A	M	E	S	

Antwerp Diamond Heist

A	N	T	W	E	R	P	D	I	A	M	O	N	D	■
B	U	I	L	D	I	N	G	■	L	E	N	■	E	G
A	M	P	■	■	A	L	O	E	■	F	I			
N	A	P	O	L	E	O	N	S	■	W	H	E	E	L
D	■	I	D	O	L	■	E	E	W	■	U	L	N	A
O	■	L	O	C	K	M	E	C	H	A	N	I	S	M
N	■	Y	U	K	■	I	D	■	I	V	D	■	E	O
E	S	■	R	E	A	L	■	S	C	O	R	E	■	N
D	E	I	S	T	■	L	■	T	H	I	E	V	E	S
■	L	D	■	P	I	T	A	■	D	D	E	■	T	
N	E	I	G	H	B	O	U	R	S	■	H	E		
■	C	O	M	B	I	N	A	T	I	O	N	S	■	R
A	T	T	■	A	■	R	E	T	U	R	N	S		
M	E	I	■	C	A	M	E	R	A	S	■	V	I	A
■	D	C	■	K	I	A	■	S	E	N	S	O	R	S

American Museum of Natural History

D	E	L	O	N	G	S	T	A	R	R	U	B	Y
N	A	I	L	■	A	T	A	R	U	■	D	U	O
A	G	E	■	A	L	A	R	M	S	■	R	U	G
■	L	■	S	A	R	G	■	H	U	N	G	R	Y
J	E	W	E	L	■	O	E	R	■	N	■	L	S	P
■	D	■	■	C	F	T	E	■	D	L	A	E	S
H	I	B	A	C	H	I	■	S	P	E	A	R	L	Y
C	A	P	T	A	I	N	■	E	E	R	■	Y	V
I	M	P	O	U	N	D	I	N	G	■	I	T	E	M
■	O	■	H	E	I	S	T	■	C	H	O	S	E
A	N	T	S	■	S	A	■	M	S	O	■	O	■	T
L	D	I	H	■	E	■	H	E	A	L	■	L	A	H
A	■	G	A	L	■	W	I	N	D	O	W	S	■	O
R	■	E	R	A	S	E	■	T	H	U	R	■	A	D
M	U	R	P	H	T	H	E	S	U	R	F	■	A	S

Schiphol Airport Diamond Heist

S	C	H	I	P	H	O	L	A	I	R	P	O	R	T
E	A	■	D	I	A	M	O	N	D	S	■	R	E	U
T	R	E	A	T	S	■	T	T	E	■	O	F	■	L
■	G	■	H	A	T	H	A	W	A	Y	■	F	R	I
N	O	L	O	■	A	■	E	L	■	M	■	E	■	P
A	T	■	A	U	T	H	O	R	I	T	I	E	S	■
M	E	A	N	T	■	N	■	P	S	P	L	U	T	O
T	R	I	■	J	■	B	■	T	■	L	O	I	N
A	M	S	T	E	R	D	A	M	■	V	I	S	T	A
R	I	■	R	■	E	R	I	K	■	O	■	U	V
U	N	C	O	M	P	A	S	S	I	O	N	A	T	E
■	A	P	P	E	A	L	■	S	A	L	S	■	I	R
U	L	■	E	N	T	E	R	I	N	G	■	B	O	A
P	■	I	■	S	T	R	I	N	G	A	L	O	N	G
S	U	N	D	A	Y	S	■	G	S	■	A	X	■	E

Graff Diamonds

```
I  N  S  T  I  T  U  T  E  #  #  #  F  W  P
S  O  U  P  #  W  G  #  M  U  #  S  O  A  R
S  U  N  S  #  E  G  O  #  #  P  A  R  L  O
U  N  #  #  I  N  #  V  I  E  R  #  E  L  F
E  #  D  I  E  T  Y  E  D  #  O  #  M  N  E
D  I  I  #  #  Y  O  R  E  #  S  H  O  U  S
#  M  A  K  E  -  U  P  A  R  T  I  S  T  S
#  P  M  #  S  T  #  O  #  #  H  #  T  R  I
B  O  O  #  S  H  O  W  E  R  E  D  #  E  O
E  R  N  #  E  R  I  E  #  S  T  O  L  E  N
L  T  D  #  N  E  A  R  S  #  I  #  Y  #  A
I  A  S  #  T  E  #  E  #  S  C  H  O  O  L
E  N  #  S  I  #  B  D  S  M  #  O  N  E  #
V  C  #  P  A  B  A  #  A  M  U  S  I  N  G
E  E  #  F  L  Y  I  N  G  S  Q  U  A  D  #
```

Carlton International Hotel

```
A  L  F  R  E  D  H  I  T  C  H  C  O  C  K
B  O  R  E  D  #  F  S  H  #  M  A  #  O  O
A  P  E  N  S  #  C  R  I  M  I  N  A  L  #
N  O  N  E  #  S  #  A  E  #  N  G  L  C  #
D  I  C  E  #  C  H  E  F  #  M  E  N  E  U
O  #  H  #  J  A  I  L  #  B  A  S  I  C  S
N  E  R  #  E  P  #  I  R  O  N  #  #  T  T
E  D  I  #  W  E  D  #  A  D  #  O  L  I  O
D  I  V  #  E  #  U  N  D  E  R  W  O  O  D
#  B  I  L  L  I  O  N  A  I  R  E  #  N  Y
S  L  E  E  R  Y  #  #  N  #  O  #  S  #  #
T  E  R  R  Y  #  C  H  #  O  B  J  E  C  T
R  #  A  A  #  G  O  O  S  E  B  U  M  P  S
A  M  #  #  C  O  N  S  I  D  E  R  I  N  G
P  I  N  K  P  A  N  T  H  E  R  S  #  #  #
```

Charles Ponzi

P	O	S	T	A	G	E	S	T	A	M	P	S	■	A
U	R	I	A	H	■	X	E	■	D	R	Y	I	N	G
R	E	E	N	■	A	C	C	R	U	I	N	G	■	O
C	O	R	K	■	T	H	U	N	D	E	R	I	N	G
H	■	R	E	S	T	A	R	T	E	D	■	N	O	■
A	F	A	R	■	O	N	T	■	■	C	T	R		
S	A	■	S	U	R	G	I	N	G	■	R	■	A	
E	C	T	■	I	N	I	T	I	A	T	I	V	E	S
D	E	B	T	■	E	N	I	G	M	A	T	I	C	■
■	D	U	O	■	Y	G	E	H	E	■	I	S	L	O
■	■	R	A	■	S	T	R	I	C	T	L	Y		
M	O	N	O	C	L	E	■	M	S	■	I	A	E	A
S	C	I	N	T	I	L	L	A	■	O	S	S	■	B
T	E	S	T	O	S	T	E	R	O	N	E	■	N	U
C	O	L	O	R	T	E	L	E	V	I	S	I	O	N

Lou Pearlman

T	R	A	N	S	C	O	N	R	E	C	O	R	D	S
R	E	C	O	N	■	N	O	N	K	O	S	H	E	R
U	N	C	O	O	K	E	D	■	E	M	P	O	F	■
S	T	O	N	O	G	A	■	A	S	P	■	■	R	A
T	A	U	■	P	■	R	■	W	■	A	H	E	A	D
E	L	N	■	S	A	T	I	N	■	N	E	X	U	S
E	■	T	B	■	H	N	■	B	I	F	I	D	■	
S	M	I	L	E	S	■	V	A	L	E	N	C	I	A
■	I	N	U	I	T	■	E	X	I	S	T	I	N	G
A	L	G	E	B	R	A	S	■	■	■	■	G	A	
E	L	■	■	A	C	T	U	A	T	E	D	■	I	
F	I	C	T	I	T	I	O	U	S	■	P	A	W	N
C	O	R	D	■	E	D	R	■	A	R	M	E	S	
U	N	M	■	A	G	I	S	M	■	D	O	U	S	T
■	S	■	P	S	Y	C	■	B	L	I	M	P	S	■

Reed Slatkin

S	C	I	E	N	T	O	L	O	G	I	S	T	■	A
T	O	P	A	G	A	■	I	T	■	N	C	■	E	N
O	F	A	R	■	B	L	A	C	K	V	O	M	I	T
C	O	S	T	L	I	E	R	■	V	E	R	I	G	I
K	U	S	H	I	■	A	■	H	A	S	I	■	H	D
S	N	■	L	■	U	P	S	■	S	T	A	C	T	E
■	D	R	I	P	P	I	N	G	S	■	O	S	P	
M	E	N	N	O	N	■	U	■	T	N	■	R		
I	R	■	K	N	O	W	L	E	D	G	E	S	■	E
L	■	L	■	Z	Z	■	S	C	A	L	E	S	S	
L	A	B	■	I	N	V	E	S	T	M	E	N	T	S
I	N	S	T	■	A	A	T	I	■	E	X	T	R	A
O	D	■	W	A	R	R	A	N	T	S	■	A	N	
N	■	M	I	L	K	I	N	G	■	K	E	P	T	
S	U	■	T	E	S	T	Y	■	B	L	U	E	S	S

Scott Rothstein

O	R	G	A	N	I	Z	A	T	I	O	N	S	■	B
F	L	O	R	A	L	■	T	H	O	U	G	H	■	I
F	■	R	A	C	K	E	T	E	E	R	■	A	P	R
I	D	E	A	■	U	O	■	O	A	R	E	D		
C	■	■	C	O	R	R	U	P	T	■	E	G	O	
E	M	I	T	■	B	O	N	N	E	T	■	H	■	F
R	O	N	S	■	E	P	E	T	■	E	■	O	G	P
■	R	D	■	B	Y	E	Y	O	U	R	■	L	E	A
M	O	I	■	O	■	■	N	■	O	D	O	R		
■	C	A	S	A	B	L	A	N	C	A	■	E	D	A
U	C	■	I	■	S	T	R	U	C	T	U	R	E	D
P	O	N	Z	I	■	■	N	■	S	I				
B	■	A	E	O	N	■	F	R	A	N	C	A	I	S
O	■	G	R	E	E	C	E	■	M	A	L	I	C	E
W	H	I	S	T	L	E	B	L	O	W	E	R	S	■

Greater Ministries International

```
C H R I S T I A N C H U R C H
L A O ■ C O O L ■ H I T C H ■
I N T E R N ■ I N E P T ■ U P
T D ■ T I E ■ G R E A T E R
O L ■ A P R O N ■ R A U N C H
R E S ■ T ■ D ■ A S ■ K H I
I ■ U M U ■ E B B ■ P I G S
A S P I R A T I O N S ■ O ■
M A P L E ■ E B L ■ A B B E Y
A X L E ■ D E L I V E R E R S
R ■ E ■ M I N I S T R I E S
I B M ■ I S ■ C H ■ B P ■ L
A L E ■ M O S A I C ■ E I R E
N O N ■ E W ■ L N ■ G E N E S
A C T I O N S ■ G O O ■ G P S
```

Colonial Pipeline Ransomware Attack

```
L A W E N F O R C E M E N T ■
G U A N ■ A K A O N I ■ E T C
V T ■ D E M A N D ■ S K I ■ A
■ H ■ I L E P S E ■ T I G H T
D O W N ■ D I O D E S ■ H A C
A R A G E ■ ■ M ■ A S C H
R I G ■ M A L W A R E ■ K Y
K T ■ F A ■ D A R K S I D E ■
T I ■ M S B ■ R E C O V E R Y
R E F ■ P I P E L I N E ■ E
A S E S ■ T R ■ L ■ T A I L
C ■ R A ■ C O L O N I A L ■ L
E A R P H O N E ■ E S ■ N E
R U E ■ G I G A B Y T E S ■ D
■ ■ T R A N S P O R T I N G ■
```

NASA Cyber Attack

T	H	R	E	A	T	R	E	D	U	C	T	I	O	N
H	A	I	R	Y		O		E	N	A	O	N		U
R		O		A	D	I	N	F	I	N	I	T	U	M
E	E	R	Y		O	D		E	T	A	L	E		B
E	X	T	O	R	T	I	O	N		D	E	R	B	I
	P		U	U			S	T	A	T	N	O	N	
D	O	W	N	L	O	A	D	E	D		S	A	N	G
E	R	I	G	E	R	O	N		S		T			
A	T	L	E	A	S	T		H	A	C	K	I	N	G
D		E	S	S	A		H	E	L	I	P	O	R	T
L	E	S	T		R	E	G	I	M	E	N	T	S	
I	N		B	I	O	L	O	G	I	C	A	L		
E	N	V	I	R	O	N	M	E	N	T	A	L		H
S	U	I	T	A	B	L	E		E	A	R		M	I
T	I	G	H	T	E	S	T		D	R	E	A	M	S

WannaCry Ransomware

S	H	A	D	O	W	B	R	O	K	E	R	S		T
E		N	O	P	E		O		E	Y	E		I	D
C	R	Y	P	T	O			P	R	E	V	E	N	T
U	O		E	I		W	I	N	D	O	W	S		
R	A	N	S	O	M	W	A	R	E		L	I	T	A
I	M		N		O	N	E	R	O	U	T		F	
T		C	H	E	W	I	N	G		T	Y	P	E	
Y	C	O		D	A		A		A	I		A	W	
A	L	U	M		M	I	C	R	O	S	O	F	T	
G	E	N	T	R	Y		R	E	S	I	N	I	C	E
E	V	T		I		Y	C		A		S	H	Y	
N	E	R	V	O	U	S		O		N	O	H		E
C	R	Y	P	T	O	W	O	R	M		M	I	N	I
Y	E			E		A	N	D	T	H	E	N		N
	R	E	P	R	O	C	E	S	S	I	N	G		G

Heartland Payment Systems

B	R	E	A	C	H	G	U	A	R	A	N	T	E	E
U	P	S	■	Y	A	R	N	■	U	T	E	R	U	S
S	■	Q	■	B	C	■	E	■	S	A	T	I	R	E
I	C	■	E	E	K	I	N	G	S	■	■	I	N	■
N	O	N	P	R	E	S	C	R	I	P	T	I	O	N
E	M	A	■	S	R	■	R	■	A	R	E	T	E	S
S	P	O	K	E	S	■	Y	I	N	E	■	Y	■	■
S	U	M	A	C	■	U	P	N	■	C	Q	■	A	S
E	T	■	O	U	G	H	T	S	■	I	U	■	F	P
S	E	■	A	R	C	H	E	T	Y	P	I	C	A	L
■	R	A	■	I	■	■	D	A	V	I	E	S	I	A
E	S	T	A	T	E	S	■	L	E	T	T	E	R	S
P	■	O	■	Y	■	O	■	L	S	A	■	■	C	H
I	O	N	S	■	E	D	G	E	■	T	O	D	A	Y
C	R	E	D	I	T	A	N	D	D	E	B	I	T	■

Equifax

L	I	B	E	R	A	T	I	O	N	A	R	M	Y	■
A	N	O	N	Y	M	■	N	E	A	R	E	A	S	T
T	F	■	G	R	E	E	T	S	■	T	■	L	■	■
E	O	■	L	■	R	Y	E	■	V	I	■	W	O	P
N	R	■	A	F	I	E	L	D	■	F	L	A	I	R
T	M	■	N	■	C	■	L	I	N	I	E	R	■	O
H	A	N	D	B	A	S	I	N	■	C	R	E	E	P
O	T	O	■	A	N	A	G	O	G	I	C	■	L	R
S	I	N	G	E	S	■	E	■	O	A	■	M	E	I
T	O	I	L	S	■	K	N	O	W	L	E	D	G	E
I	N	S	U	R	A	N	C	E	■	■	V	■	Y	T
L	■	S	C	■	B	E	E	H	I	V	E	S	■	A
I	■	U	O	■	U	E	■	■	S	E	N	I	O	R
T	H	E	S	I	S	■	M	I	L	I	T	A	R	Y
Y	O	S	E	■	E	C	U	M	E	N	I	S	M	■

A Busload of Kids

T	R	A	C	T	O	R	T	R	A	I	L	E	R	■
R	I	■	H	U	M	A	N	■	U	N	A	B	L	E
A	C	C	I	D	E	N	T	■	H	D	T	V	S	
F	O	O	L	S	■	S	■	Q	U	A	D	■	■	
F	■	■	D	■	T	O	F	U	■	L	E	H	A	R
I	■	B	R	O	O	M	■	A	V	E	R	A	G	E
C	V	■	E	K	■	■	M	R	■	D	■	M	E	N
K	I	D	N	A	P	P	E	R	S	■	K	B	■	T
I	C	R	■	Y	A	R	■	Y	O	S	■	U	■	
N	T	I	■	I	O	N	■	G	U	A	R	D	S	
G	O	V	E	R	N	S	■	G	■	B	U	G	L	E
■	R	E	N	G	S	T	O	R	F	F	■	E	■	■
W	I	R	E	D	■	A	G	E	■	U	G	R	I	C
E	A	■	M	A	T	T	R	E	S	S	E	S	■	O
I	N	L	A	■	R	E	E	N	T	E	R	■	N	G

Jaycee Dugard

S	E	X	U	A	L	L	Y	D	E	V	I	A	N	T
T	X	■	N	I	P	■	A	E	V	■	I	D	E	A
E	■	K	I	D	N	A	P	P	E	D	■	D	■	S
P	R	O	V	E	■	■	P	E	N	■	W	I	F	E
F	E	■	E	L	E	V	E	N	■	P	A	C	E	D
A	L	A	R	M	■	A	D	D	S	■	■	T	■	
T	A	P	S	■	E	L	■	S	U	D	S	I	N	G
H	T	E	I	■	I	E	D	■	P	A	R	O	L	E
E	I	■	T	E	N	T	■	S	P	U	R	N	E	D
R	O	S	Y	■	S	T	U	R	G	I	S	■		
■	N	A	■	I	D	■	O	I	E	H	■	G	B	
I	S	M	U	S	■	B	U	S	S	T	O	P	■	A
C	H	U	G	S	■	A	C	S	S	E	■	O	I	L
■	I	E	L	U	■	C	H	E	E	R	L	E	S	S
A	P	L	Y	E	■	K	E	D	S	S	■	M	O	A

John Paul Getty III

O	R	C	H	E	S	T	R	A	T	I	N	G		A
Z	U	R	I	C	H		S	C	U	D	D	I	N	G
A	S	I	D	E		F	A	T	H	E	R		J	O
R	S	E		R	U		I			A	A	R	O	N
K	I	D	N	A	P	P	I	N	G		N	O	R	I
	A		E		T	I	N	G	E		G	O	D	S
P	N	E	U	M	O	N	I	A		P	H	D		T
O	R	M	A			T		N	I	L	E			M
M	O	B		G	R	A	N	D	F	A	T	H	E	R
P	U	E	B	L	O		U	R		I	A	A	D	A
O	L	D	D	O	M	I	N	I	O	N		W	I	N
M	E	D		O	E		A	P		S		A	A	S
	T	I	H	M		B	V		M	M	P	I		O
E	T	N	A		J	O	U	R	N	A	L	I	S	M
N	E	G	O	T	I	A	T	I	O	N	S		M	

Charley and Walter Ross

G	E	R	M	A	N	T	O	W	N	H	O	M	E	
O	N	E	E	R		O	R		O	U	E	R	S	
F	L	E	X		F		Q	U	A	R	T	E	R	
P	O	L	I	C	I	A		B	U	S	S	T	O	P
	G		C	A	R	R	I	A	G	E		S	R	O
C	O	L	O	N	E	L		A	D	H		E	N	
O		E		D	W	A	R	F		R	U	D	D	Y
G	A	G		Y	O	G	A		C	A	M	E		T
S	N	A	P		R	O	U	G	H	W	A	T	E	R
	S	L	O	C	K		S	A	L	N	I	E	C	E
S	W	I	L	L	S	S	O	L	O		C	M	K	
S	E	Z	I	I		M	A	R	K	E	T		K	
	R	E	C	F		U		I		V	I	C	I	
I		D	E	F	O	R	M	E	D		E	V	E	N
N	V		S	A	L	T	P	E	T	R	E		G	

Nell Donnelly

K	I	D	N	A	P	P	I	N	G	■	P	■	F	B
A	■	M	O	R	A	I	N	I	■	P	E	D	A	L
N	E	A	R	E	S	T	■	T	H	O	R	E	A	U
S	Q	■	T	■	T	H	A	W	■	I	U	M	■	E
A	U	T	H	O	R	I	T	I	E	S	■	A	D	E
S	A	H	E	■	I	■	A	T	T	O	R	N	E	Y
C	L	E	A	N	E	R	S	■	N	■	D	S	E	
I	■	S	S	■	S	E	C	■	I	O	N	■	I	D
T	E	E	T	H	■	T	A	■	O	U	■	G	■	
Y	■	■	D	I	S	G	U	S	T	I	N	G		
C	H	A	U	F	F	E	U	R	■	P	E	T	E	R
R	A	N	S	O	M	■	■	E	C	L	A	I	R	S
I	■	E	X	A	G	G	E	R	A	T	E	■		
M	E	I	■	E	■	E	S	S	E	N	T	I	A	L
E	N	F	O	R	C	E	M	E	N	T	■	■	N	O

Printed in Great Britain
by Amazon

54217132R00123